IO499909

- Descriptions in this manual are based on the Android 8.0/8.1 (Android Oreo or Android O). However, people using older versions of Android will find some benefits reading this manual.

- All information supplied in this guide is for educational purpose only, and users bear the responsibility for using it.

- Because of the differences that exist between Android phones from different brands, some of the settings/options/features mentioned in this book may not be completely the same with what you have on your phone. For example, if I ask you to tap **Lock screen and security**, you may not see this exact phrase and you may instead see **Security & Location**. In addition, if I ask you to tap **Delete**, you may not see this exact word but see a word like **Remove.** When something like these happen, simply tap the phrase or word that has the closest meaning to what I ask you to do/tap. Alternatively, if the instruction has to do with phone settings, you can simply use the search bar located at the top of the settings' screen to find what you are looking for.

- The screenshots/pictures used in this book may be different from what you see on your phone. This is because phone manufacturers usually customize Android OS to their taste and this affects the way phone options/settings are presented on the screen. Therefore, it is quite difficult (if not impossible) to have a screenshot that represents what is found on every Android phone. However, the differences are not usually much.

- Some features or options discussed in this book may not be found on all Android phones. For example, not all Android phones have fingerprint options.

- All information supplied in this guide is what was available as at the time of writing this guide, and it may not be 100% accurate again if there is a major software update to the Android Operating System, apps or features mentioned in this book.

- Depending on your local network service provider or your location/region, some of the features discussed in this guide may not be available on your Android Phone.

- Although I took tremendous effort to ensure that all pieces of information provided in this guide are correct, I will welcome your suggestions if you find out that any information provided in this guide is inadequate or you find a better way of doing some of the actions mentioned in this guide. All correspondences should be sent to pharmibrahimguides@gmail.com

About This Guide

Finally, a simplified guide on Android Phones is here– this guide is indeed a splendid companion for phones using Android OS 8.0/8.1 (Android Oreo).

This is a very thorough, no-nonsense guide, useful for both experts and newbies. This guide contains a lot of information on Android Phones.

It is full of actionable steps, hints, notes, screenshots and suggestions. This guide is particularly useful for newbies/beginners and seniors; nevertheless, I strongly believe that even the techy guys will find some benefits reading it.

Enjoy yourself as you go through this very comprehensive guide.

PS: Please make sure you do not give the gift of an Android Phone without giving this companion guide alongside with it. This guide makes your gift a complete one.

Table of Contents

How to Use This Guide (Please Read!)

This guide is an unofficial manual for Android Phones running Android 8/8.1 (Oreo) and it should be used just like you use any reference book or manual.

To quickly find a topic, please use the table of contents. In addition, you can use the index section to search for any word or phrase in this guide. This would allow you to quickly find information and save time.

When I say you should carry out a set of tasks, for example, when I say you should tap **Settings > Sound > Notifications & actions**, what I mean is that you should tap on **Settings** and then tap on **Sound**. Lastly, you should tap on **Notifications & actions**.
In addition, if I ask you to tap "Notifications & actions" or "Notifications", what I mean is that you should tap "Notifications & actions" and if you don't see "Notifications & actions", tap "Notifications".
Finally, when a function is enabled or turned on, the status switch will appear bold and colored. On the other hand, when a function is disabled or turned off, the status switch will appear gray.

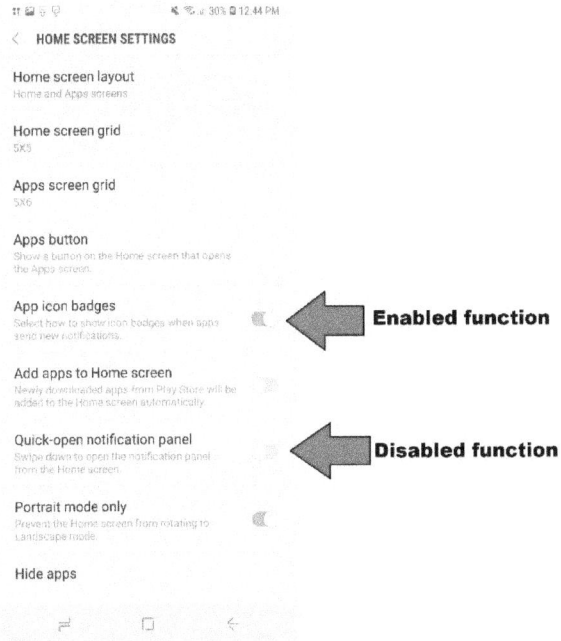

I hope this guide helps you get the most out of your Android phone.

Getting Started with Your Phone

What Is Android Operating System

Android Operating System (Android OS) is an operating system developed by Google. This OS is based on modified version of Linux Kernel. The OS is used in phones, tablets among others. The latest Android OS released as at the time of writing this guide is Android 8.1 (Oreo).

Hint: To know the Android OS of your phone, swipe down from the top of the screen and tap the settings icon ⚙ . Scroll down and tap **About Phone**, or tap **About Device.** If you can't still see your Android verson, tap **Software Information** or **System**…

Turning Your Phone On/Off and Setting Up Your Phone

Turning on your Android phone is as simple as ABC. To turn on your phone, press and hold the power button until you notice a small vibration. If you are turning on your phone for the first time, please carefully follow the on-screen instructions to set it up. Usually, you will have the option to connect to a wireless network during the setup, to learn more about connecting your phone to Wi-Fi, please see page 392. In addition, I advise that you insert the SIM Card before switching on your Android phone. To learn more about inserting the SIM card, please see page 19.

For many Android phones, the power button is located at the side or upper edge of the screen.

To turn off your phone, press and hold the power button and select **Power off/Shutdown/OK.** If necessary, select **Power off/Shutdown/Ok** again to confirm.

Hint: If you don't feel like switching off your phone again and you want to dismiss the power off screen, simply tap the back button. Alternatively, tap anywhere outside the onscreen icons. *Please note that this approach may not work on all Android phones.*

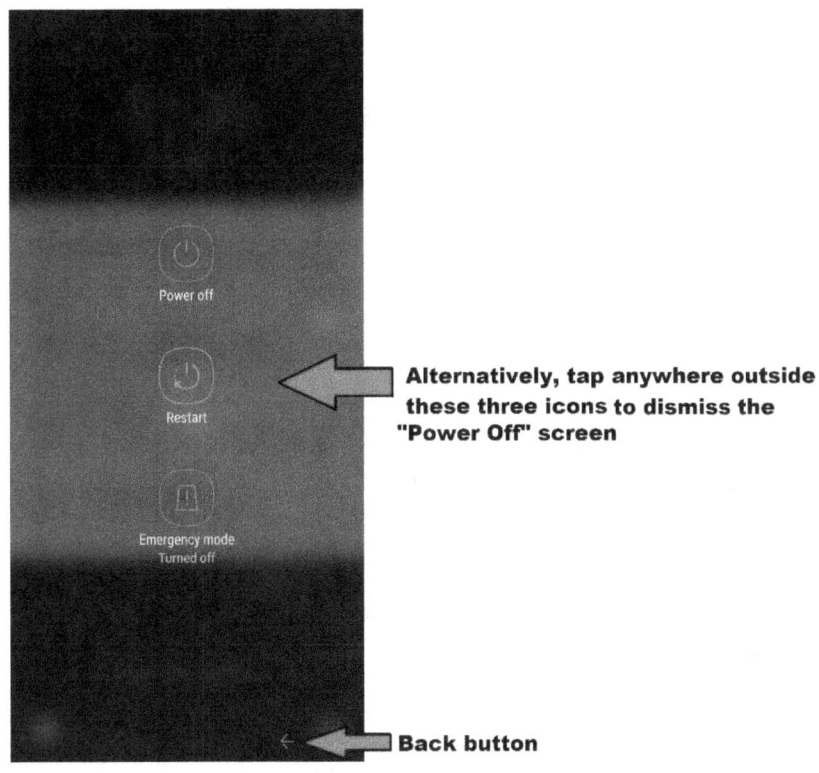

Alternatively, tap anywhere outside these three icons to dismiss the "Power Off" screen

Back button

In addition, if you are using an Android phone for the first time, remove any protective nylon from the surface of the phone.

Please do not vex if you find it unnecessary reading about how to on/off your device. I have included it, in case there may be someone reading this guide who is a complete novice and knows close to nothing about smartphones.

Tips:

- Some network provider may require you to enter a PIN when you switch on your phone. You can try entering **0000.** This is the default PIN for many network providers. If you have problem entering the correct PIN, please contact your network service provider.

- For many Android phones, during the setup, you may skip a process by tapping **Skip/Next** or by tapping the **X** icon. Usually, you will have the option to perform this process in the future by going to your phone settings.

- While using your Android phone for the first time, you may have the option to transfer your contents from your old phone to your Android phone. Just carefully follow the onscreen instructions to do this. If you skip the process of content transfer during the phone setup, and you will like to perform the transfer now, please see page 37 to learn how to go about this.

- Because of software updates and installations, it is likely that your Android phone will consume a large amount of data during the setup, I would advise that you connect to a wireless network if you can. Using a mobile network during the setup might be expensive.

- When you start using your Android phone, you would probably notice that its screen locks within some seconds after you finish interacting with it. To allow the screen stay longer before it locks, change the screen timeout setting. To do this:

  o Swipe down from the top of the screen and select the settings icon ⚙ .

  o Tap **Display** > **Screen Timeout.** Then choose an option. Alternatively, tap **Display** > **Advanced** > **Sleep** and then choose an option. For other Android phones, tap **Display** > **Sleep** and then choose an option.

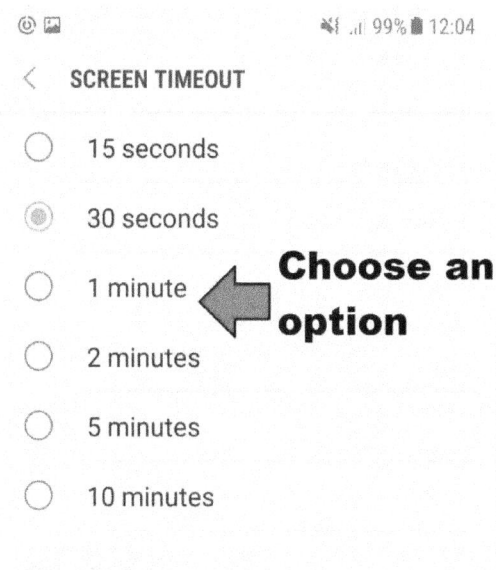

Please note that selecting a longer timeout would make your battery discharge faster.

Do you need to charge your Android phone before first use?

To the best of my knowledge, it is not necessary. If you charge it before the first use, that is cool. But if there is no way to charge it, then you can use it straightaway without charging it. I have learnt that the new lithium batteries used in smartphones don't really need to be charged before the first use (provided that the battery still has power).

Swiping the Screen Properly

From time to time, you would need to interact with the touchscreen of your Android phone by swiping it with your finger. If you don't swipe it properly, you may not get the expected result. You can swipe to perform the following actions:

1. **Access the notification menu/quick settings**

To access the notification menu/quick settings, swipe from the top of the screen. Please make sure you are starting from the top of the screen (around the earpiece/receiver area) to get the expected result. See the picture below.

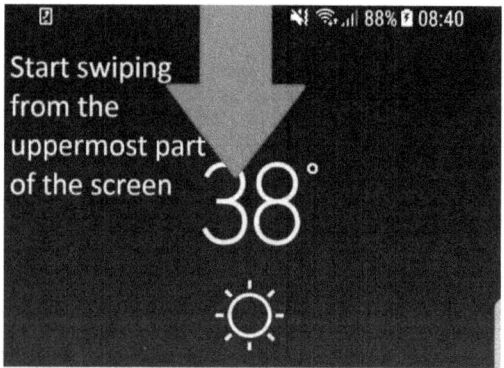

2. **Accessing the app screen**

On supported Android phones, to access the applications screen, swipe up from the lower part of the screen. See the direction of the arrow below.

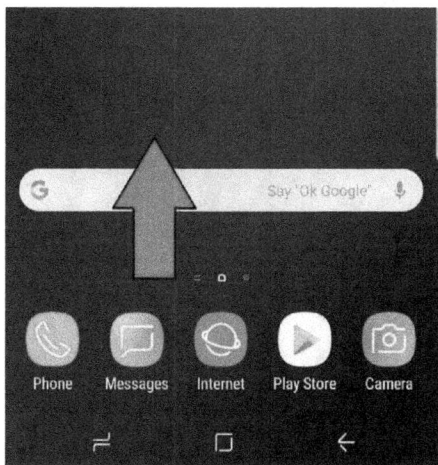

Tip: To go back to the home screen while on the applications screen, just swipe up or down from the middle (or around the middle) of the screen.

Get to Know Settings Tab

I am talking about settings tab under this section because I will be referring to this tab a lot.

The settings tab of an Android phone has many subsections and because of this, I would advise that you use the **Search** menu (denoted by the lens icon 🔍) to quickly find what you are looking for. To use the settings' search feature, swipe down from the top of the screen and tap the settings icon (see the picture below).

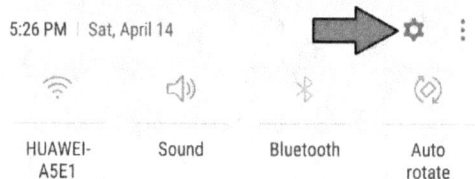

5:26 PM | Sat, April 14

🛜	🔊	∗	⟨⟩
HUAWEI-A5E1	Sound	Bluetooth	Auto rotate

Then tap on the search icon and type a keyword corresponding to the setting you are looking for. For example, if you are looking for a setting relating to battery, just type **Battery** into the search bar. The result filters as you type.

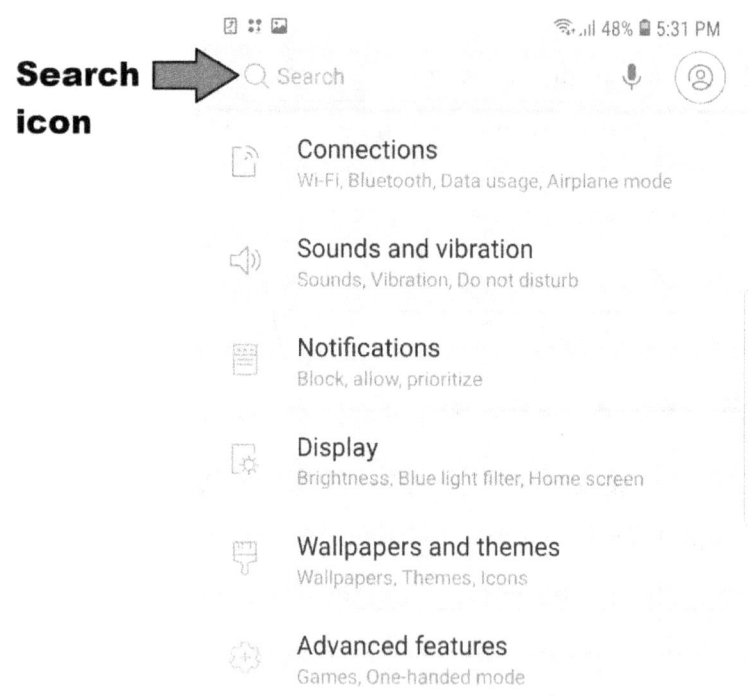

Search icon

🎵 ∷ 🖼   🛜 �📶 48% 🔋 5:31 PM

🔍 Search   🎤 ⓐ

Connections
Wi-Fi, Bluetooth, Data usage, Airplane mode

Sounds and vibration
Sounds, Vibration, Do not disturb

Notifications
Block, allow, prioritize

Display
Brightness, Blue light filter, Home screen

Wallpapers and themes
Wallpapers, Themes, Icons

Advanced features
Games, One-handed mode

Tip: For some Android phones, you can search the settings with your voice instead of typing. This appears cool and smart. To use this feature, just tap the microphone button (located on the search bar) and then say a word or a phrase. For example, you may say **battery** if you want to search for settings relating to battery.

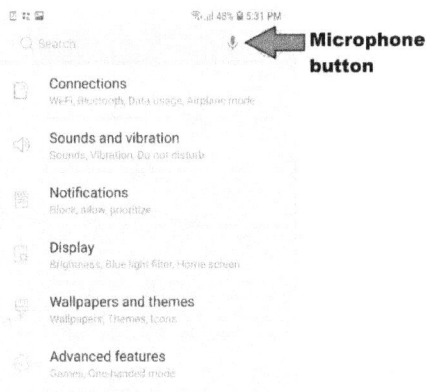

To perform another voice search, simply tap the **X** icon next to the present word/phrase, tap the microphone button again and say the new phrase/word.

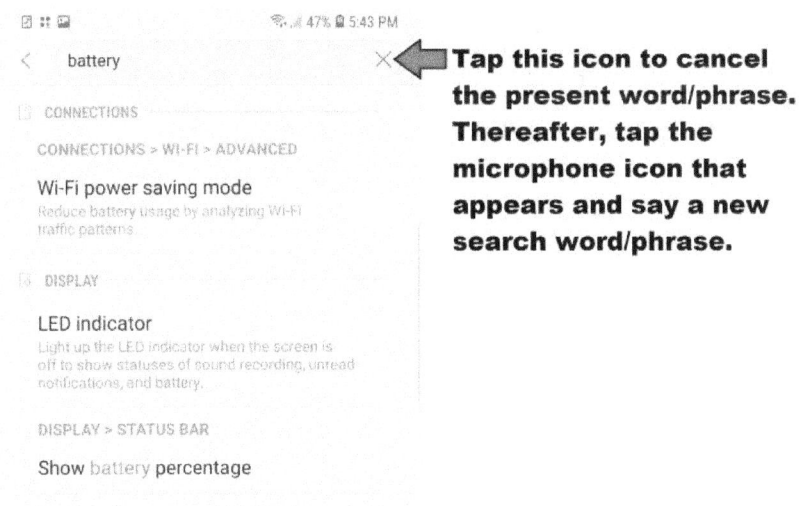

Please note that the option of *voice settings search* is not available on all Android phones.

Charging Your Device

If you are using your Android phone more often (especially if you use Wi-Fi more frequently), you may realize that you need to charge your phone every day. One of the coolest times to charge your device is when you are taking a shower, as you are not likely to be using it at the time.

Do you need to charge your phone before the first use?

Please see the answer on page 5.

To learn more on how to use your phone for a longer time on battery, please go to page 421.

To charge your Android phone:

1. For many Android phones, when you first open your product box, you will notice that the power cord consists of two parts (i.e. the USB cable and the USB power adapter), connect these two parts together. See the picture below.

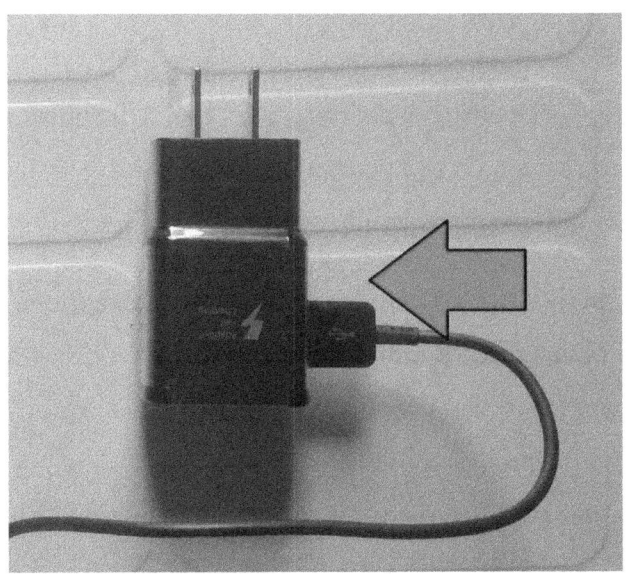

2. Connect the end of the USB cable to the charging port of your device, making sure that both the charging cable and the charging port on your device make a good and firm contact.

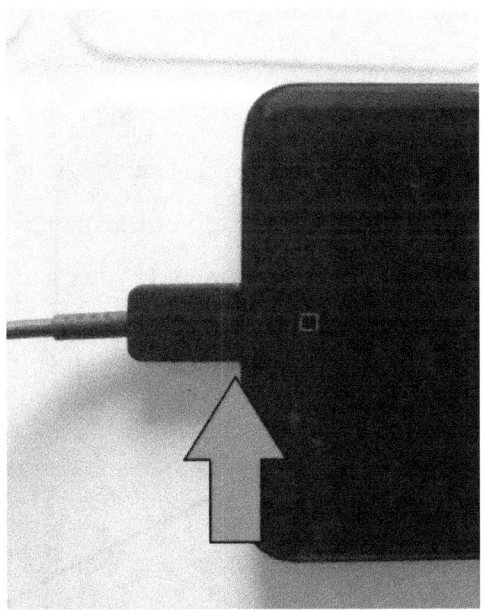

3. Plug the power adapter to an electrical outlet. When your phone is charging, a charging icon ⚡ will appear at the top of the screen. When your phone is fully charged, the battery icon should appear solid/full.

Note: For many Android phones, you may need to apply a small force to remove the USB cord from the phone after charging it. Please be careful so that the phone does not mistakenly drop from your hand in the process.

- To know the estimated charging time remaining, swipe down from the top of the screen and then tap **Settings** ⚙ > **Device Maintenance > Battery**. If you don't see "Device Maintenance", tap **Settings** ⚙ > **Battery**.

- Alternatively, tap **Settings** ⚙ and tap the search icon located at the top of the screen. Then begin to type **Battery** until you see **Battery** at the top of the menu. Tap it. The charging time may be longer if you are using your device while charging it.

Tips:

- To extend the power of your device substantially, swipe down from the top of the screen and then tap **Settings** ⚙ > **Battery**. Tap the status switch next to "Power saving mode", "Ultra power saving mode" "Stamina Mode" or "Battery saver".

Alternatively, if you are using a Samsung phone, swipe down from the top of the screen and then tap **Settings** > **Device Maintenance > Battery**. Under **Power saving mode** tab, tap MID or MAX and then tap **APPLY**.

- There are some apps that consume a lot of processing power. To access and manage these apps, swipe down from the top

of the screen and then tap **Settings** > **Battery**. Tap the menu icon located at the top of the screen and select **Battery optimization** or **Battery saver**. If you see an app that is not optimized, tap the app, tap **Optimize** and then select **Done.**

Alternatively, if you are using a Samsung phone, swipe down from the top of the screen and then tap **Settings** > **Device Maintenance > Battery**. Under **App power monitor.**

For some Android phones, you may be able to access battery tab by swiping down from the top of the screen and tapping battery icon .

In addition, if you are using a Samsung phone, you can give an unrestricted battery power usage to a selected app. To do this, swipe

down from the top of the screen and then tap **Settings** > **Device Maintenance > Battery**. Tap **Unmonitored apps** (located at the bottom of the screen) and then tap **Add apps**. Select the app you want, and tap **DONE** located at the top of the screen.

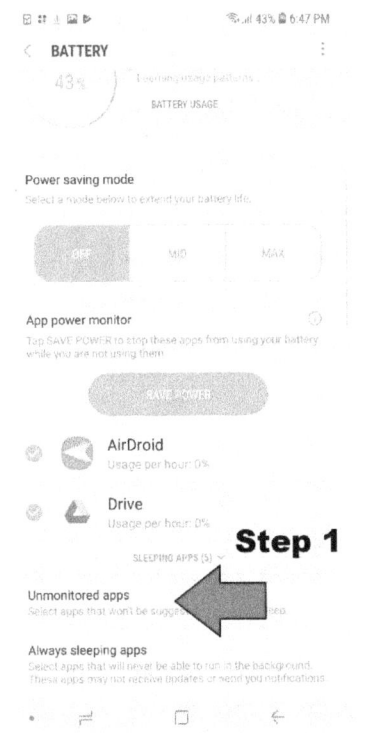
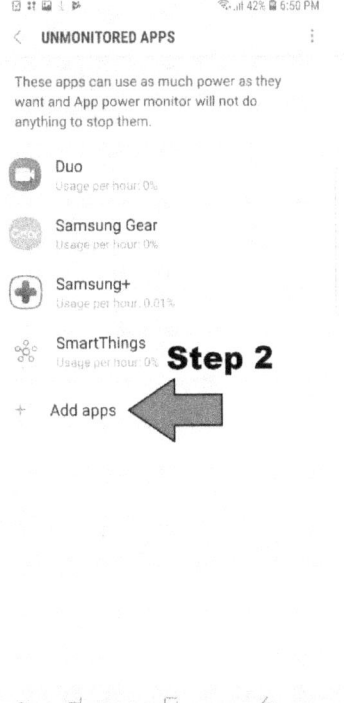

To remove an app from **Unmonitored apps** tab, swipe down from

the top of the screen and then tap **Settings** > **Device**
Maintenance > **Battery** > **Unmonitored apps.** Then tap and hold
the app(s) you want to delete. Tap **Delete** (located at the top of the
screen) to remove the app from Unmonitored apps tab. Note that the
app is not removed from your device, it is only removed from those
apps that have unrestricted access to your battery.

Warning: If your phone is water resistant, please note that it is not advisable to use the multipurpose port (charging port) while it is wet. If your phone has contact with water or any watery substance, please make sure you dry the multipurpose port before using it. Although some Android phones are water resistant, it is not advisable at all to charge them while they are wet. This may cause an electric shock or damage your device.

Using the Fast Charging Feature

Many recent Android phones are built with a battery charging technology that charges the battery faster by increasing the charging power. For some phones, this feature can allow you to charge the device up to 50% in about 40-50 minutes. Please refer to your device's owner or customer support to know if your device supports fast charging.

Please note that some Android phone manufacturers called fast charging different name, for example, Motorola called it Turbopower™.

To use fast charging feature, simply connect your phone to the power adapter that came with it.

Please note that using your phone while charging may affect the time your phone would take to make a complete charging cycle.

Please note that if your phone supports fast charging, you might not still be able to use this feature when you charge the battery using a standard battery/phone charger. To use "Fast Charging" on your device, you will need to connect it to a battery charger that supports fast charging like the one that came with your device. To know if a battery charger supports this feature, please refer to the manufacturer manual/information.

Tip: If you are using a Samsung phone, you can enable or disable

the fast charging settings by going to settings  > **Device**

Maintenance > Battery. Then tap on menu icon located at the top of the screen. Select **Advanced Settings > Fast cable charging**.

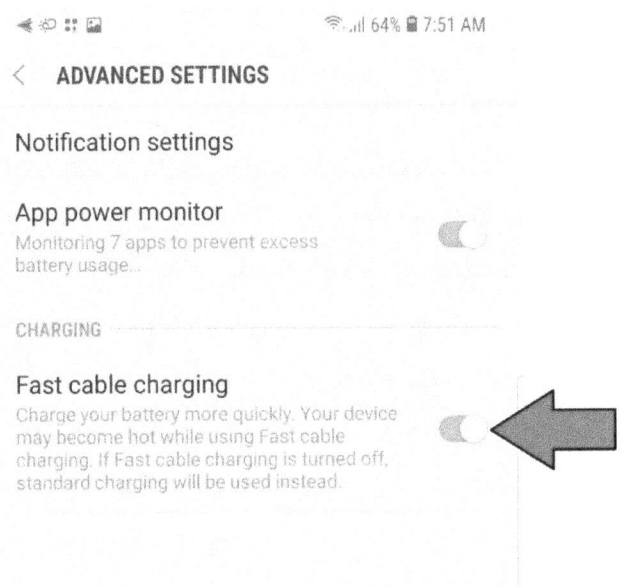

If you are not using a Samsung phone, you can try typing **Fast cable charging** into the search bar of your device's "Settings" and see if you can get the fast charging option(s).

Although the fast charging technology on Android phones is a cool feature, it may still be affected by factors like the temperature of the phone. If the device heats up for one reason or the other, the charging speed may decrease.

What About the Wireless Charging?

Some Android phones have a built-in wireless charging feature and this means that you can charge your device's battery using a wireless charger (usually sold separately). Please refer to your device's owner or customer support to know if your device supports wireless charging.

To charge your device wirelessly:

- Connect the power adapter that came with your wireless charger (sold separately) to the charging port on your wireless charger. Thereafter, plug it to a wall socket.

- If you are using your wireless charger for the first time, remove any protective nylon from the surface of the wireless charger. Then, place your mobile Android device on the wireless charger following the instructions provided by the manufacturer of the wireless charger.

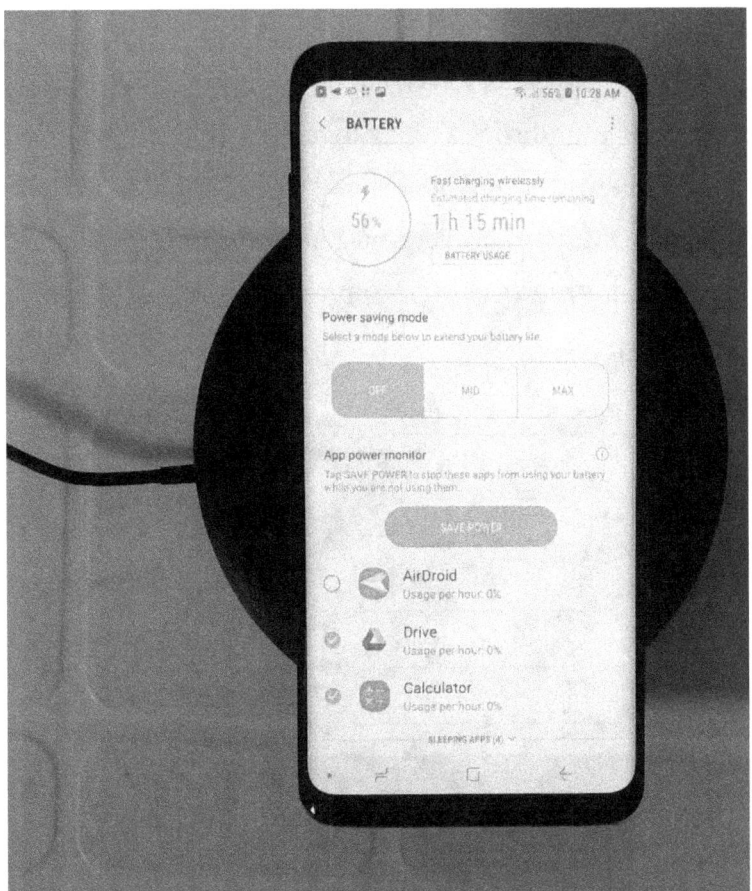

Depending on the type of the wireless charger/Android phone you are using, charging wirelessly may take a longer time when compared to using a cable. This means that if you want to charge your device faster, consider using a cable.

Inserting and Managing SD Card/SIM Card

Many Android phones support the use of external memory card.

To insert memory card or SIM Card:

1. Locate the SIM and SD Card tray on the top/side or bottom edge of your device and gently insert the eject tool usually included with your phone into the eject hole (located on the SIM/SD Card tray). Then push until the tray pops out. *Please note that you may need to apply small force before the tray pops out.*

2. Pull out the tray gently from the tray slot and place the SIM Card on its tray and the SD Card on its tray. Make sure the metallic contacts on the SIM and the SD Card are facing down. It is possible there are Android phones that require that their SIM cards face up, if this is your condition, please insert the SIM card facing up.

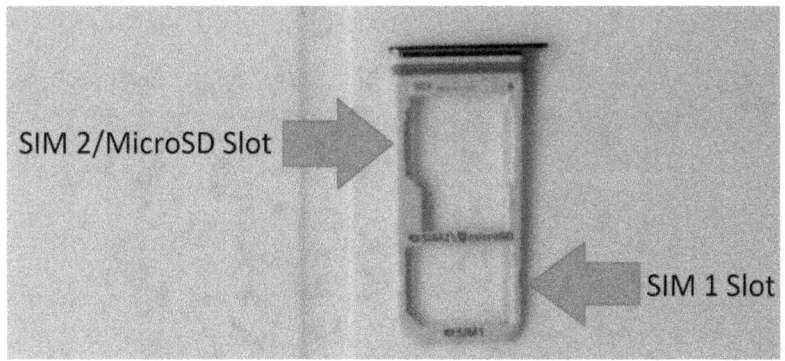

SIM 2/MicroSD Slot

SIM 1 Slot

3. Slide the card tray back into the slot.

4. Please note that if the SIM Card or the memory card is not inserted properly, your phone might not recognize it. Please endeavor to follow the instructions above to avoid this.

5. To locate the memory card after inserting it, swipe down from the top of the screen and then tap settings and tap "Storage" or "Storage & USB". Locate and tap the inserted SD card.

Note: If your Android Phone is water resistant, you may be tempted to drop it in water at one time or the other. Please make sure that you fully insert the card tray into the tray slot before dropping the phone inside water to prevent liquid from entering your device.

As a rule, you must always make sure you prevent water from entering the inner compartment of the phone. Therefore, please make sure you properly close any slot you have opened on your phone before inserting it into water.

Hint: When the memory card is properly installed, you should see the memory card icon on the status bar at the top of the screen.

To remove the SD Card:

It is important to unmount your SD card before removing it to avoid losing your files. To eject or unmount your SD card:

1. Swipe down from the top of the screen and select the settings

   icon ⚙ .

2. tap "Storage" or "Storage & USB".

3. Locate and tap the inserted SD card.

4. Tap **Unmount/Eject** ▲ next to the SD card.

If you are using a Samsung Android phone, try following the steps below to eject your memory card.

1. Swipe down from the top of the screen and select the settings icon .

2. Tap **Device Maintenance**

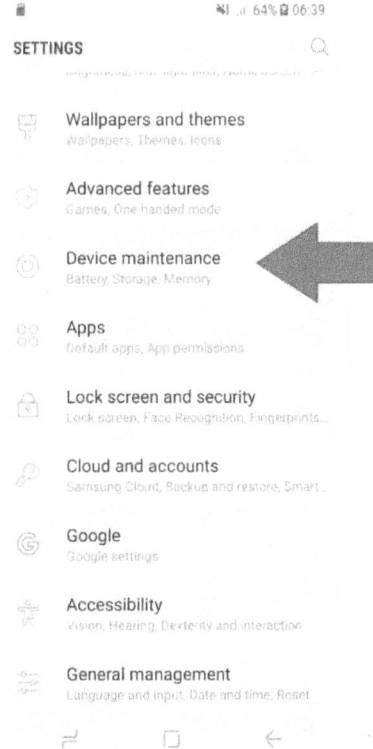

3. Tap **Storage.**

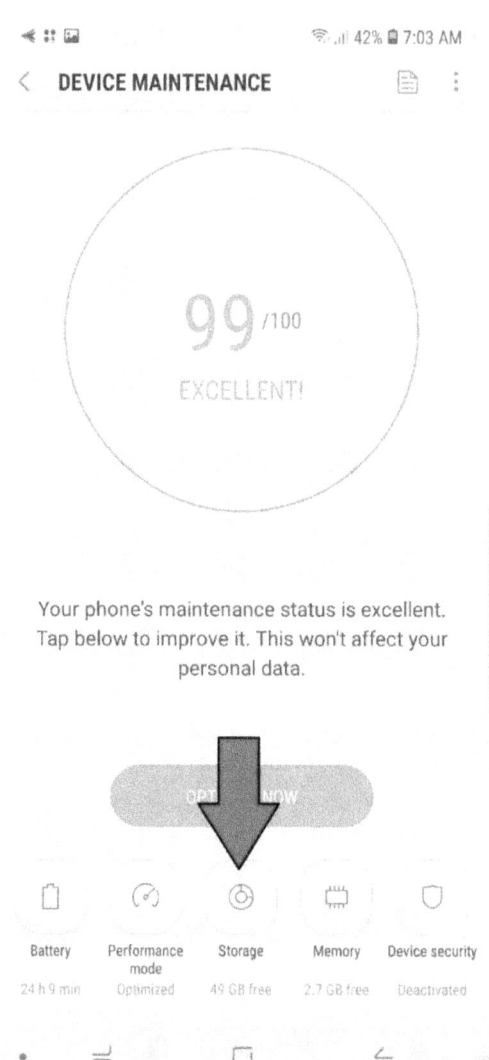

‹ **DEVICE MAINTENANCE**　　　🗎 ⋮

99 /100

EXCELLENT!

Your phone's maintenance status is excellent.
Tap below to improve it. This won't affect your
personal data.

OPTI　　NOW

Battery	Performance mode	Storage	Memory	Device security
24 h 9 min	Optimized	49 GB free	2.7 GB free	Deactivated

4. Tap the **menu icon** (the three dots icon located at the top of
the screen).

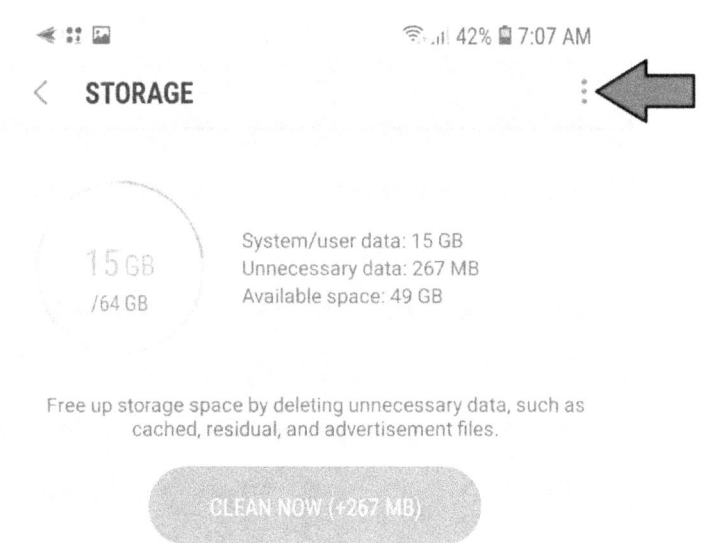

5. Tap **Storage settings**

6. Tap **Unmount icon** and gently open the SD Card slot using the ejection pin (as you have done above on page 20). Close the SD Card slot when you are done removing the memory card.

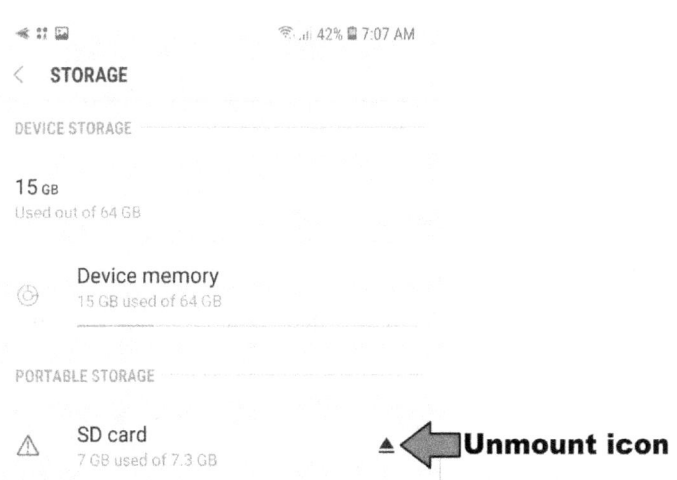

Please note that if you unmount the memory card without removing it from your device, you would need to mount it before it can be accessed again. To mount your memory card, follow the steps one to five above and then tap **Unmounted** and then select **Mount** when prompted.

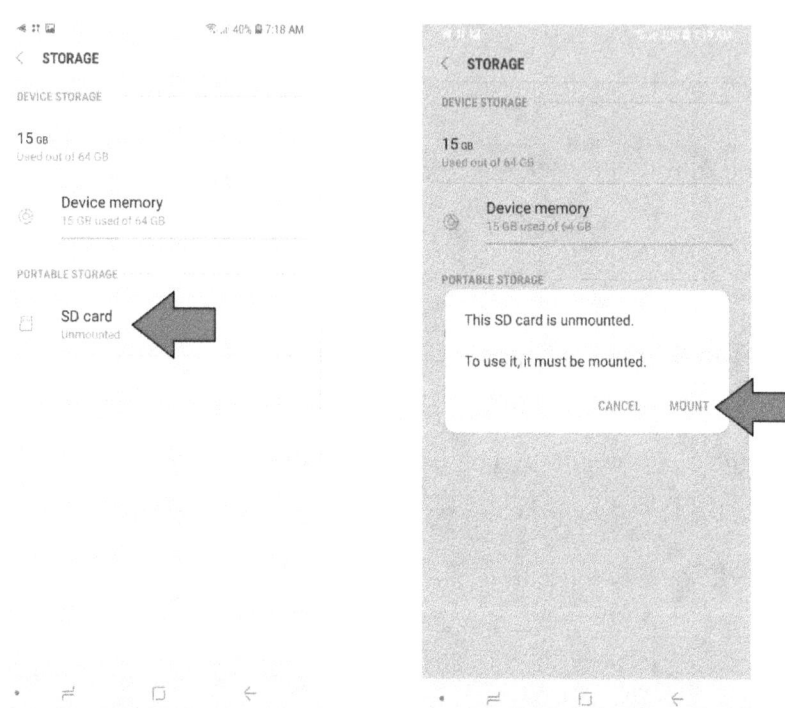

Formatting the memory card

To completely erase your memory card:

1. Swipe down from the top of the screen and select the settings

    icon ⚙ .

2. Tap **Storage & USB**. If you don't see "Storage & USB," tap **Storage**.

3. Tap the SD Card.

4. Tap the menu icon ⦙ usually located at the top of the screen and tap **Settings**.

5. Tap **Format** and then tap **Erase & format.**

Please note that formatting a memory card will cause you to lose all the files stored on the memory card and you may need to backup your files before initiating this process.

Tip: Some Motorola phones allow you to format a memory card as internal storage. This would allow you to use your memory card like the way you use your phone internal memory. To use a memory card as internal storage on a Motorolla phone, repeat step 1 to 4 above and select **Format as internal**.

If you are using a Samsung Android phone, try following the steps below to format your memory card.

a) Swipe down from the top of the screen and select the settings

icon  .

b) Tap **Device Maintenance**.

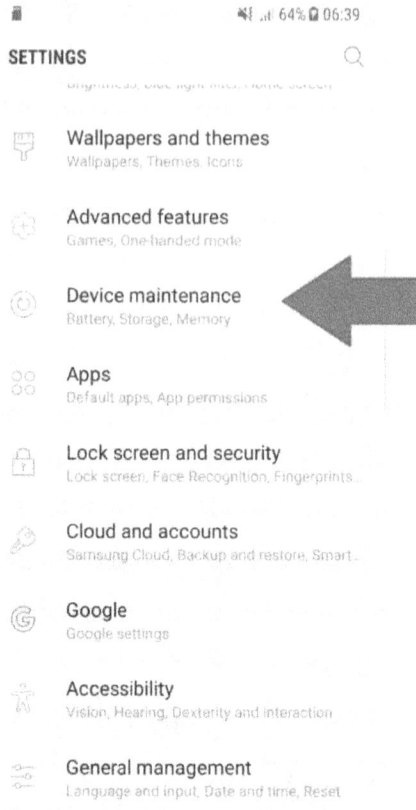

Wallpapers and themes
Wallpapers, Themes, Icons

Advanced features
Games, One-handed mode

Device maintenance
Battery, Storage, Memory

Apps
Default apps, App permissions

Lock screen and security
Lock screen, Face Recognition, Fingerprints

Cloud and accounts
Samsung Cloud, Backup and restore, Smart

Google
Google settings

Accessibility
Vision, Hearing, Dexterity and interaction

General management
Language and input, Date and time, Reset

c) Tap **Storage.**

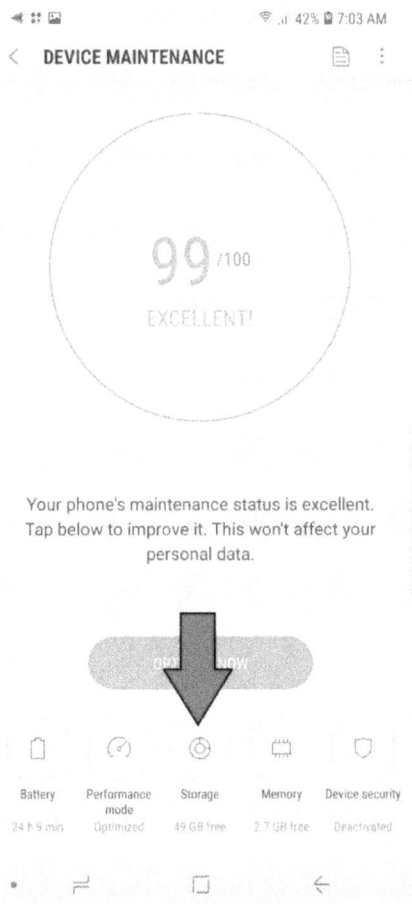

d) Tap the **menu icon** (the three dots icon located at the top of the screen)**.**

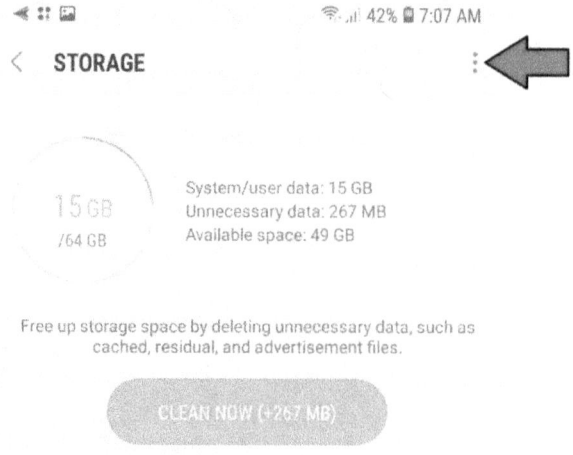

e) Then select **Storage settings**.

f) Tap **SD card**. (Please make sure you are tapping SD card and not the unmount icon next to it).

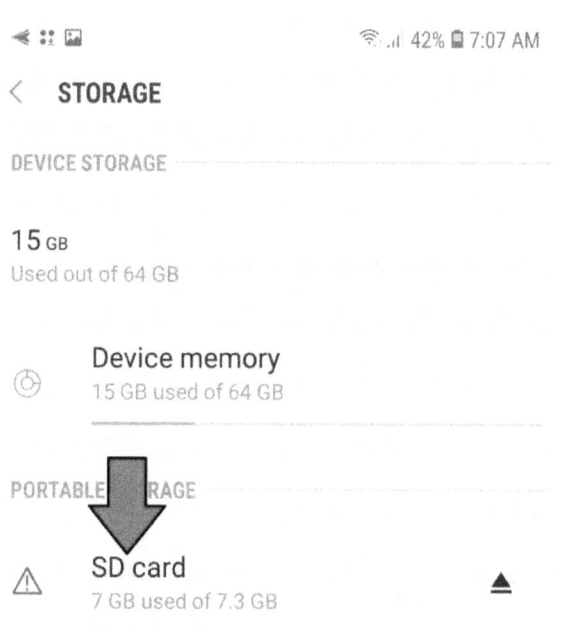

g) Tap **Format**, read the onscreen information and then tap **Format**.

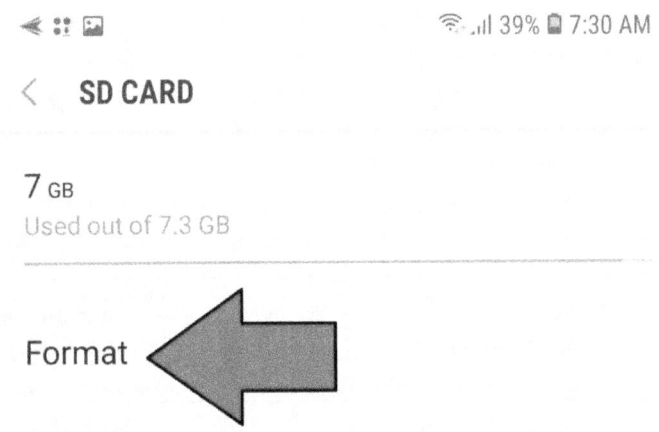

Please note that formatting a memory card will cause you to lose all the files stored on the memory card and you may need to backup your files before initiating this process.

To transfer apps from internal storage to SD Card:

1. Swipe down from the top of the screen and tap settings ⚙ .

2. Tap **Apps**.

3. Tap the app you want to transfer.

4. Select **Storage** from the options that appear.

5. Next to the name of the app you want to transfer or under "Storage used", tap **Change**.

Please note that this option may not be available for all apps. In fact, I have noticed that the "change" option is not available for most of apps that came with the phone.

6. Tap **SD card**.

7. Tap **Move** and follow the onscreen instructions to complete the transfer process.

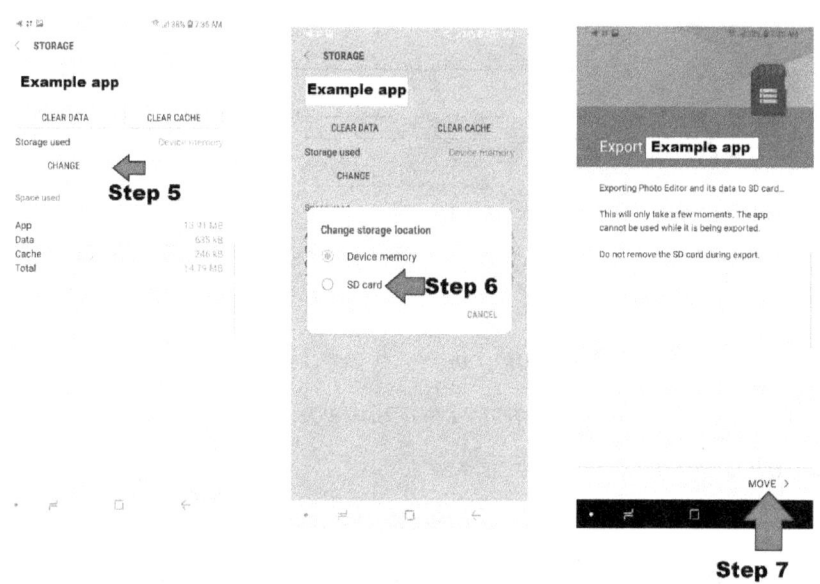

To transfer files from internal storage to SD Card:

1. Swipe down from the top of the screen and select the settings icon ⚙ .

2. Tap **Storage & USB**. If you don't see "Storage & USB," tap **Storage**.

3. Tap **Internal storage**.

4. Select the file category you want to move.

5. Touch and hold the file you want to move to select it.

6. Tap the menu icon ⋮ and select "Copy to…"

7. Tap the SD Card and follow the prompts.

For some Sony Andriod phones, you can transfer files from internal storage to SD card by performing these actions:

- Swipe down from the top of the screen and select the settings

  icon ⚙ .

- Tap **Storage**.

- Tap **Transfer data to SD card**.

- Select the files you want to transfer.

- Tap **Transfer** and follow the prompts.

Tip: You may consider removing temporary files from your device or clear the cache memory for all applications to free up space.

Swipe down from the top of the screen and tap settings ⚙ > "Storage & USB" or "Storage" > "Free Up Space" or "Clean Now". If you are using a Samsung Android phone, try following the steps below to remove temporary files. From the home screen, swipe up from the bottom of the screen and tap **Settings** ⚙ > **Device Maintenance**. Tap **Storage** and tap **Clean Now**.

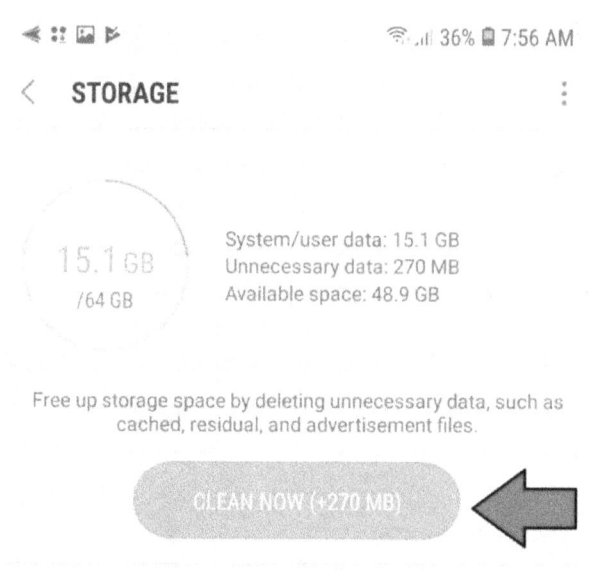

Please note that using this method may clear cached data for all apps. In a layman language, a cached data is an information stored by an app on your device to serve you faster.

If your phone is hanging or misbehaving, consider cleaning the memory. You can clean the memory of some Android phones by following the steps mentioned above.

On the other hand, if you are using a Samsung Android phone, you may follow the steps below to clean your memory.

From the home screen, swipe up from the bottom of the screen and tap **Settings** > **Device Maintenance**. Tap **Memory** and tap **Clean Now.**

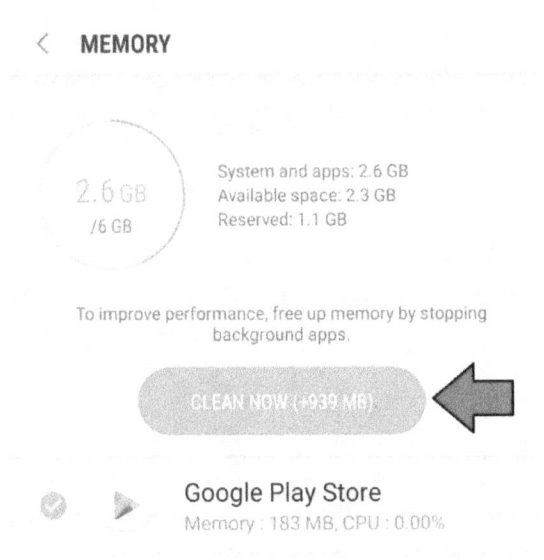

System and apps: 2.6 GB
Available space: 2.3 GB
Reserved: 1.1 GB

To improve performance, free up memory by stopping background apps.

CLEAN NOW (+939 MB)

Google Play Store
Memory : 183 MB, CPU : 0.00%

Maintaining the Water and Dust Resistance

If your Android phone is water and dust resistant, there are few things you have to put at the back of your mind so that you don't spoil your phone. Some of the things you have to know are discussed below:

- Many "water resistant Android phones" have IP68 rating and this means that you can't immerse the device in water deeper than 1.5 m and/or keep it submerged for more than 30 minutes.

- The screen of your "water resistant Android phone" may not respond properly while under water or when wet. I would advice that you clean it with a dry towel to get the full functionality.

- It is not advisable to put your "water resistant Android phone" under water moving with force such as tap water. This is because water may get into the inner part of your device in the process.

- While the Android phone's screen is wet, you may not enjoy the optimal function of your device as you should. Clean it with a dry towel to make it work properly.

- To avoid electric shock, please don't charge your "water resistant Android phone" while it is wet or while it is under water.

- Avoid putting your "water resistant Android phone" in a liquid other than water. In addition, avoid putting your phone inside salt water or ionized water.

Note: Don't forget that it is not advisable to drop your "water resistant Android phone" inside water while the SIM/memory slot is opened. In addition, please don't charge your phone while it is wet or under water to avoid electric shock.

Moving Your Items from Your Old Phone to Your Android Phone

You can move your files to your new phone by following the step(s) mentioned below:

1. For many recent Android phones, you will have the options to copy items from your old phone to the new phone during the setup. All you need to do in a situation like this is to simply follow the onscreen instructions during the setup. If you skip the data transfer during the phone setup and you want to return to it, go to the phone settings and tap "Finish setup" (usually located at the bottom of the screen).

2. If using a Samsung Android phone, you can transfer items from your old phone (Android Phone or IOS Phone) to your new Samsung Android phone using USB connector (On-the-Go (OTG) connector) and a USB cable. To use this method, please follow the instructions below:

Please make sure you download and install Smart Switch app on your old phone before you begin the transfer process. Smart Switch can be downloaded from Google Play store. In addition, this method of data transfer consumes large amount of energy, make sure your phone is fully charged before initiating this process.

To transfer content via cable:

- Plug the USB connector (On-the-Go (OTG) connector) that came with your device into the multipurpose jack of your device.

 **OTG Connector**

- Then connect your device and the old phone using a USB cable. Please note that you are to select Media device (MTP) option on your old phone if prompted. The whole connection will look like this (see below). *Please note that you may need to download, install and open Samsung Smart Switch Mobile on your old phone to complete this process.* **Samsung Smart Switch Mobile** app can be downloaded from Google Play store.

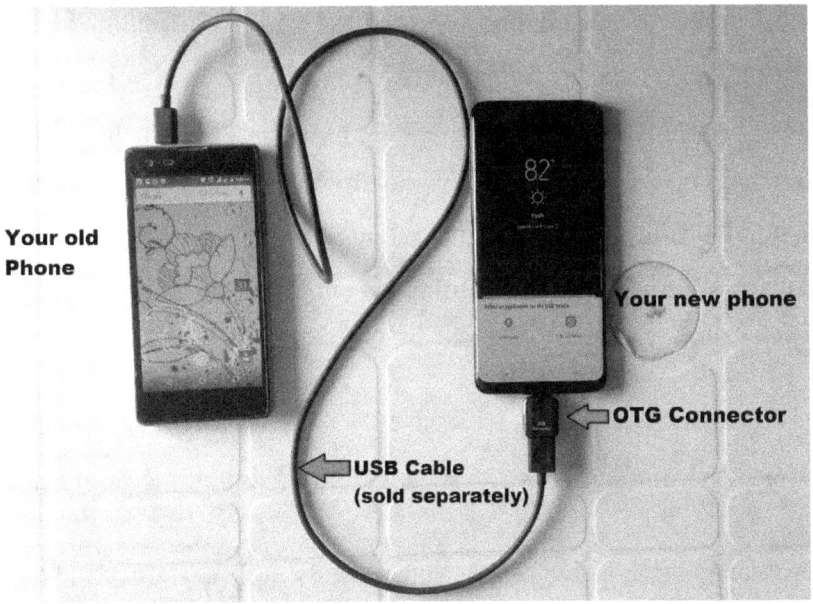

Your old Phone

Your new phone

OTG Connector

USB Cable (sold separately)

- When prompted, tap **Smart Switch** and then select **Just Once**. If you are not prompted, disconnect the cable, then reconnect.

- Tap **Start**.

- Tap **Agree** if you agree with the terms/conditions.

- Read the onscreen information and tap **OK** if you agree with the information.

- On the old phone, open **Samsung Smart Switch Mobile** app and follow the prompts.

- Tap **Receive** on your Samsung Android Phone.

- Your device will recognize the old phone and a list of data you can transfer would appear. Select what you want to transfer and tap **Transfer.**

- Follow the on-screen instructions to complete the data transfer process.

Alternatively, if USB connector and the USB cable are not accessible, you can send items from your old phone to your new Samsung Android phone wirelessly using Smart Switch app. Please note that you will need to download and install **Samsung Smart Switch Mobile** app on your old phone to complete this process. **Samsung Smart Switch Mobile** app can be downloaded from Google Play store.

To transfer content wirelessly:

- On your device, swipe down from the top of the screen and

  tap settings icon , tap **Clouds and Accounts** and then tap **Smart Switch**. Thereafter, tap **Start > Agree > OK > Wireless > Receive > Android**.

- Open the **Smart Switch** app on your old phone.

- Tap **Start** and tap **Agree**.

- Tap **Wireless.** Then the Smart Switch app should try to establish connection. If prompted, tap **Accept.**

- On your old phone, select those items you want to transfer, and tap **Send**.

- Follow the on-screen instructions on both your Samsung phone and the old phone to complete the transfer process.

- When the transfer process is complete, tap **Close App**.

3. I would like to mention that you can also transfer items from your old phone to your new Android device using memory card. All you have to do is to insert a memory card into your old phone, transfer your content to the memory card, remove the memory card and then place it inside your Android phone.

4. If you have backed up your data to Google cloud, you can transfer the backups to the new Android phone by simply signing into your Google account using the new Android phone.

5. Lastly, you can transfer your items from your old phone to your new phone by using cloud storage. For example, you can use OneDrive app. To do this, add files to OneDrive app on your old phone so that you can access them from your Android phone. To move a file to OneDrive, just drag and drop or send the files to your OneDrive folder. The files will be uploaded to OneDrive when you have an internet connection on that device.

Once the files are on your OneDrive, you can access them on your Android phone by opening OneDrive app. To avoid any problem while trying to access your files, please ensure that you are connected to a browsing network while trying to access OneDrive. Please note that you may need to download OneDrive app to your phones to use this method.

Using the Touch Screen

Your Android phone's touch screen allows you to easily select items and perform functions. With the touch screen, you may operate your phone like a pro.

Notes:

- Do not press the touch screen with your fingertips, or use sharp tools on the touch screen. Doing so may cause malfunctioning.

- Do not allow the touch screen to come into contact with other electrical appliances. This may cause the touch screen to malfunction.

- When the touch screen is wet, endeavor to clean it with a dry towel before using it. The touch screen may not function properly when wet.

- For optimal use of the screen, you may need to remove screen protector before using it. However, a good screen protector should be usable with your Android phone.

You may control your touch screen with the following actions:

Tap: Touch once with your finger to select or launch a menu, application or option.

Tap and hold: Tap an item and hold it for more than a second to open a list of options. In addition, you can tap and hold the touchscreen to activate the selection mode to select multiple items in a list.

Tap and drag: Tap, hold and drag with your finger, to move an item to a different location in the application grid/list.

Pinch: Place two fingers far apart, and then draw them closer together.

Swiping/Scrolling: Swipe or scroll to see other parts of the touch screen.

Flicking: This happens when you quickly swipe the screen. For example, you can dismiss a notification by flicking the screen. To do this, swipe down from the top of the screen and flick the notification you want to dismiss.

Hint: If you are using an Android phone with a screen protector, you may consider increasing the touch sensitivity of your phone for optimum usage. To do this on compatible phones, swipe up from the bottom of the screen and tap **Settings** > **Advanced Features** > **Touch sensitivity.** Then tap the indicator switch next to **Touch sensitivity**. If the instruction above does not work for you, you may search for "Touch sensitivity" using the search bar on settings screen.

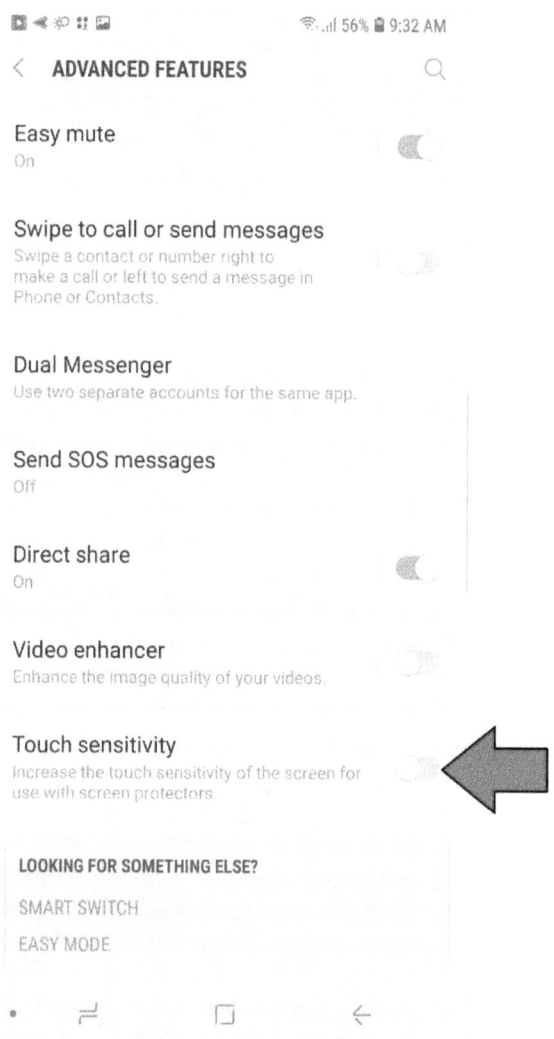

Tip: Some Android phones allow you to control the screen with just one hand when you enable one-handed mode. To enable this mode:

1. Swipe down from the top of the screen and tap settings icon

.

2. Tap "Display".

3. Tap "One Handed Mode".

If you don't see "One Handed Mode" using the method above, you can try searching for the phrase "one handed mode" using the search bar on the settings tab.

> **To Lock or Unlock the touch screen**

When you do not use the device for a specified period, your device turns off the touch screen and automatically locks it. This is to prevent any unwanted device operations and save battery. To manually lock the touch screen, press the power key.

To unlock, turn on the screen by pressing the power key (or double tap the home button for supported Android phones) and then swipe in any (or required) direction. If you have already set a lock screen password, you will be prompted to enter the password instead of swiping.

Note: You can change the lock screen method on your phone, please refer to page 136 to learn how to do this.

Rotating the touch screen

Andriod phones have a built-in motion sensor that detects its orientation. If you rotate the device, the screen should automatically rotate according to the orientation.

➢ To activate or deactivate screen rotation

To quickly disable or enable screen rotation, swipe down from the top of the screen and tap 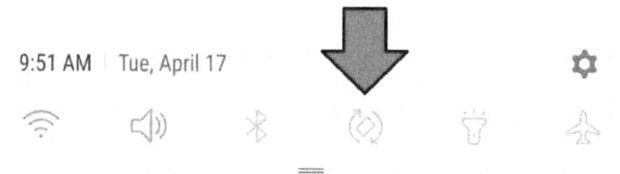. Please note that when the screen rotation icon appears grey (or light colored), then screen rotation is disabled.

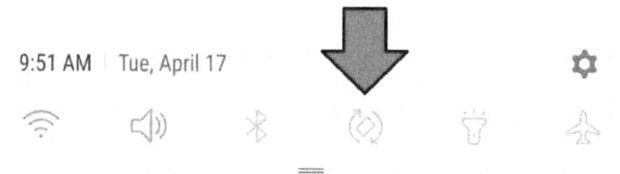

Using the Dedicated Back Button

You may use the dedicated back button (see the picture below) to view the previous page or go back to a previous menu. Back button can also be used to close a dialog box, menu, or keyboard.
In addition, you may use the dedicated back button on your device to get out of any page when you are done with the page and you don't see the done option.

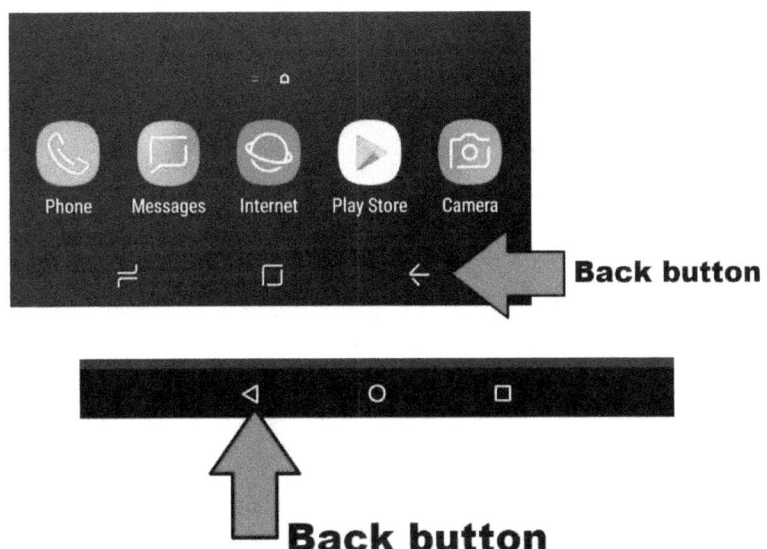

Back button

Back button

Hint: Back button is one of the components of the navigation bar. To learn how to manage navigation bar like a pro, please go to page 98.

Using the In-APP Back Button

There are some apps that give you the opportunity to go back to the previous screen using the in-app back button ⟨ or ← . When available, this button can be found at the upper left part of the screen.

In-App Back Button

✖ .ıl 100% 📱 15:10

‹ ACCESSIBILITY   Q

CATEGORIES

Vision

Hearing

Dexterity and interaction

MORE SETTINGS

Text-to-speech

In-App Back Button

Getting to Know the Menu Icon

The menu icon is the three dots icon ⋮ that usually appears at the top of the screen when you open an app. This icon can also be called **hidden options icon**. This is because it contains more options about an app or item.

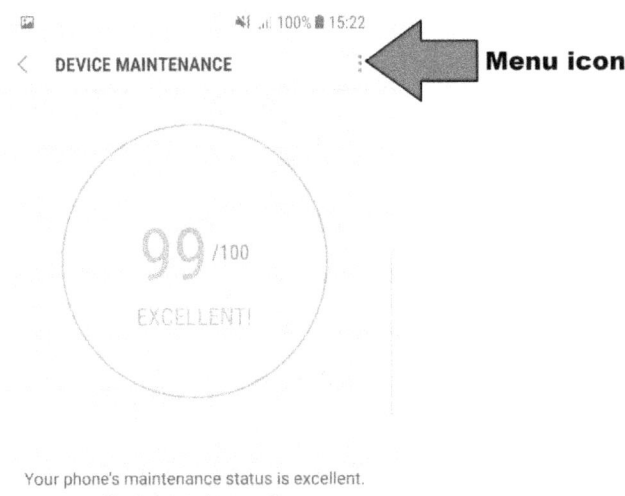

Your phone's maintenance status is excellent.
Tap below to improve it.

Hint: Whenever you are thinking of accessing more options when using an app/item, or you are thinking of using an app in a new way, just tap on the menu icon.

Special Information for LG Android Phone Users

Some LG Android phones using Android 8.0 have many of their settings options under **General** tab. Settings like Apps & Notifications, Accessibility, Lock screen & Security among others can be found under **General** tab. I would advise that you check "General" tab whenever you don't see a setting. Alternatively, you can use the search bar located at the top of the screen on the settings page to find what you are looking for.

Getting to Know and Use the Home Screen

From your home screen, you can view your phone's status and access applications. Scroll left or right to see different apps on the home screen. Please note that the home screen usually has many screens and you can add more screens to it by tapping on +. More on this shortly.

Home Screen Layout:

Because of the differences that exist among Android phones, the home screen on your Android phone may be slightly different from what is shown here. Nevertheless, I believe the information provided below should be of help in managing your home screen.

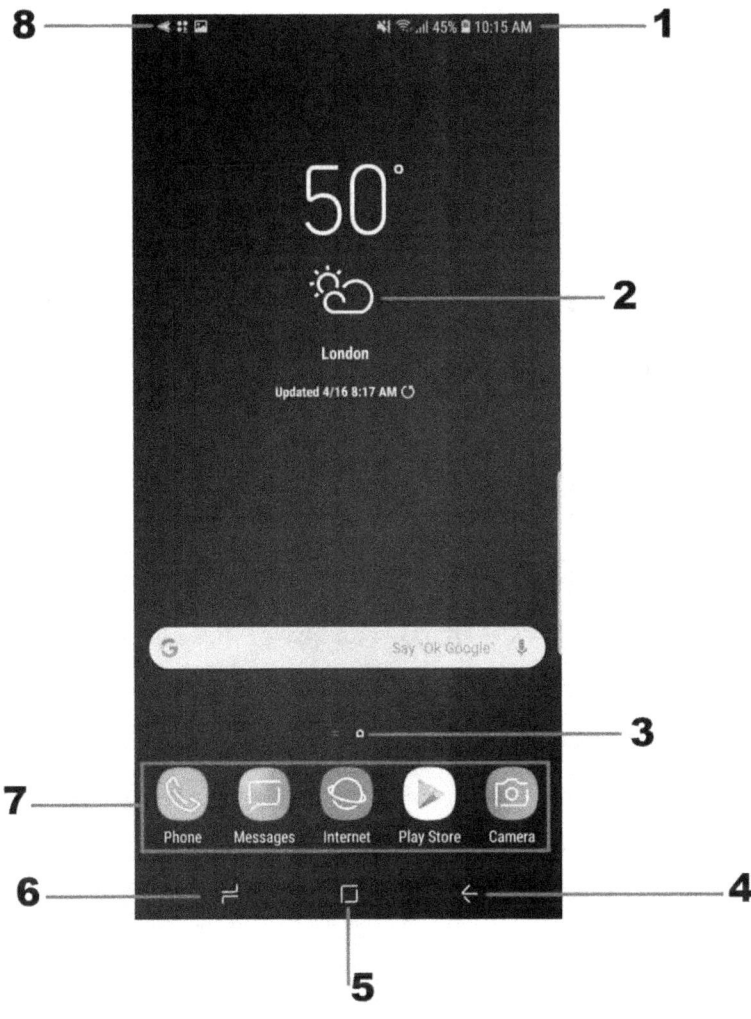

Number	Function
1.	**Status icons**: These icons tell you more about your device. For example, if the Wi-Fi is turned on, you would see the Wi-Fi status icon on this part of the screen. *This part of the screen is also called status bar.*

2.	**Weather widget**: This widget may not be visible if you have not allowed it, to make weather widget visible, while on the home screen, tap and hold the screen and select **Widgets.** Swipe the screen until you see **Weather** and tap it. Then tap and hold **Weather** widget and move it to the desired home screen.
3.	**Home Screen Indicator:** This indicates which home screen is currently visible
4.	**Back Button**.
5.	**Home Button**
6.	**Recent App button**
7.	**App shortcuts**: Tap any of these icons to launch the corresponding app.
8.	**Notification icon**: When you see a notification icon appearing at the top left part of the screen, simply swipe down from the top of the screen to learn more about this notification icon.

Managing the Home Screen

To get more out of the home screen, you will need to perform some tweaks. To customize the home screen to your taste:

- While on the home screen, tap and hold an empty space on the home screen or place your two fingers on the screen and then move them closer. To go to the home screen from any screen, press the home button or .

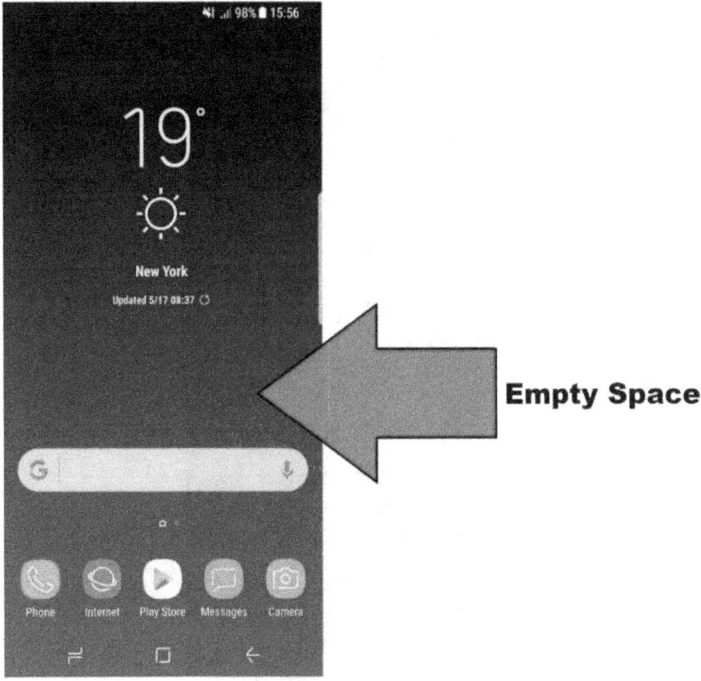

Empty Space

- Then you would see a screen that looks like the one below.

- You can perform any of the following actions:
  - **Add a screen**: To do this, swipe right or left until you see the plus/Add **(+)** icon. Tap this icon to add a new screen.

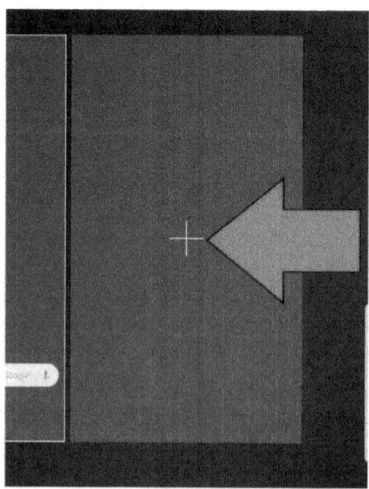

In addition, you can add app icons to a home screen. To do this, tap and hold an app icon on the applications screen and then drag it to the home screen you want. Lift your finger. Alternatively, tap and hold an app icon on the applications screen and select **Add to Home**. This second option may not be available on your phone. If this is the case, use the first option.

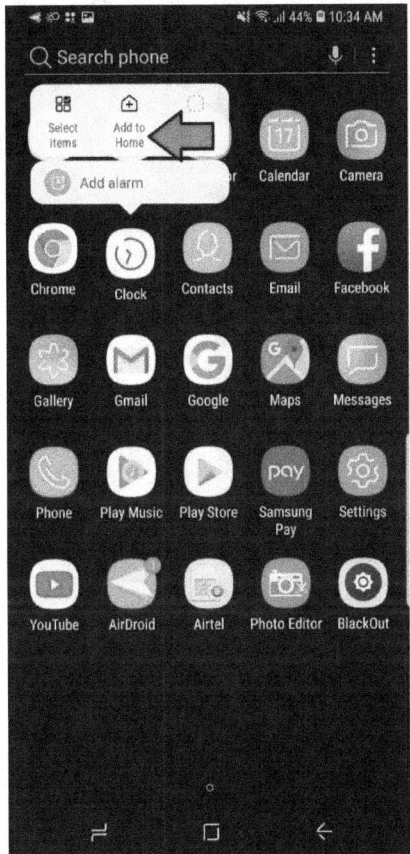

To move an app icon from one home screen to another, tap, hold and drag the app icon to the edge of the screen and wait

for the screen to turn. Do this until you get to the desired
screen and then lift your finger.

Tap and hold the app icon you want
to move, then move it to the right
edge or left edge of the screen
until the page turns. When the app icon
is in right position, lift your finger.

○ **Remove a screen/pane**: To do this, swipe left or right
until you see the home screen you want to remove. Then
tap the Delete icon 🗑 or "**X**" located on top of the
screen/pane you want to delete.

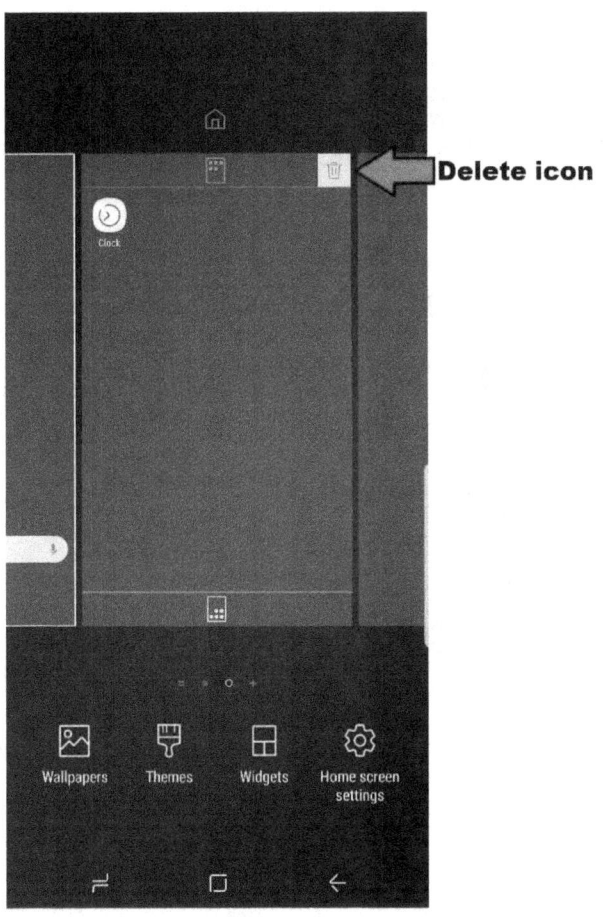

Delete icon

o **Change the order of the home screens:** To do this, tap and hold a screen and drag it to the edge of the screen until the page turns. When the home screen is in the right position, lift your finger.

Tap and hold the screen you want to move, then move it to the right edge or left edge of the screen until the page turns. When the screen is in right position lift your finger.

To easily access a home screen, you may consider setting it as your **main** home screen. Please see below.

o **Set a screen as the main home screen:** To do this, swipe left or right until the screen you want to set as the main home screen is visible. Then tap the **Home button** located at the top of the screen. When a screen is your main home screen, the home screen button appears bold.

Tip: To access the home screen at any point in time, press the dedicated home button ⬜ or ⚫.

Hint: To move out of a setting when you are done, tap the back button.

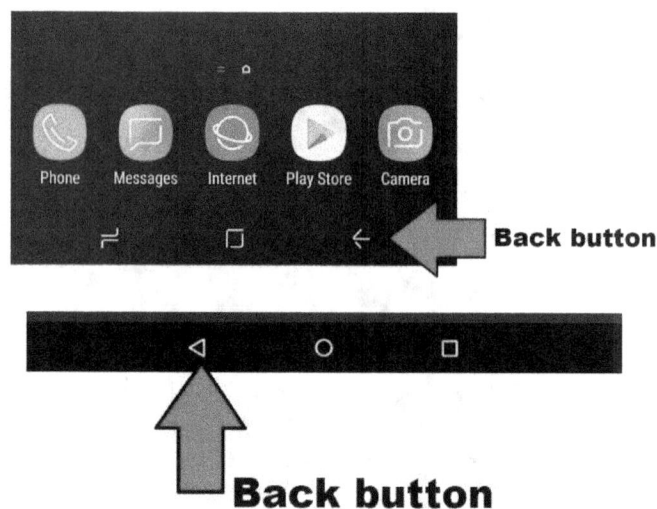

Back button

Back button

Suggestion: Do you want to increase or decrease the number of apps that appear in a row on the home screen? If yes, go to page 74 to learn more.

Add/Remove an app shortcut to the home screen

You can add apps/items to the home screen so that you can easily access them anytime.

To do this:

1. Access the app screen by swiping up the screen while on the home screen. Alternatively, tap the all app icon to access the app screen.

2. While on the app screen, tap and hold an app icon, and then select **Add to Home**.

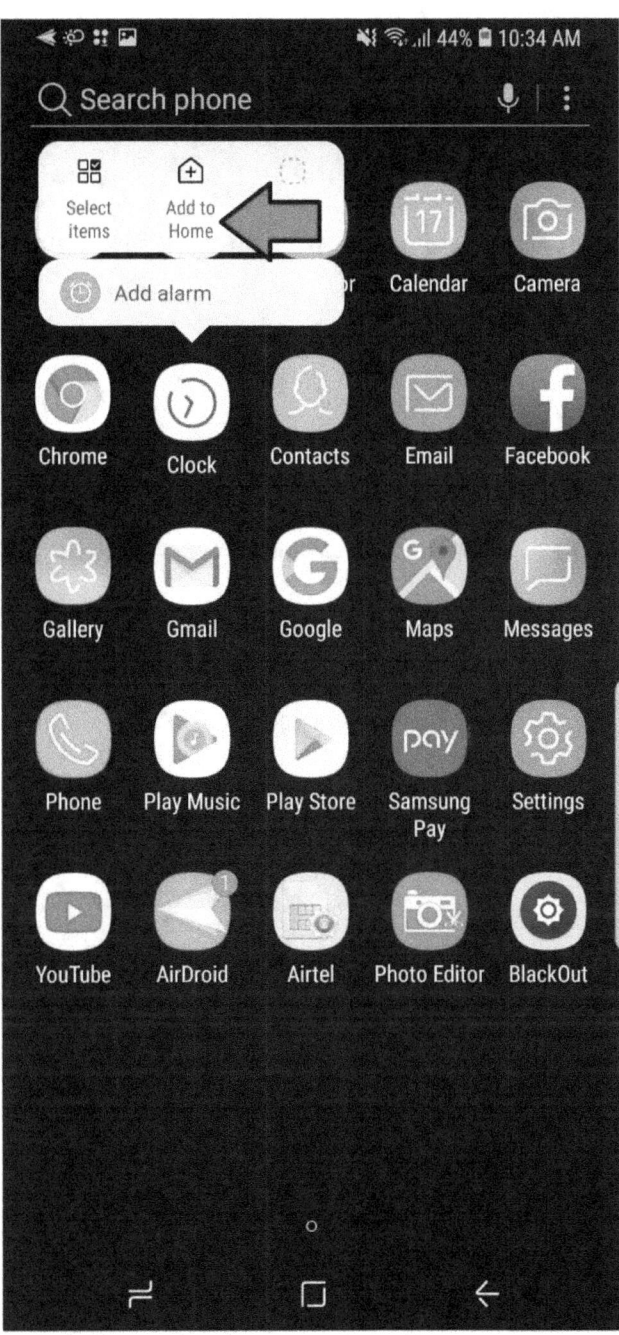

If this option is not available on your Android phone; tap, hold and drag the app you want to add to the top of the screen. You will then see images of each home screen. Move the app to the home screen of your choice. Lift your finger.

3. To move an app icon to a new location on the home screen, simply tap, hold and drag it to that location.

4. To remove an app icon from the home screen, tap and hold the app icon you want to remove and then select **Remove from Home**.

If this option is not available on your phone, tap and hold the app you want to remove. Then drag it up to "**X Remove**". Please note that removing an app icon from the home screen does not uninstall the app (unless you select uninstall), it merely removes it from the home screen.

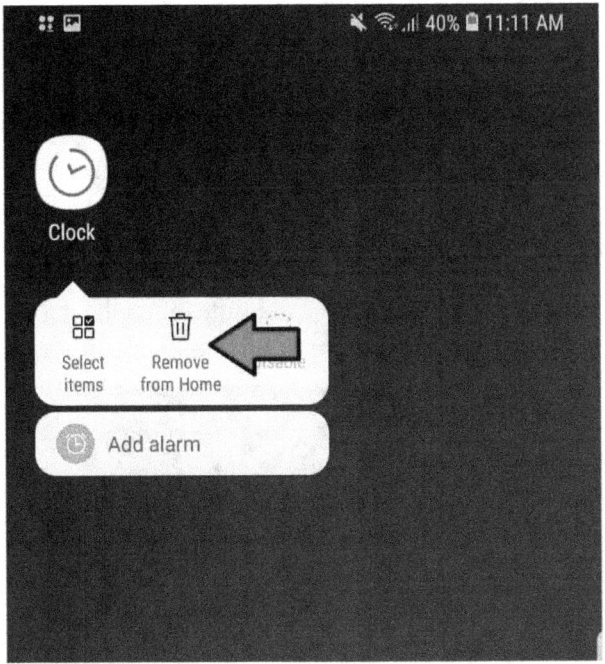

Tip: On supported Android phones, you can add an app shortcut to the home screen instead of adding the whole app. For example, in the picture shown above, you can add an "alarm" shortcut instead of adding "Clock". To add/remove an app's shortcut, follow step 1-4 above, but choose the shortcut you want to add instead of the app. Note, if you tap and hold an app and you don't see any shortcut list being displayed to you, then the chosen app does not have a shortcut.

Managing the home screen widget

Widget is a small item that allows you to control an app in a special way. Widgets display information and invite the user to act in special ways.

To add a widget to a home screen:

1. While on the home screen, tap and hold an empty space on the home screen or place your two fingers on the screen and then move them closer. To go to the home screen from any screen, press the home button  or .

2. Tap on **Widgets** located at the bottom of the screen.

3. Swipe left or right to see the available widgets and select the one you like. Tap and hold a widget from the list of the widgets that appear, drag it to a home screen and release it.

4. To move a widget to a new location, tap, hold and drag the widget to the desired location. Tap outside the widget to save the changes. To move a widget to another home screen, tap and hold the widget and drag it to the edge of the screen until the page turns. When the widget is on the right home screen, lift your finger.

5. To remove a widget from the home screen, tap and hold the widget and then select **Remove from Home screen**. Alternatively, tap and hold the widget and drag it up to "X Remove" or "Remove from the home screen".

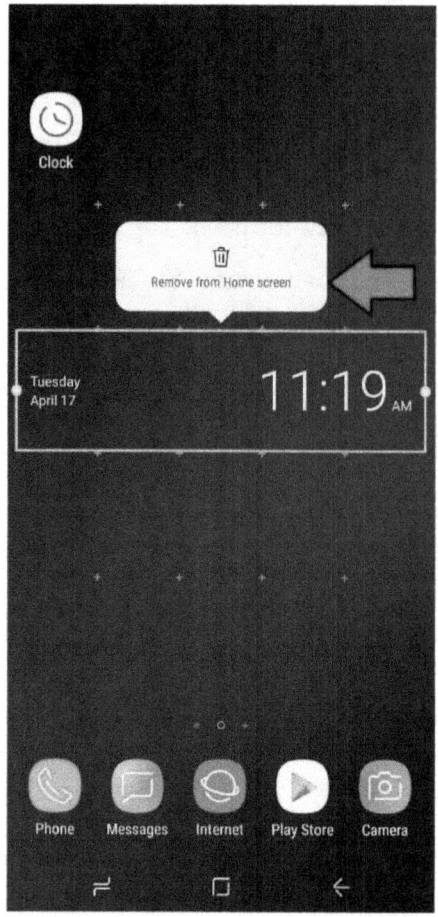

6. To resize a resizable widget, touch and hold, then release the widget. Then drag the dots that appear on the rectangular outline. Tap outside of the widget to save the changes. *Please note that you may not be able to resize all widgets.*

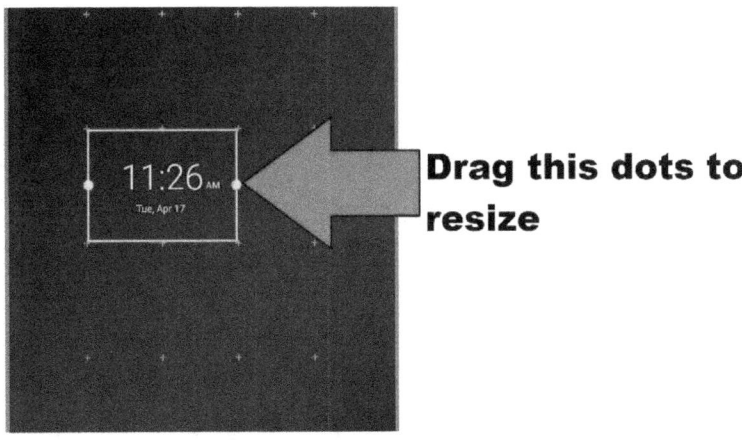

Drag this dots to resize

In addition, please note that you may not be able to adjust the size of some widgets vertically.

Managing the home screen theme

1. While on the home screen, tap and hold an empty space on the home screen or place your two fingers on the screen and then move them closer. To go to the home screen from any screen, press the home button ⬜ or ⚫.

2. Tap **Theme** located at the lower side of the screen and follow the prompts.

3. Choose a theme. *Please note that you may need to agree to Terms and Conditions before you can access themes.*

4. To search for themes, tap the search icon $\mathcal{Q}$ located at the top of the screen. Type a search phrase and hit the search icon $\mathcal{Q}$ on the virtual keyboard.

5. When you have seen the theme you like, tap the theme, and tap **Install/Download**.

6. Wait for the theme to finish downloading and tap **Apply** (See below). If you are taken to Google Play store to download your chosen theme, tap the back button until you see the theme screen.

7. To change the theme to the default one, open themes as described in steps 1 and 2 above. Then tap the default theme and tap **Apply**.

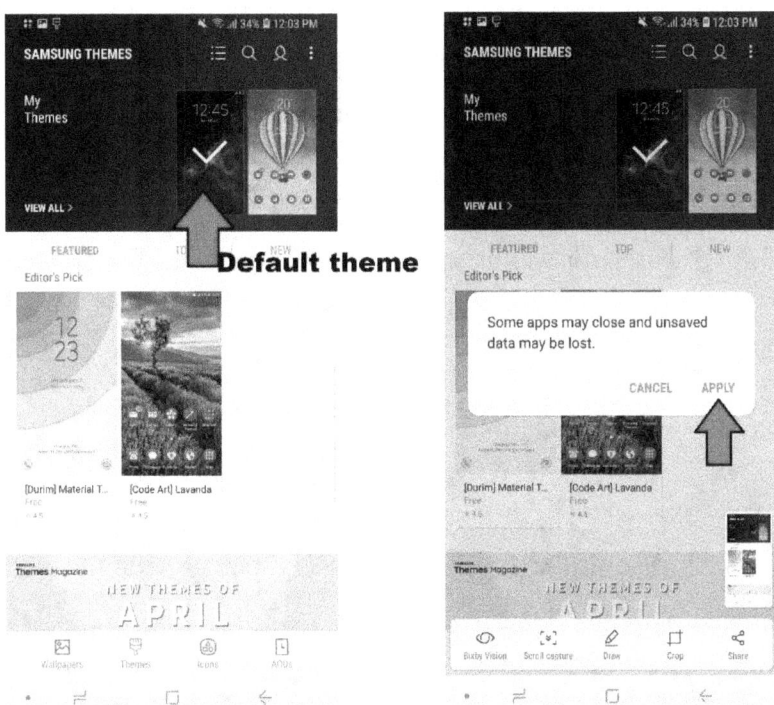

Please note that visual elements such as colors, icons, and wallpapers, may change depending on the selected theme.

Managing the home screen wallpaper

This option allows you to change the wallpaper settings for the home screen and the locked screen.

1. While on the home screen, tap and hold an empty space on the home screen or place your two fingers on the screen and

then move them closer. To go to the home screen from any

screen, press the home button  or .

2. Tap on **Wallpapers**.

3. To search for wallpapers, tap the search icon located at the top of the screen. Type a search phrase and hit the search icon on the virtual keyboard. *Please note that the search feature may not be available on some Android phones.*

4. Choose a wallpaper and if necessary, tap **Download** and then tap **Apply**.

5. Choose whether you want the wallpaper to appear on the **home screen, lock screen, or home and lock screens**.

Some phones give you the opportunity to add motion effect to your wallpaper. If your phone supports this feature, tick **Motion Effect** to give your wallpaper a motion effect.

Please note that "motion effect" may not be available if you choose "lock screen" in step 5 above.

6. Tap **Set as Wallpaper**.

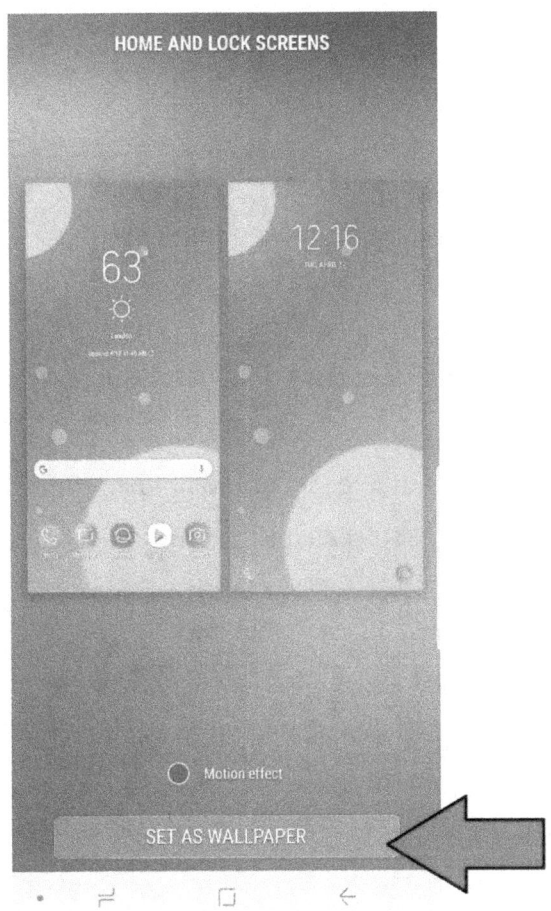

Please note that you may be prompted while trying to apply a wallpaper, just read the information shown to you and agree if you like.

To change wallpaper on Sony Android phones:

1. Repeat steps 1 and 2 above.

2. Tap "Lock screen" or "Home screen." Please omit this step 2 if you want to choose the same wallpaper for both lock screen and home screen.

3. Choose a wallpaper for your chosen screen and tap "Select" and then "Apply".

What about the screen grid?

The screen grid option allows you to choose the number of app icons that is displayed in a row on your home screen.

1. While on the home screen, tap and hold an empty space on the home screen or place your two fingers on the screen and then move them closer. To go to the home screen from any screen, press the home button or .

2. If you see "Grid," tap it. If not, tap "Home screen settings" or "Settings" located at the lower part of the screen and then tap "Home screen grid" or "Grid".

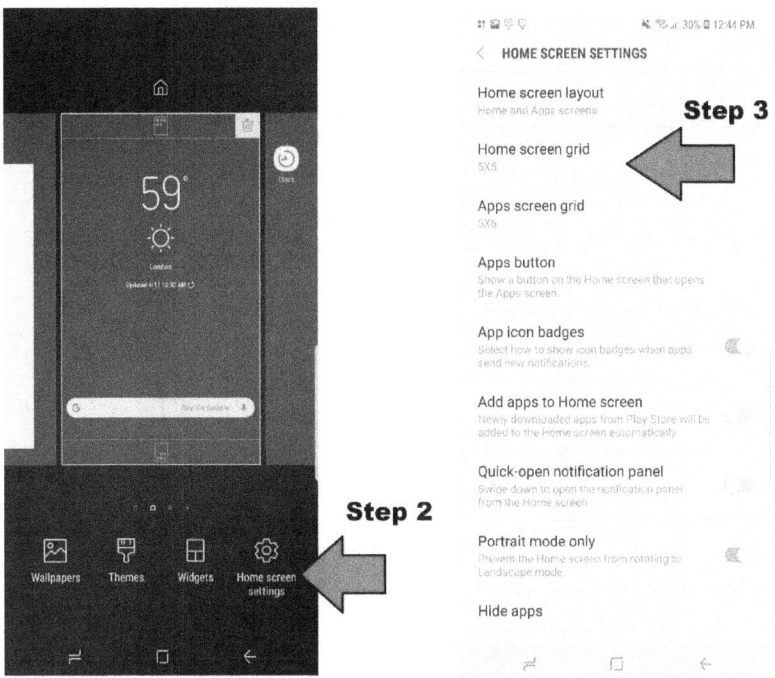

3. Choose a dimension. For Samsung Android phones, 4x5 means there are four apps in a row and five apps in a column; 4x6 means there are four apps in a row and six apps in a column; 5x5 means there are five apps in a row and five apps in a column; and 5x6 means there are five apps in a row and six apps in a column.

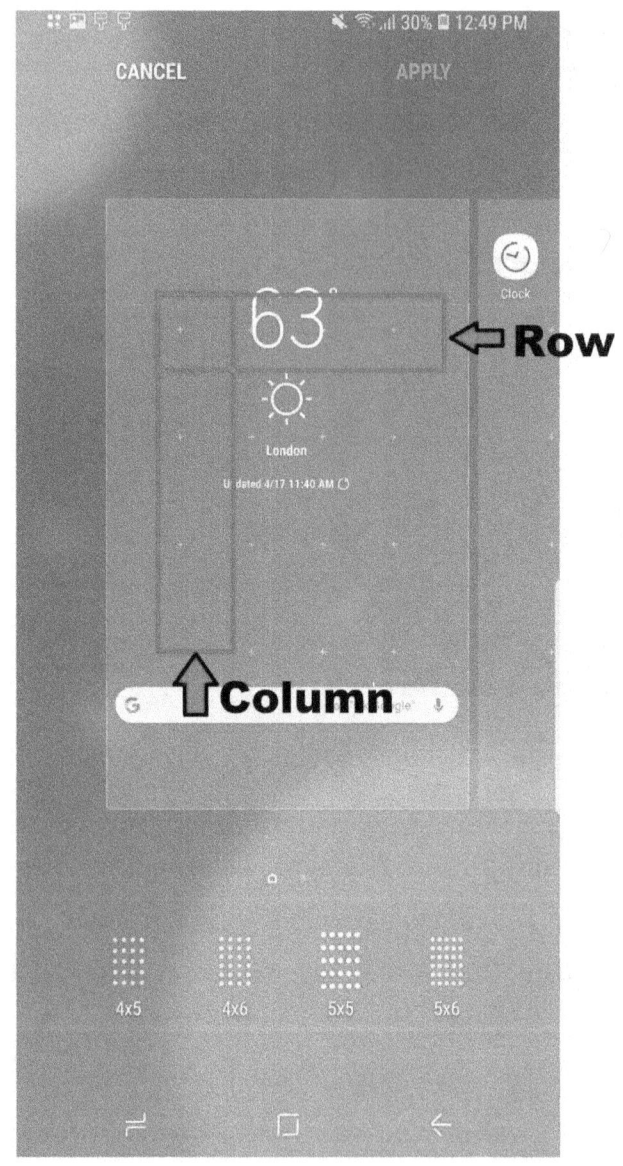

4. When you are done picking a dimension, tap **Apply**.

Tip: Alternatively, for some Android phones, you can access the **home screen settings** by performing the following actions:

- While on the home screen, swipe up the screen to access the applications screen.

- Tap the menu icon and select **Home screen settings**.

Creating a folder of items/apps on the home screen

1. From the home screen, tap and hold an app, then drag and drop it onto another item/app's icon to create a folder.

2. Tap the created folder, tap "Enter folder name" or "Unnamed folder" and enter a name.

3. To change the color of the folder, tap the color icon ⬛ and select a color. The option to change the color may not be available on some Android phones.

4. To add another app, tap **ADD APPS** located at the bottom of
   the screen. If this option is not available on your phone;
   simply tap, hold and drag an app to a folder to add another
   app/item.

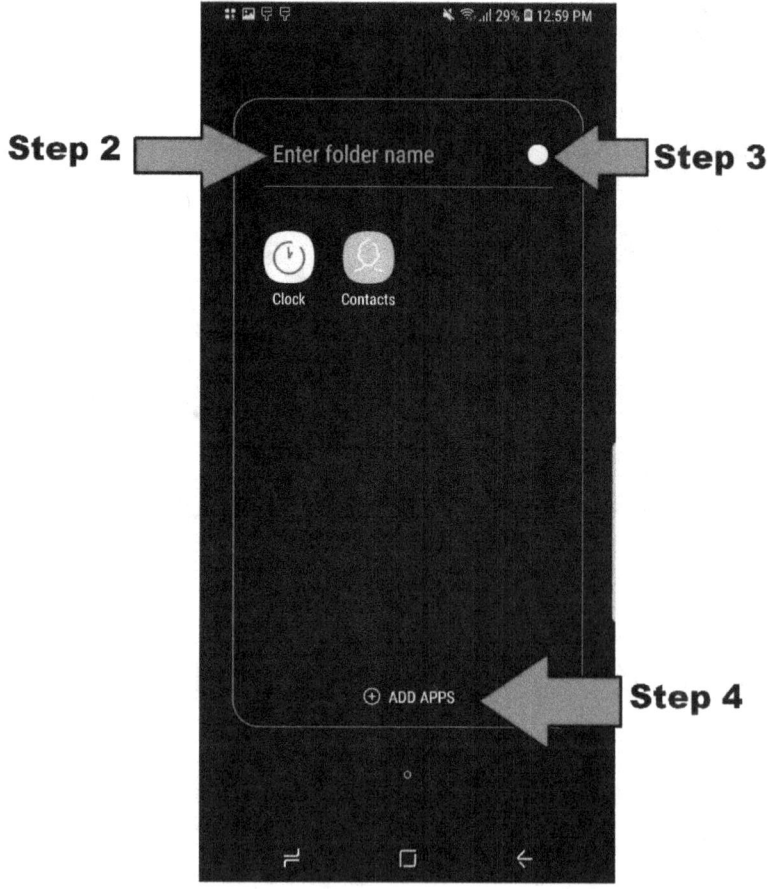

5. When you are done customizing a folder, tap the **Done**
   button (the checkmark button) on the virtual keyboard or tap
   the back icon ← or ◁.

6. To remove an app from a folder, tap the folder, and then long-tap the app you want to remove and drag it out of the folder. Lift your finger.

    Please note that the folder is automatically deleted when it remains only one app in the folder.

Accessing and Managing Applications

To open an app:

1. Go to applications screen.
2. Tap the app of your choice.
3. To go back to the app grid screen, press the back button

    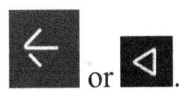 or .

Accessing Recently Opened or Running Applications

1. Tap on the recent button  or  to show the recent apps window. This contains the list of all opened/running apps.

    On supported Android phones, to quickly switch between recently used applications, double tap the recent button

    or .

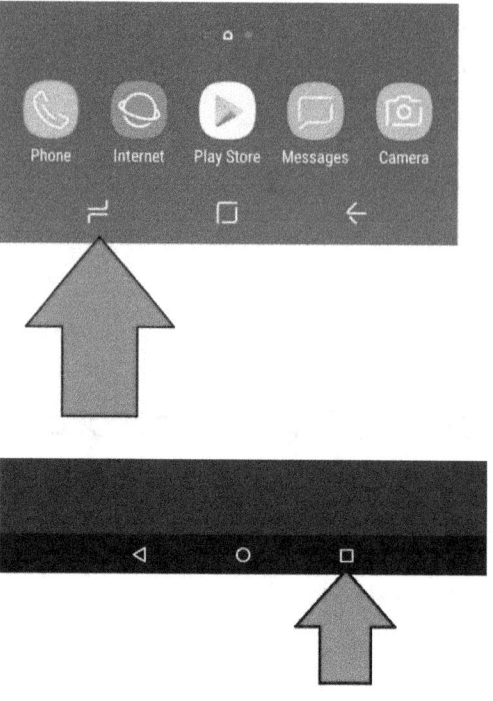

2. Tap an app to launch it or tap the **X** icon to close it. To close
   all opened apps, tap "Close All" located at the bottom of the
   screen. If you don't see "Close All," tap "Clear All" or delete

   button 🗑 located at the top or bottom of the screen.

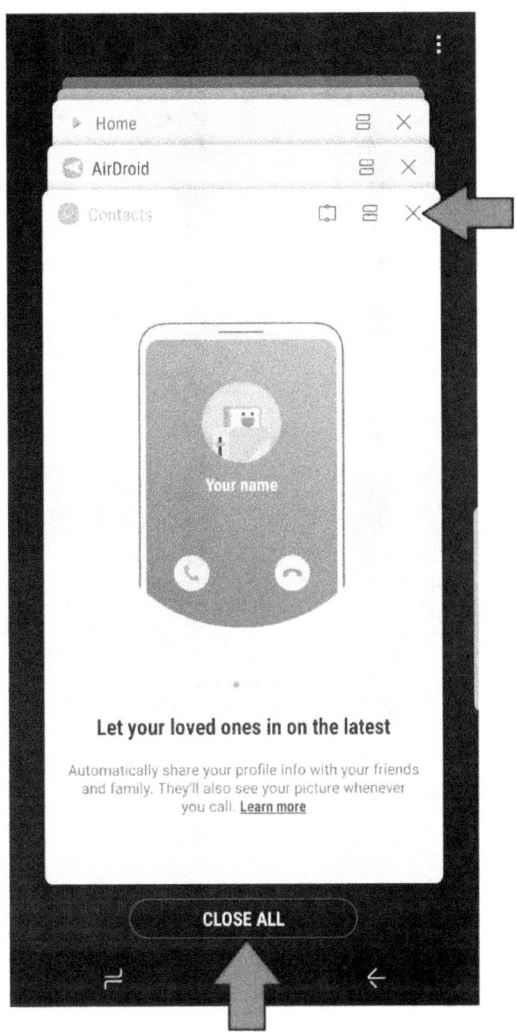

Tip: On supported Android phones, you can lock an app so that it does not get closed when you tap **CLOSE ALL.** To do this, tap the recent button ![recent button icon] or ![recent button icon] and select the menu icon located at the top of the screen. Then select **Lock apps.**

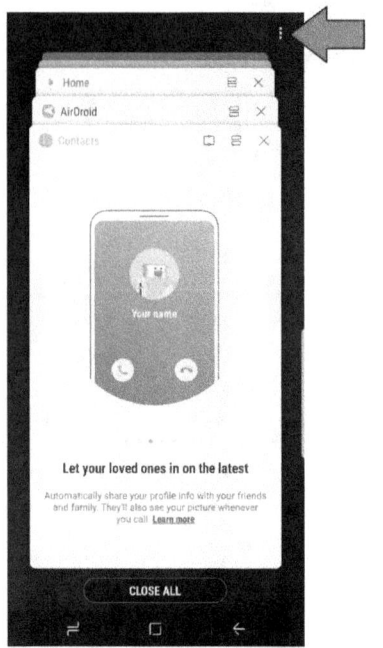 

Tap the padlock icon next to the app window you want to lock and
select **DONE.** When the padlock icon is closed then the app window
is locked.

*Please note that although a locked app window is not closed when you tap **CLOSE ALL**, you can still close it by swiping it to the right or left.*

Advice: Although Android Phones can run many apps at a time, multitasking may cause memory problems, or additional power consumption. To avoid these, end all unused programs by closing the app(s).

Managing the applications screen

Selecting apps

On supported Android phones, you can select many apps to perform an action on all of them at the same time. To do this:

    1. Tap and hold an app, and then tap **Select items.**

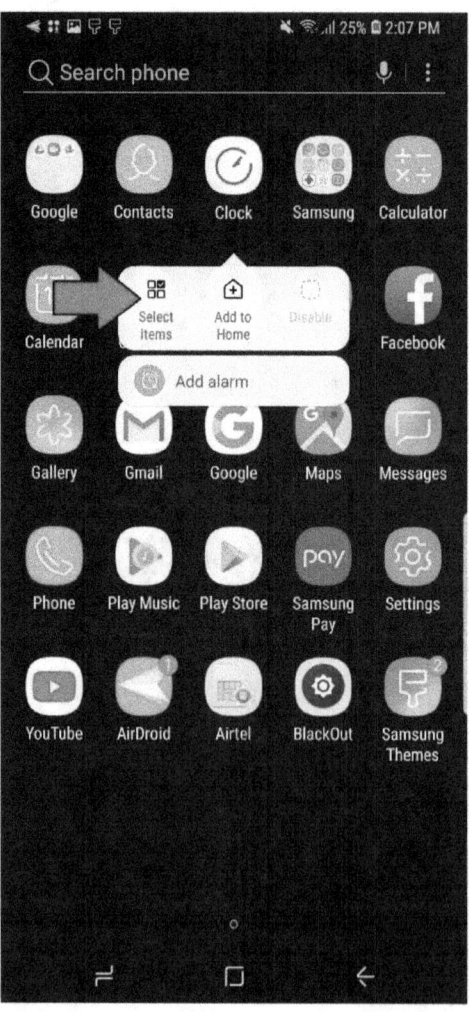

2. Then select all apps you want and choose an option at the top of the screen. If an option appears grey that means you can't use the option. For example, if your selection contains a folder, then the **Create folder** icon will appear grey because you can't put a folder inside another folder. Also, you can tap and hold an app in your selection to move them to another part of the screen. Or you can drag the selected apps up the screen to move them to the home screen and make them shortcuts.

 **Choose an option**

Tip: On some Android devices, when there is an app notification, a badge/dot appears on the corresponding app icon. If an app has a badge/dot, you can clear it by following the method below:

- Swipe down from the top of the screen to access the notifications screen.

- Dismiss the corresponding notification on the notification screen to clear the badge/dot. For example, if AirDroid app has a badge, you will dismiss this badge when you dismiss its notification on the notification screen. You can dismiss a notification by swiping the notification towards right or left.

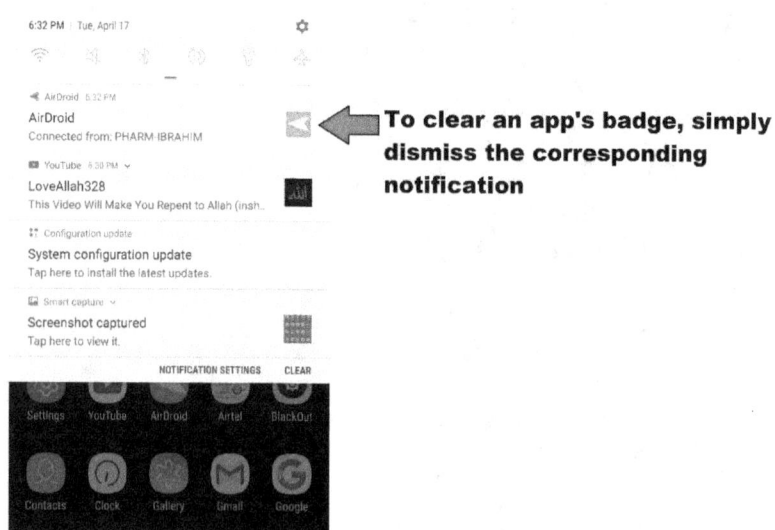

Please note that a badge is a notification number or dot displayed on

an app icon, e.g.

Tip: To customize *app icon badges* settings, swipe down from the top of the screen and tap settings icon 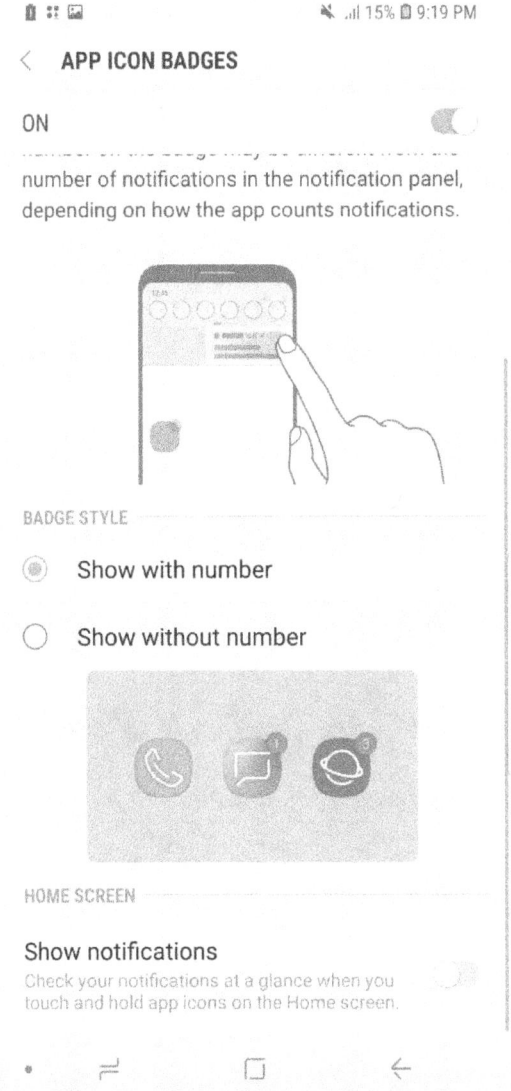 . Type in "app icon badges" or "notification dots" into the search bar located at the top of the screen. The results filter as you type. Tap "app icon badges" or "notification dots" from the results that appear.

If the instruction above does not work for you, try the following:

Go to **Settings** ⚙ > **Apps & notifications** > **Notifications** > **Allow notification dots**.

Showing the apps button

If you are using a Samsung Android phone and the apps button ⊞ is not shown on your home screen by default, you can enable it by following the steps below:

You can choose to show the apps button ⊞ on the home screen. To do this:

1. While on the home screen, swipe up the screen to access the applications screen.

2. Tap the menu icon ⋮ and select **Home screen settings**.

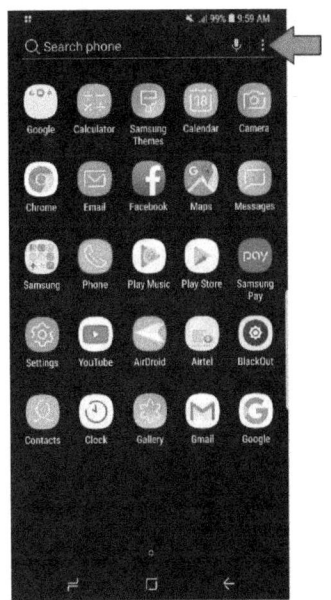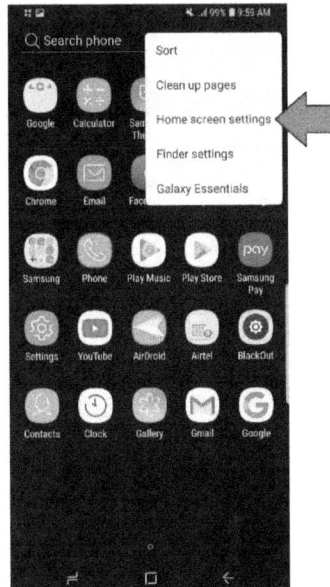

3. Tap **Apps button** and then choose **Show Apps button.** Then tap **APPLY** located at the top of the screen.

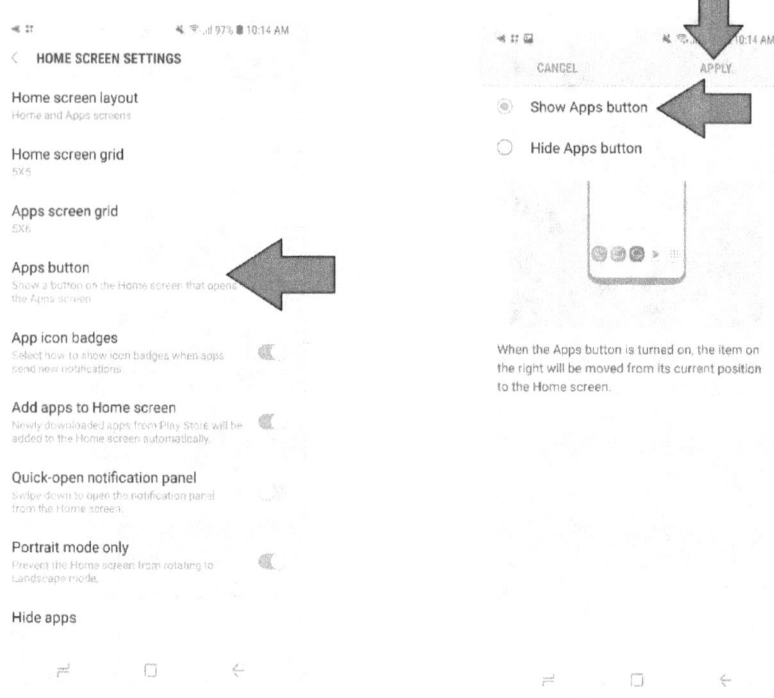

Arranging Application Alphabetically

1. Open the applications screen.

2. Tap the menu icon ⋮ next to the search bar.

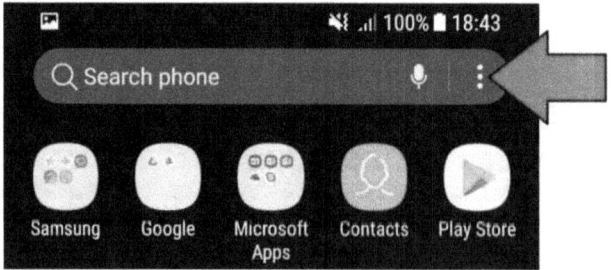

3. Tap **Sort** and choose an option.

Note: If you choose to arrange your apps/folders alphabetically, the folders may appear first.

Hiding applications

If you don't want your kid to access sensitive apps on your phone, you can hide them (this feature may not be available on all Android phones). For example, if you don't want your children to access your shopping app, you can hide it. However, please note that people may still be able to see your hidden apps, if they are tech savvies and they know the way.

To hide apps on supported Android phones:

1. Open the applications screen.

2. Tap the menu icon ⋮ and select **Home screen settings**.

3. Tap **Hide apps.** Then select the apps you want to hide, and tap **APPLY** located at the top of the screen.

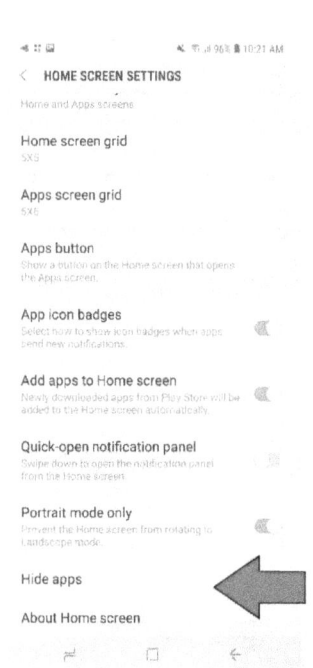
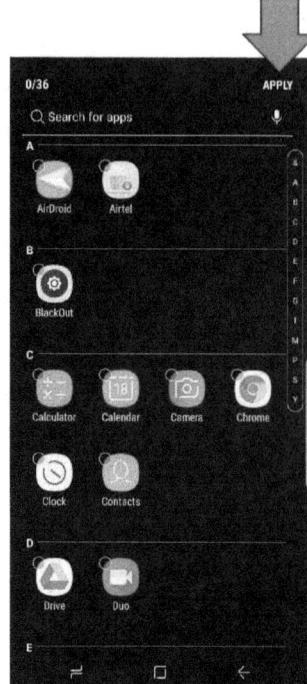

4. To unhide the apps, just repeat the steps 1 to 3 above and unselect the apps you have selected before. Then tap **APPLY** located at the top of the screen.

Managing applications

You can force-stop a misbehaving app. In addition, you can clear cache/data to clear errors in an app or to save phone memory.

To force-stop an app:

1. Swipe down from the top of the screen and tap settings icon
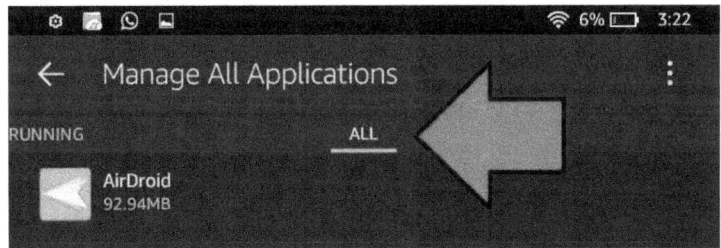.

2. Swipe up and tap "Apps".

   If you don't see "Apps", tap "Apps & Notifications" and then "App info" or "Apps".

   Please note that if you are using an LG Android phone, you may need to tap **General** tab, before you see "Apps & notifications."

3. Tap the app you want to manage.

   Note: If "All apps" is not selected, tap the small dropdown icon (v-like icon) located at the top of the screen and select "All apps" to see all the apps installed on your device. For some Android phones, you may need to swipe left to access the "All apps" screen.

4. To disable an app, tap **DISABLE.** Disabling an app may make such an app unavailable and clear its data. To enable an app, repeat steps 1 to 3 above and tap **ENABLE.** *Please note that you may not be able to disable some apps on your*

phone. For example, you may not be able to disable some apps that came with your phone.

5. To force-stop an app, tap **FORCE STOP.** Force-stopping an app is useful when an app is misbehaving or when it refuses to close. To access a force-stopped app again, just relaunch the app from the applications screen.

6. To clear the cache or data of an app, tap **Storage** and then tap **CLEAR DATA or CLEAR CACHE.** *Please note that clearing data may cause you to lose settings, files and all other stored information on the app. Only clear the data of an app if you want to start using it as a new app.*

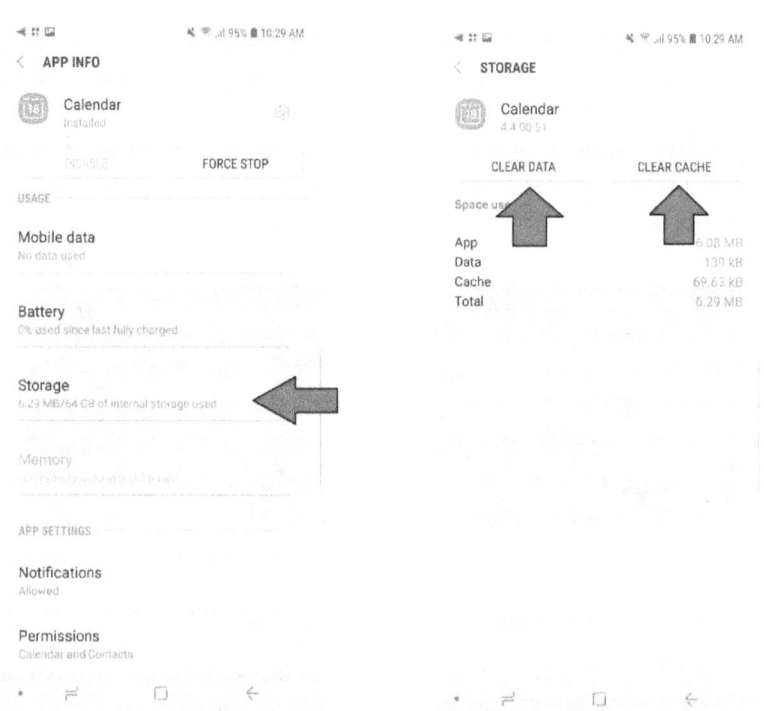

Tip: If you don't see **Clear Data** in the step 6 above, then choose **Manage Storage** (or Storage & Memory). When you choose **Manage Storage** option, you should be able to access Clear Data tab. If you can't still access Clear Data tab, then this option may not be available for the chosen app or service.

7. To manage the notification of an app, tap **Notifications** and choose an option.

8. To manage the permissions you have given to an app, scroll down and tap **Permissions** and choose an option.

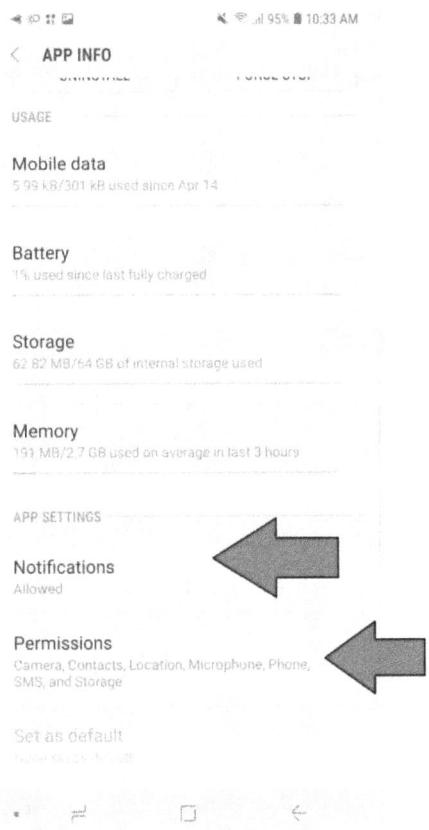

Hint: If an app is disturbing you with notifications and you want to quickly manage notification settings, just swipe down from the top of the screen and tap "Notification Settings". Then use the status switch next to each app to manage their notifications.

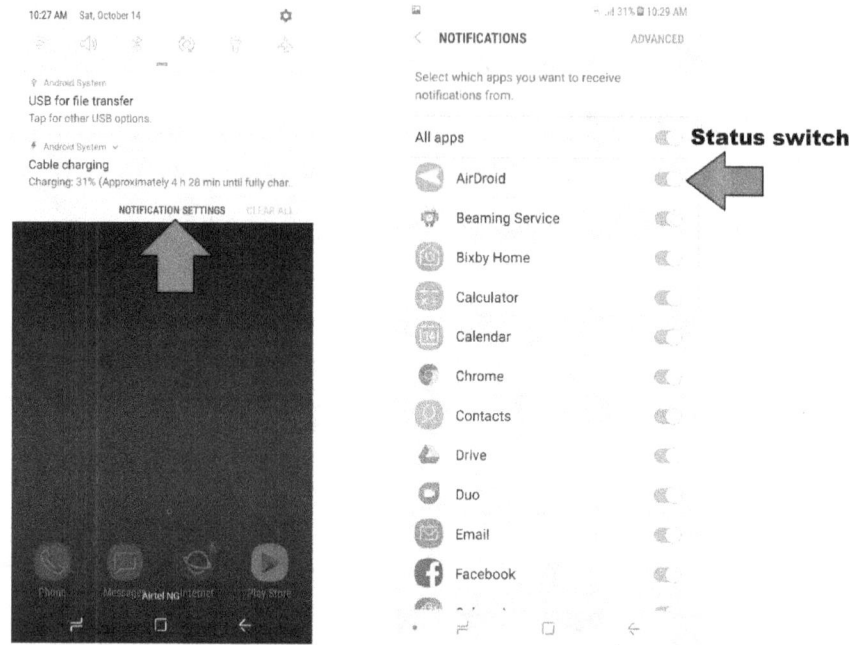

If you can't see "Notification Settings", swipe down from the top of the screen and tap and hold the notification you want to manage.

Then tap the status switch or the more info icon ⓘ to enable or disable this notification. Alternatively, swipe down from the top of the screen and slowly/slightly drag a notification to the side. Then tap the settings icon ⚙ to access the notification settings screen.

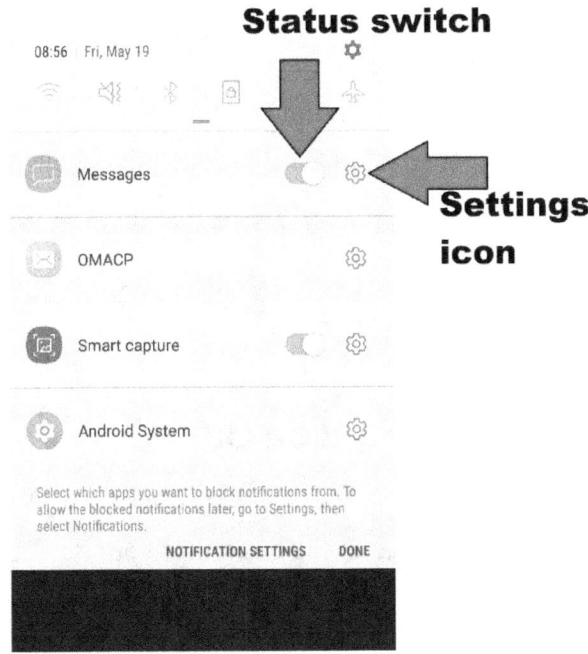

Status switch

Settings icon

To learn more about phone notifications, see page 100.

Uninstalling/Deleting an App

If you don't need an app again, you can uninstall it. To do this:

1. From the applications screen, locate the app you want to uninstall. Tap and hold this app and then select **Uninstall** or **Delete.** Tap **OK** or **Uninstall/Delete** to confirm.

2. Alternatively, tap and hold the app you want to uninstall and drag it over **Delete** or **Uninstall** (located at the top of the screen).

3. Alternatively, follow steps 1 to 3 under **Managing Applications** (See page 92), and select Uninstall under the app you want to delete.

Please note that you might not be able to uninstall some apps that come preloaded on your Android phones.

Tip: If you are using an LG Android phone, you might be able to reinstall an uninstalled app within 24 hours of uninstallation. To access this feature, go to application screen and tap **Management**. Then tap **App trash**.

Managing the Navigation Bar

The navigation bar is the bar at the bottom of your device screen. This bar comprises the back icon, the home icon and the recent apps icon.

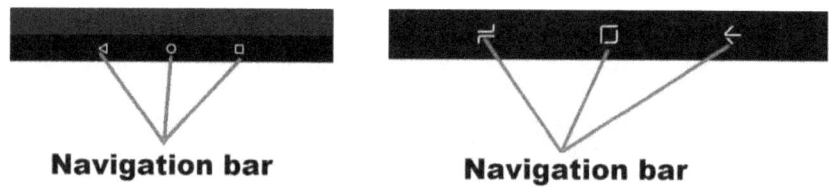

Navigation bar   **Navigation bar**

On Android phones, the middle navigation button is usually the home button, while the side button is either the back button or recent button (the opened-app button).

Tip: On some Samsung Android phones, you can hide or unhide navigation bar. To do this:

1. Swipe down from the top of the screen and tap settings icon

2. Then tap on the search icon.

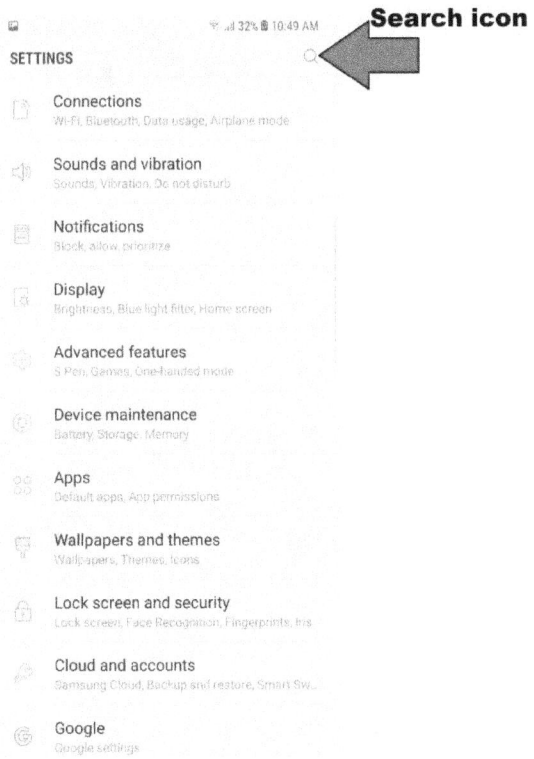

Search icon

3. Type in **Navigation bar** into the search bar. The result filters as you type. Tap **Navigation bar** from the results that appear.

4. Choose an option from the Navigation bar settings screen.

5. To enable the **Show and hide button**, tap the status switch next to **Show and hide button.** When this is enabled, you should be able to quickly hide or show the navigation bar by double tapping the small dot icon.

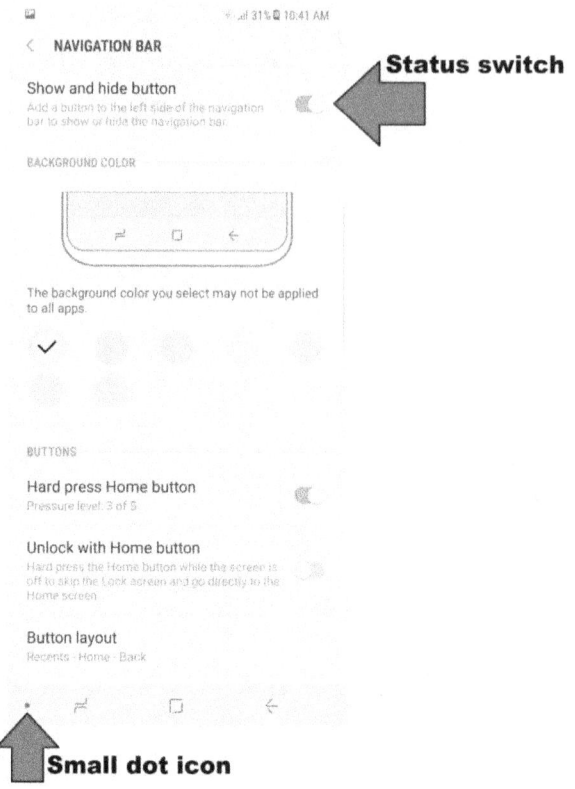

To show the navigation bar after hiding it, swipe in from the bottom of the screen.

Managing Phone Notifications

Notifications consume battery and it may be a source of disturbance occasionally. To manage notifications:

1. Swipe down from the top of the screen and tap settings icon

2. Tap "Apps & notifications" and then tap "Notifications" or "Notifications management". If you don't see "Apps & notifications," tap "Notifications."
   Please note that if you are using an LG Android phone, you may need to tap **General** tab, before you see "Apps & notifications."

3. Tap "App notifications" (if available).

4. To manage notification for an individual app, tap an app and then use the status switch to disable or enable it.

5. To further manage your device's/app's notifications, use the onscreen notifications settings.

6. For Samsung phones, you can have an advanced management of notifications by tapping **ADVANCED** and then choosing an app. You can use the advanced settings to manage apps that can give you notifications while Do Not Disturb (see page 360) is active.

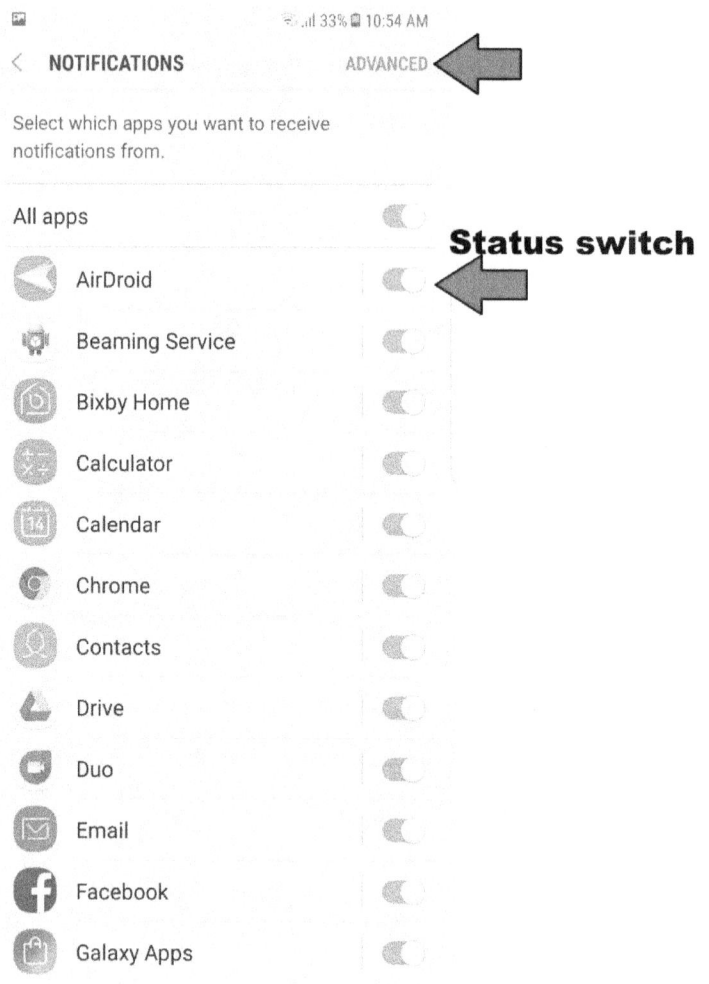

Tips:

- To manage notification sound on an Android phone, swipe

  down from the top of the screen, and tap **settings** ⚙ >

  Sound > Advanced > Default notification sound. Then

  choose a sound and tap **Save/Done.**

If you are using a Samsung Android phone, you can follow these steps instead. Swipe down from the top of the screen and tap **settings** ⚙ > **Sounds and vibration** > **Notification sounds**. Then select **Silent** if you don't want a notification sound. To change your selection, choose a notification sound**.**

- To change the ringtone on an Android phone, swipe down from the top of the screen, and tap **settings** ⚙ > **Sound** > **Phone ringtone**. Then select **None** or **Silent** if you don't want a ringtone. To change your selection, choose a notification sound**.** Tap **Save/Done** to save the changes.

- You can manage a notification badge or dot that appears on your device. To learn how to do this, please see the "Tip" on page 86.

- You can quickly block a notification from the quick action menu. To do this, simply swipe down from the top of the screen, tap and hold a notification. Then tap the status switch to block notifications from the app in question. Thereafter, tap **Save** to register the changes. To view the detailed settings of a notification, select "DETAILS", "All Categories" or ⓘ .

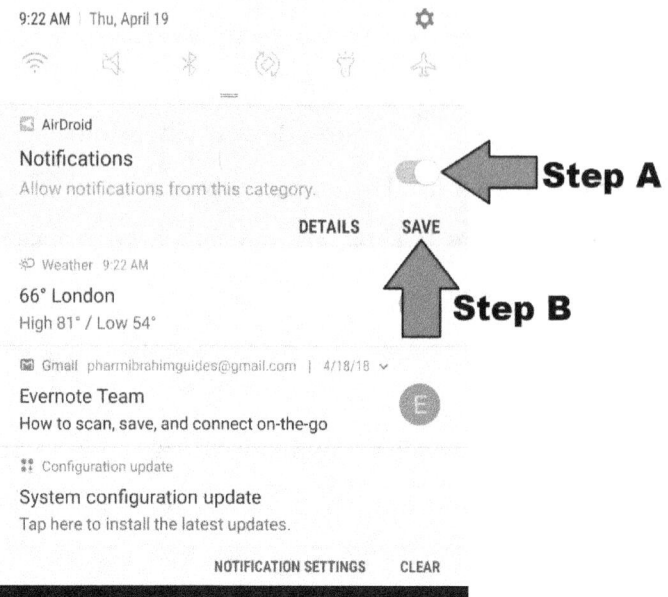

If the method above does not work for you, swipe down from the top of the screen and slowly/slightly drag a notification to the side. Then tap the settings icon ⚙ or the more info icon ⓘ to access the notification settings screen.

- You can snooze a notification for a specified time, to do this, swipe down from the top of the screen and slowly/slightly drag a notification to the side. Tap the snooze icon (the clock icon). Then tap the dropdown arrow icon "**V**" and pick a length of time.

Troubleshooting Tip: If you are not getting notification from an app (for example, if you are not getting notifications from Email app), these are the things to check:

1. Check whether you have not blocked/disabled notifications from the app. You can know this by following the steps on page 100 to 101.

2. Go to **Settings** 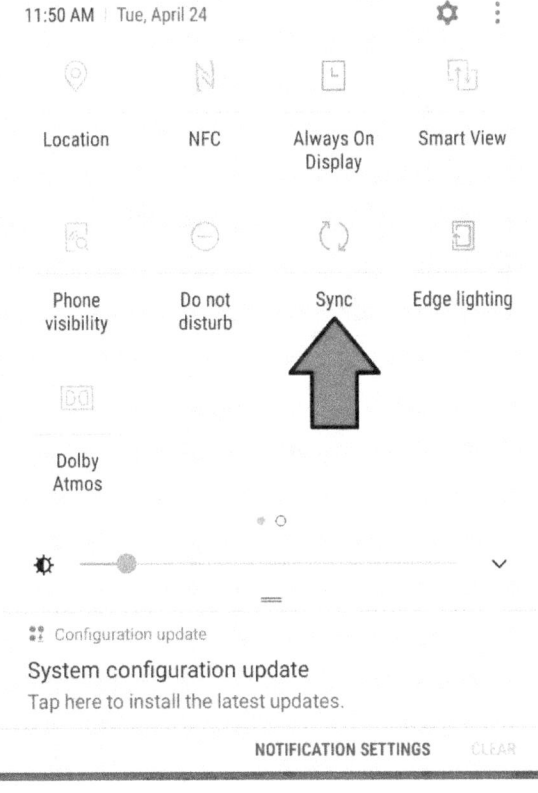 > **Users & account**. Then make sure "**Automatically sync data**" is enabled.

   If you can't see "Users & accounts" or "Automatically sync data," then try this. Swipe down from the top of the screen with two fingers. Swipe left and see if **Sync** appears bold. If it appears bold, then it is enabled. Please note that if *Sync* is disabled you may not get some notifications.

3. If the first two steps above do not work, then make sure your phone is not restricting the app's battery usage. Restricting the battery usage for an app may affect the ability of the app to get sync or use data. On some Android phones, you can know if an app has a restricted battery usage by doing the following:

Go to **Settings** 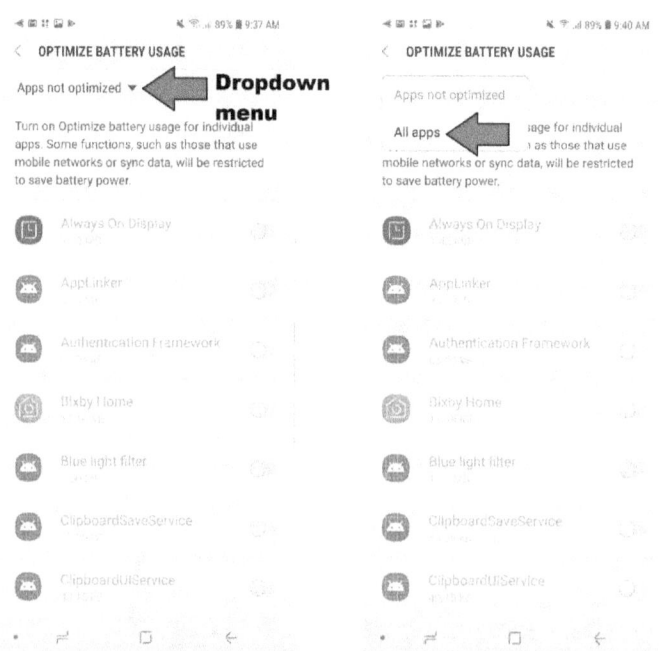 > **Apps** > **menu icon** (located at the top of the screen) > **Special access** > **Optimize battery usage**. Tap the dropdown menu and select **All apps**. Locate the app in question and make sure the indicator switch next to it is turned off.

Using the Multi Window/Split-Screen Function

Multi window is one of the coolest features of Android Phone. Multi window allows you to put two apps side by side. *However, it is important to note that not all apps support the multi window feature.*

Using the Multi Window/Split-Screen Feature

1. Open an app that supports multi-screen.

2. Touch and hold the recent button ⊐ or ▣. The app will be assigned to the first part of the split screen. Then tap **Apps List** and choose an app from the list that appears. If you don't see "Apps List," select the second desired app from the thumbnail list. You may need to swipe up or down (if necessary) to select the second app.

   Please note that for some Android phones, you may need to make sure that the two (or more) apps you want to use in the split screen mode are opened and running in the background before you tap and hold the recent button ⊐ or ▣.

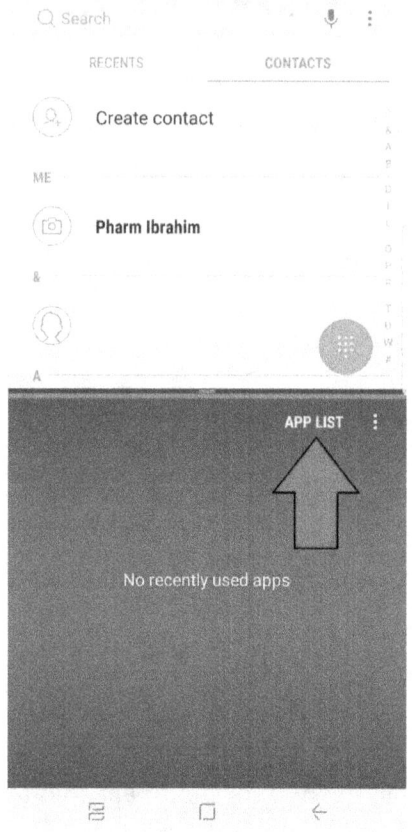

If this step 2 does not work for you, please try this. Touch and hold the app you would like to open in the split screen. Then drag the app to "**Drag here to use the split screen**" located at the top of the screen. Then select the second app to view.

3. To adjust the size of an app window, tap the middle of the dividing line between the app windows (i.e. the straight line

that appears between the two app windows) and drag it up or down. See the picture below.

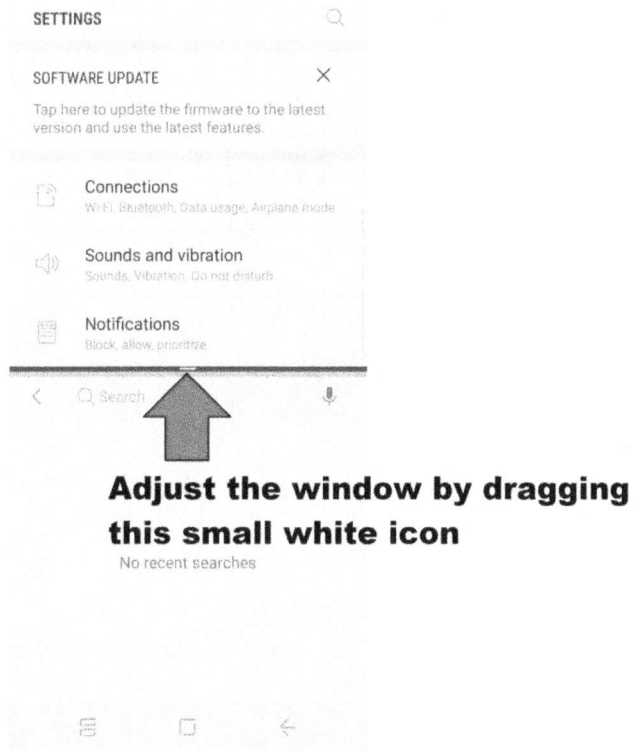

4. To close an app opened in the split-screen, tap the split-screen icon ⊞ and then tap the **X** icon next to the app you want to close. See below.

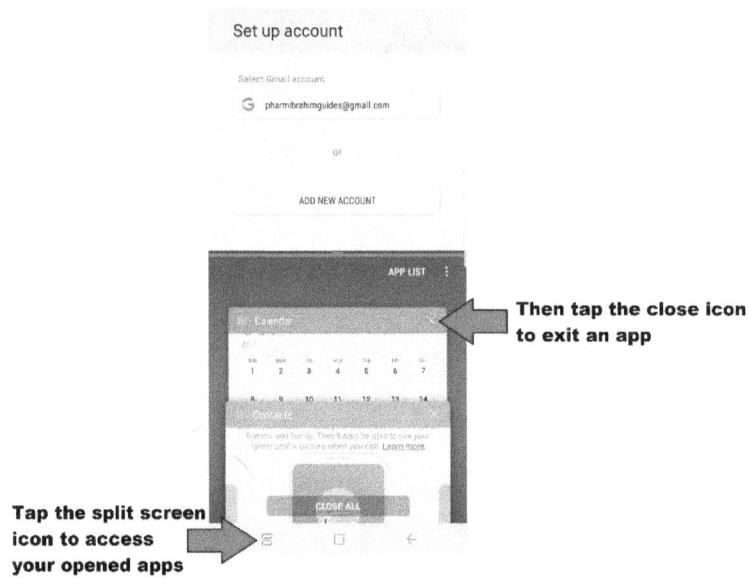

Then tap the close icon to exit an app

Tap the split screen icon to access your opened apps

If you can't see the **X** icon, the app may be locked. To unlock the app, tap the padlock icon.

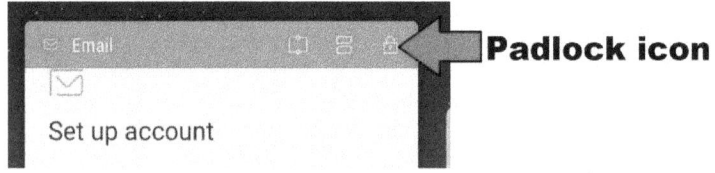

Padlock icon

5. To open another app in the split-screen, tap the split-screen icon , tap **Apps List** and choose an app from the list that appears. If you don't see "Apps List," select the second desired app from the thumbnail list.

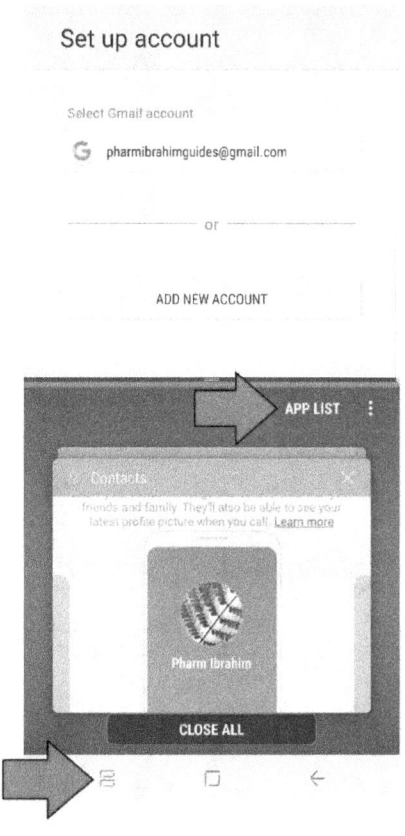

6. To exit the multi window view, tap and hold the split-screen

   icon 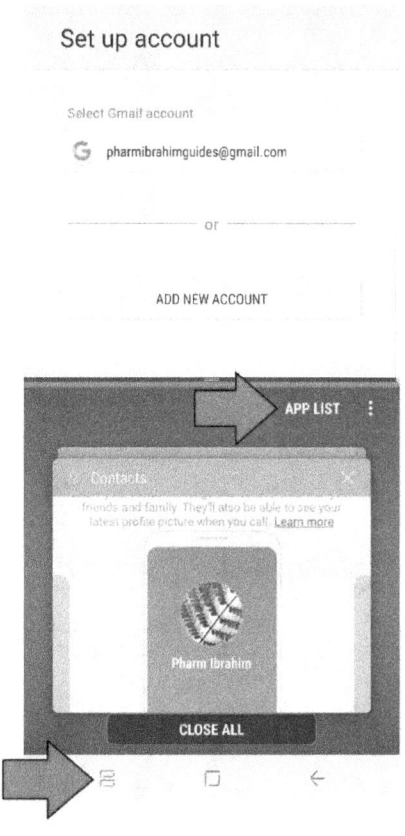 (located at the bottom of the screen).

Note: If you are using a Samsung Android phone, you may need to enable *Use Recents button* feature to be able to use Recents button

to access the multi-window/split-screen. To do this:

1. Swipe down from the top of the screen and tap settings icon

.

2. Tap **Advanced features**.

3. Scroll down and tap **Multi window**.

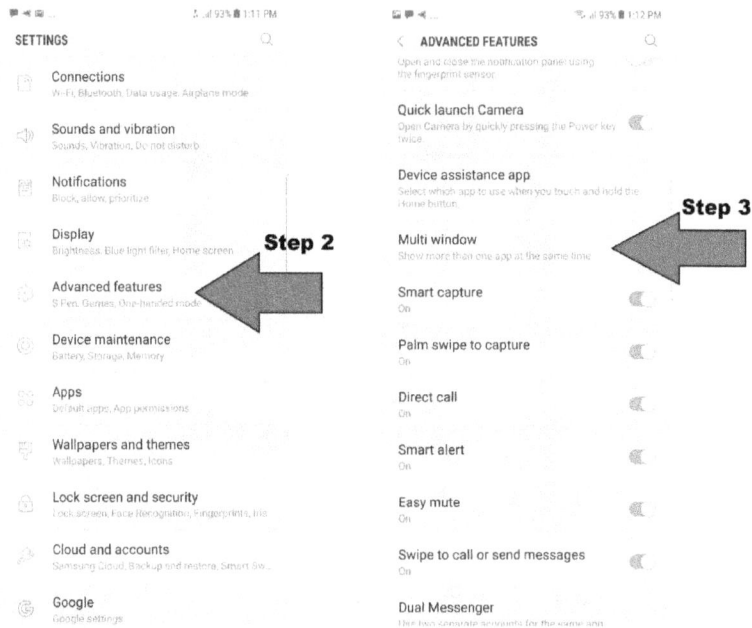

4. Tap the status switch next to **Use Recents button.**

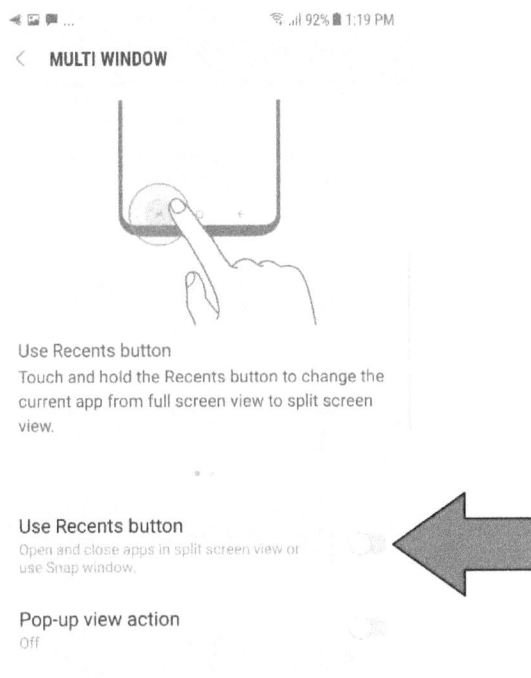

Use Recents button
Touch and hold the Recents button to change the
current app from full screen view to split screen
view.

Use Recents button
Open and close apps in split screen view or
use Snap window.

Pop-up view action
Off

Note that when this option is enabled, you will be able to change the
current app from a full screen view to a split-screen view by pressing
and holding Recent button ⊐.

Using the Multi Window Controls

When using apps in the split screen view, tap the middle of the
dividing line between the app windows to access multi window
options.

Note: *It appears that not all Android phones support this feature.*

Tap this

To dismiss the multi window screen controls, tap the back button ←.

The Multi Window Options

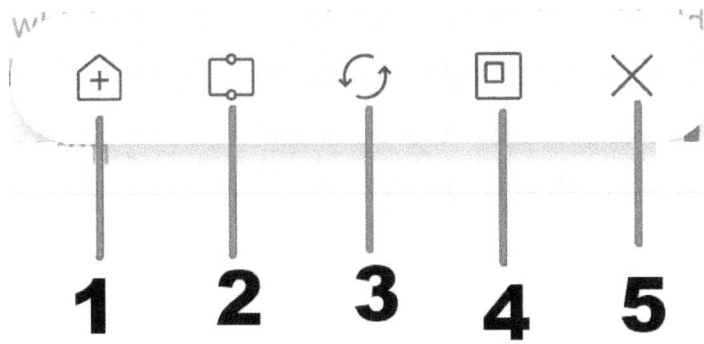

1   2   3   4   5

Icon	Function
1.	Tap this button to add the current app pair (i.e. the current two apps you are viewing) to the home screen. This will allow you to quickly access the two apps in the future.
2.	Tap this icon to move an app window to another part (usually the top part of the screen). When you tap this icon, a blue outline will appear. Adjust this blue outline as you wish to resize the window. When you are done resizing, tap **DONE** to effect the changes.
3.	Tap this icon to switch window positions i.e. move a lower app window to upper part of the screen and vice versa.
4.	Tap this to open an app in a pop-up windows or minimize an app.
5.	Tap this icon to close the currently active app and

exit the multi windows screen.

Using the minimize button:

Some Android phones allow you to customize the split screen with a

minimize button 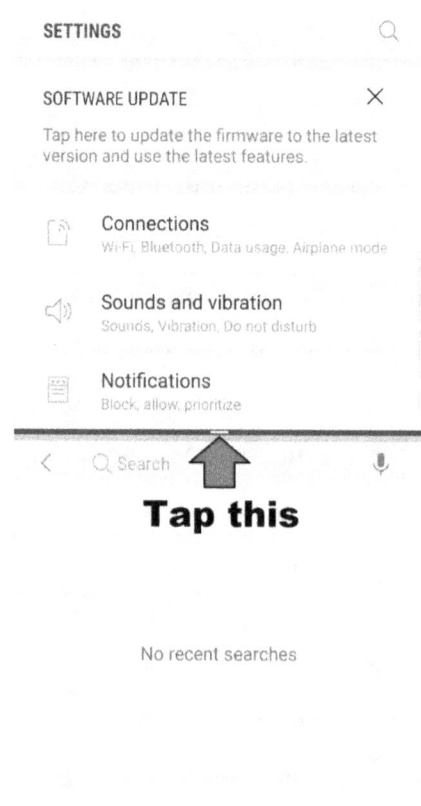. To use this button:

1. When using apps in the split-screen view, tap the middle of the dividing line between the app windows to access multi-window options.

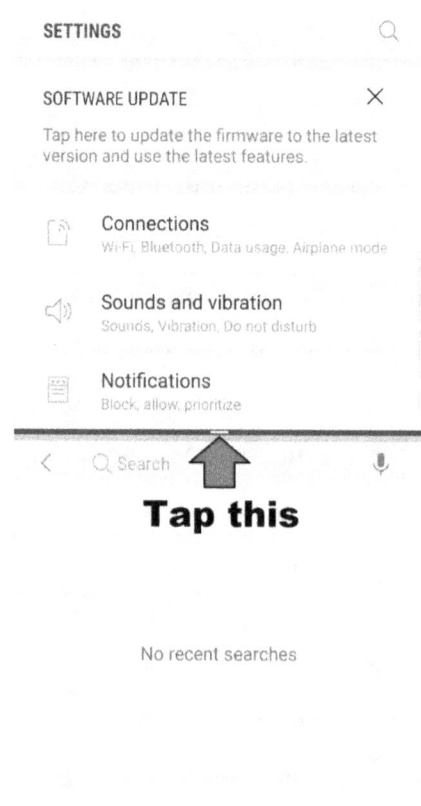

2. Tap the minimize icon 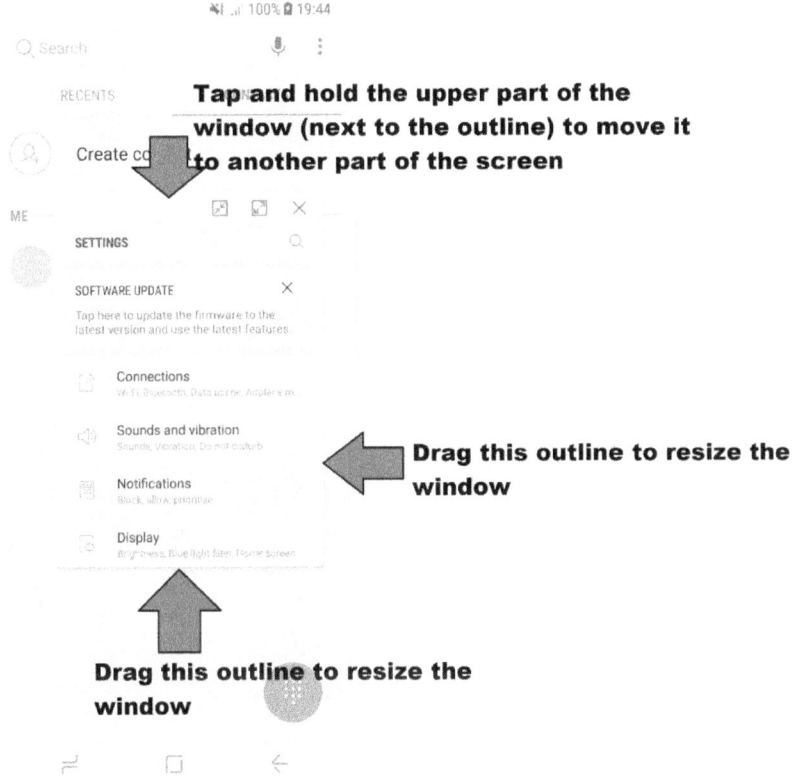 to minimize the currently active app; then tap and hold the upper part of the window next to the outline to drag the window from one part of the screen to another. To resize it however, tap, hold and move the outline as you wish.

3. Tap to minimize the app window to a small icon. This small icon can be dragged from one part of the screen to another when you tap, hold and move it.

4. To maximize the window to a full screen, tap the corresponding small icon and then tap [icon] . For example, if the app in question is settings app, tap the small icon [icon] representing the settings app and then tap the maximize button [icon] .

Understanding the Quick Settings Menu

The Quick settings panel present on the notification panel provides a quick access to device functions such as Wi-Fi, allowing you to quickly turn them on or off.

Tip: Usually, the app icon that is currently active in Quick settings menu will appear bold, so if you want to know whether you have enabled a feature or not, just check its boldness. For example, if you want to know if Bluetooth is on, swipe down from the top of the screen and see if the Bluetooth icon appears bold.

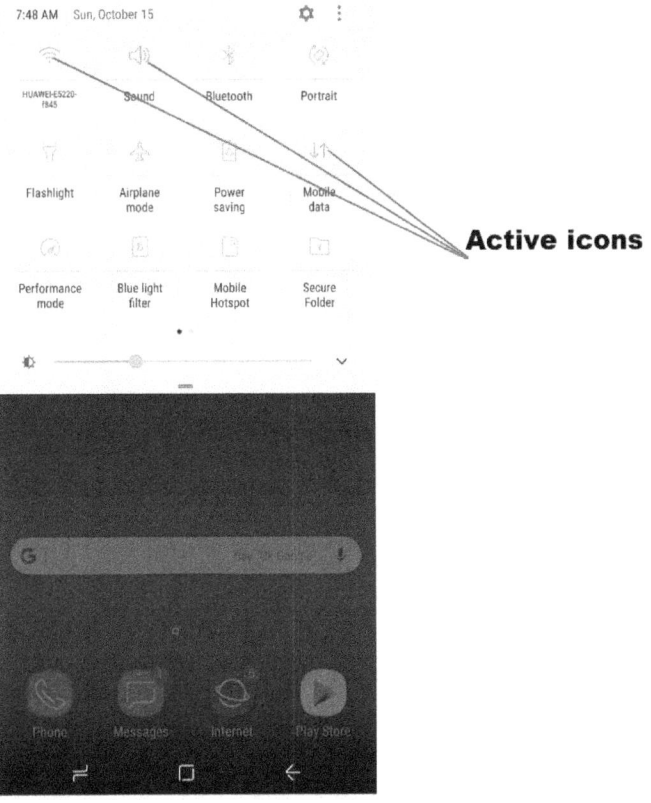

Active icons

To view additional Quick settings:

1. Swipe down from the top of the screen using two fingers to see all the active Quick settings icons.

2. Alternatively, swipe down from the top of the screen to display the Notification panel. Then drag down the double dash == icon or the small "V" icon to see more icons.

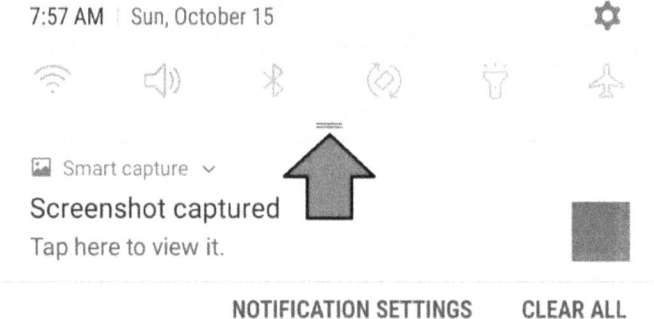

To customize the Quick settings icons:

1. Swipe down from the top of the screen using two fingers.

2. To enable or disable a setting, tap the setting icon once. To view the details of a setting, tap and hold the setting's icon.

3. Tap the pen icon ✐ . If you don't see the pen icon, tap the menu icon ⋮ located at the top of the screen and then tap **Button order**.

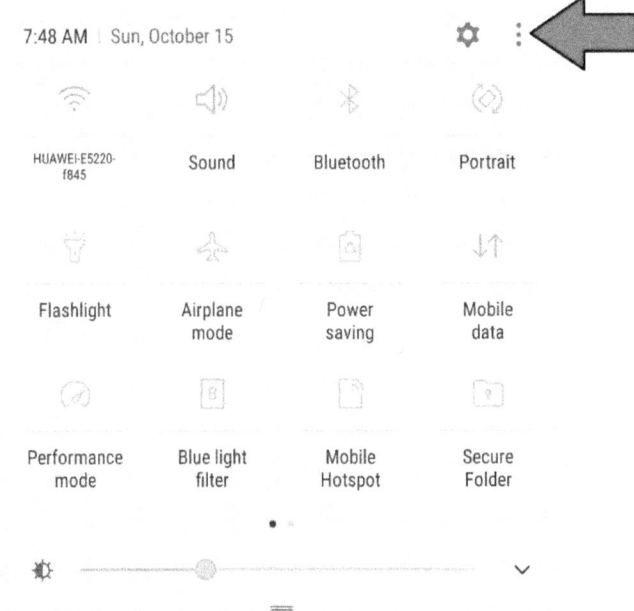

4. Tap, hold and drag any of the icons to change their positions.

5. To add an app to the Quick settings panel, drag the app from the lower section of the screen (the gray area) to the top section of the screen.

6. To remove an icon from the Quick settings panel, drag the app icon to the lower section of the screen (the gray area).

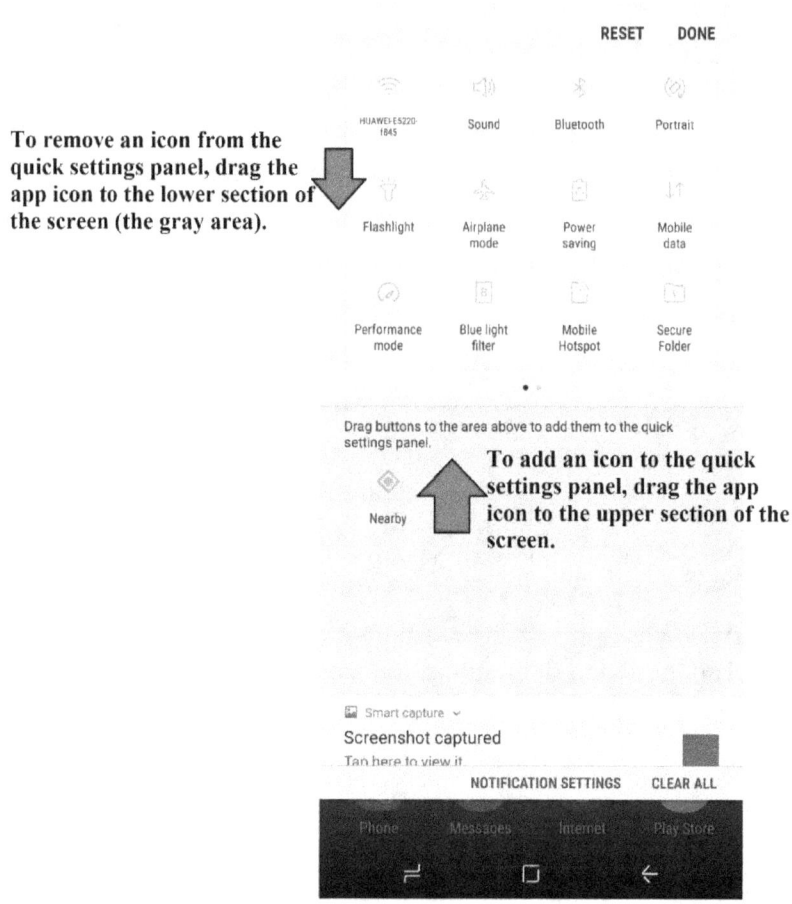

To remove an icon from the quick settings panel, drag the app icon to the lower section of the screen (the gray area).

To add an icon to the quick settings panel, drag the app icon to the upper section of the screen.

7. Tap **DONE** located at the top of the screen to save the changes. If you don't see Done, tap the back arrow 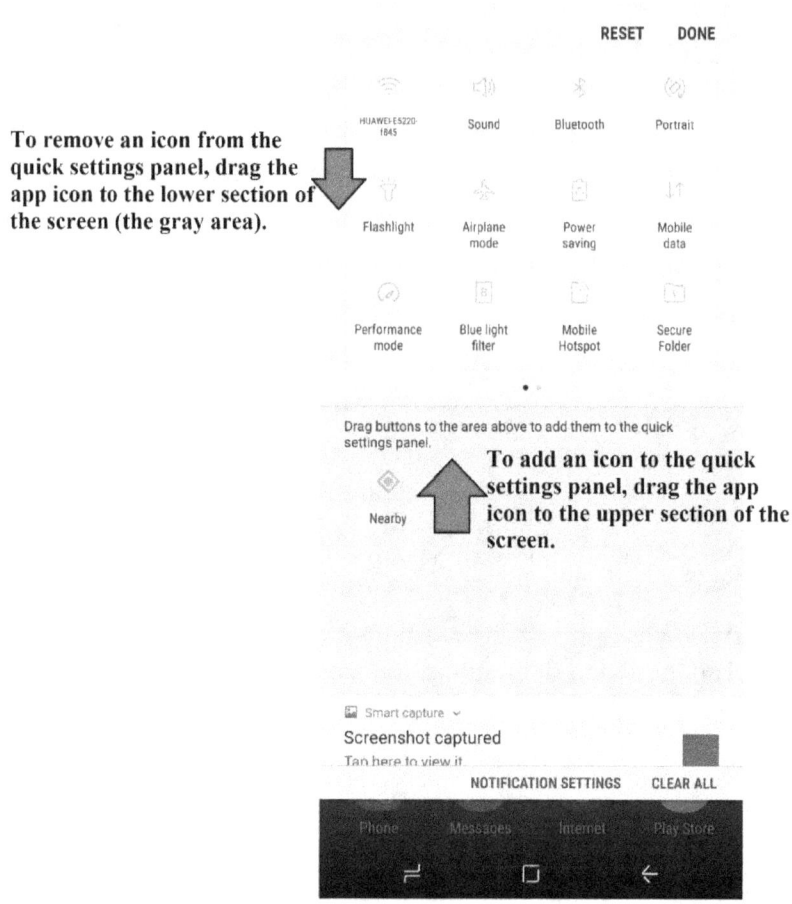 (located at the top of the screen).

Hint: Some Android phones allow you to restore the icons' arrangement to the default arrangement. To do this, tap **RESET** (see the screenshot above) and then tap **DONE**.

Tip: On supported Android phones, you can change the number of app icons that appear in a row/column in Quick settings menu. To do this, swipe down from the top of the screen using two fingers. Tap the menu icon ⋮ located at the top of the screen and then select **Button grid.** Choose an option.

Customizing Your Android Phone

You can get more done with your phone by customizing it to match your preference.

Changing Your Language

1. Swipe down from the top of the screen and select settings icon ⚙. Then scroll down and tap "General management," "General" or "System".
2. Tap **Language and input.**
3. Tap **Language(s)**.
4. Tap **Add language**.
5. If supported on your Android device, tap the menu icon ⋮ and then tap **All languages** to access a more robust list of languages.

6. Select a language from the list. If your chosen language is spoken in more than one country/region, select a country/region for your chosen language.

7. Using the v-like icon (or the two/four lines ▬ icon) next to a language, tap and drag your preferred language to the number one position in the language list. Then tap **Apply** (if available) to set the language as the default language.

CANCEL   APPLY   **Tap APPLY to save changes**

Add multiple languages below so that, if an app
does not support your default language (at the
top of the list), the next supported language in the
list will be used instead. Move a language to the
top of the list to set it as the default.

1   Français (France)   ◊

2   English (United States)   ◊

3   Português (Guiné-Bissau)   ◊

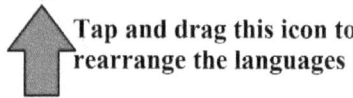

**Tap and drag this icon to
rearrange the languages**

8. To delete a language, tap the menu icon ⋮ (located at the
   top of the screen) and select "Delete" or "Remove." Tap the
   language you want to delete. Then select delete icon and tap
   "Ok".

   Alternatively, on supported Android phones, tap "Delete"
   located at the top of the screen and tap the language you want
   to delete. Then select "Delete" and tap "Ok".

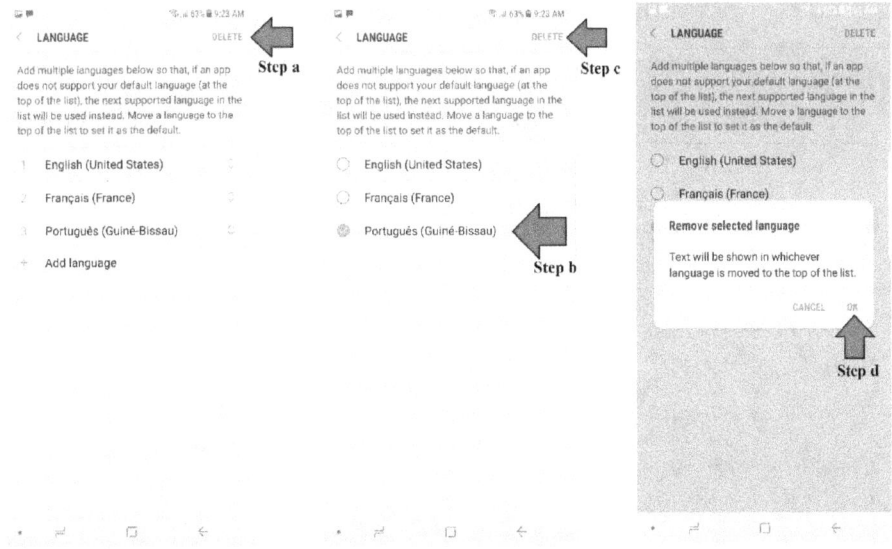

Downloading More Virtual Keyboards from Google Play Store

If want to explore more keyboard options, you can go to Google Play store to download more keyboard(s). Just open the Google Play store app and search for **Keyboard.** Then choose a beneficial keyboard from the options that appear. After you have downloaded and installed a keyboard, then perform the following actions:

1. Swipe down from the top of the screen and select settings

   icon 🛠. Then scroll down and tap "General management" or "System".

2. Tap "Language and input".

3. Tap "Virtual Keyboard" or "On-screen keyboard".

4. Tap "Manage keyboards".

5. Tap the status switch next to the keyboard you just installed to enable it. In this case, I have just downloaded and installed **SwiftKey Keyboard** from Google Play store.

6. Then tap a text input field to display the virtual keyboard. (For example, you may open a message app and tap the text input field to display the virtual keyboard). Thereafter, tap the keyboard icon ⌨ located at the lower right corner of the screen. Then choose your newly downloaded keyboard to begin to use it.

Keyboard icon

Tip: If you are using a Samsung Android phone, you can do the

following to choose a default keyboard. Go to **Settings** ⚙ >
General management > **Language and Input**. Then tap **Default**
Keyboard and choose an option.

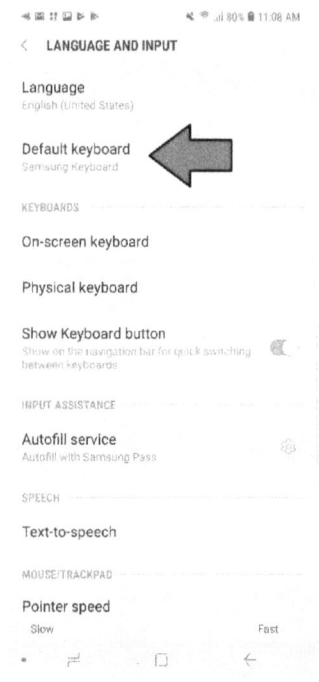
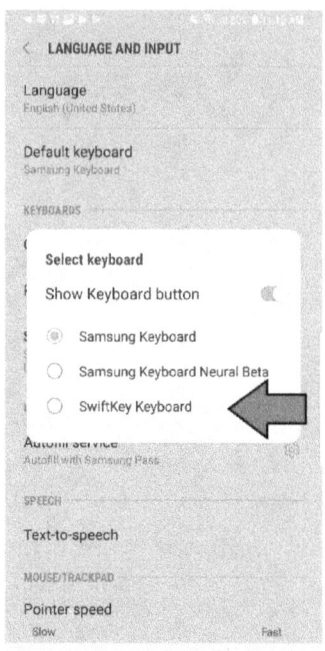

Hint: Usually, your device comes preloaded with a virtual Keyboard, to customize this keyboard to your taste:

1. Swipe down from the top of the screen and select settings icon 🔧 . Then scroll down and tap "General management" or "System".
2. Tap "Language and input".
3. Tap "Virtual Keyboard" or "On-screen keyboard".
4. Tap a keyboard. Then tap any of the on-screen options to begin the customization. I would advise that you go through these options one-by-one to have the best keyboard experience.

In addition, you can allow your chosen keyboard to support more languages. To do this:

1. Repeat steps 1 to 3 above.
2. Tap a keyboard and tap "Language" or "Languages and types".
3. If available, tap "Manage Input Languages".
4. Then tap the status switch next to all the languages you want the keyboard to support.

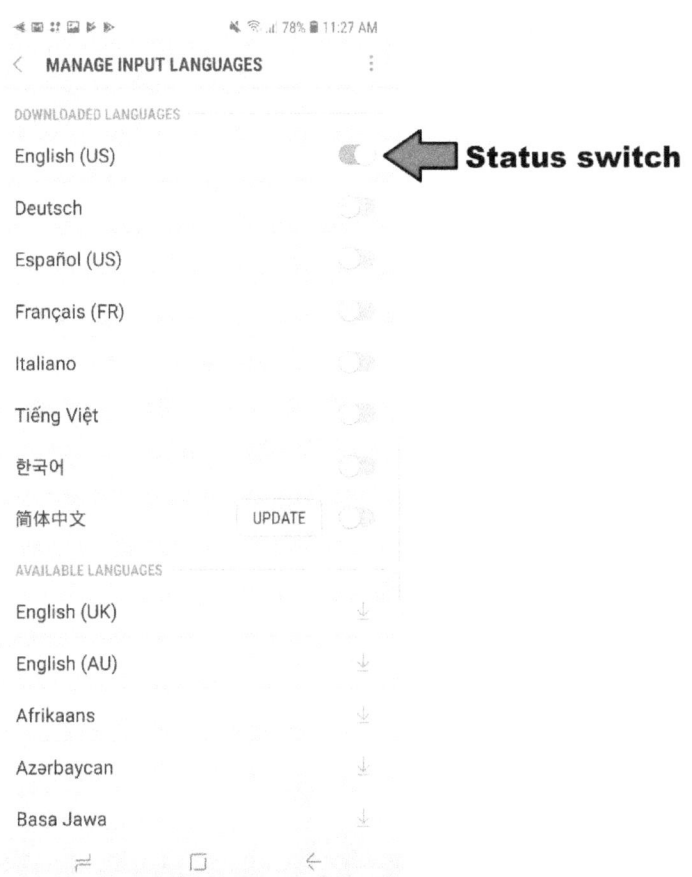

On supported Android phones, to change the keyboard language to any of the ones selected above, swipe the space bar on the virtual keyboard to right or left until you see the language of your choice.

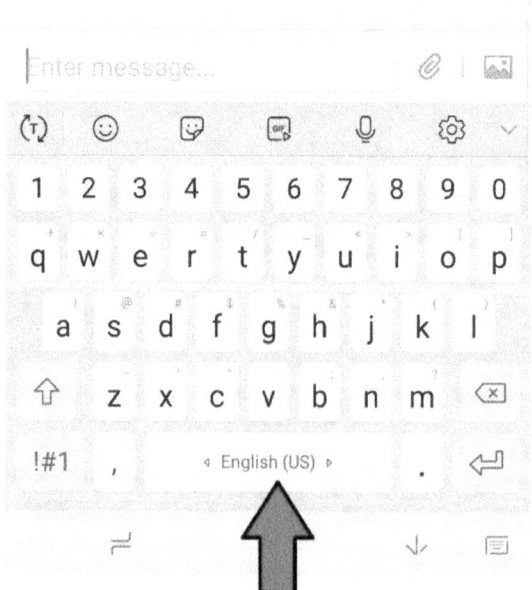

Swipe this to right or left

Set the Current Time and Date

Your device is built to update its time automatically, but you may need to manually set your time for one reason or the other. To manually set the time and date:

1. Swipe down from the top of the screen and select settings

    icon ⚙ . Then scroll down and tap "System". If you don't see "System", tap "General management".

2. Tap **Date and time**.

3. To ensure that the time on your device is updated automatically, enable the status switch next to **Automatic date and time.** Please note that when this status switch is enabled, it would appear bold.

4. To set the time on your device manually or prevent your device from updating the time automatically, disable the status switch next to **Automatic date and time**, and then edit the time and date as you desire.

5. To manage the time zone settings, disable the status switch next to **Automatic date and time** or **Automatic time zone** and then tap **Select time zone**.

6. To use a 24 hours' time setting for your device, enable the status switch next to **Use 24-hour format**.

Note: When the status switch is on, it will appear bold.

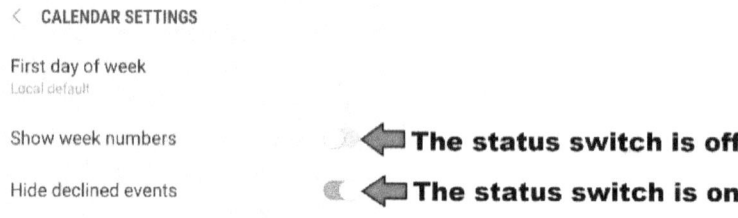

Controlling Sounds and Vibrations

1. Swipe down from the top of the screen and select settings

   icon  .

2. Tap **Sound** or **Sounds and vibration** and tap an option.

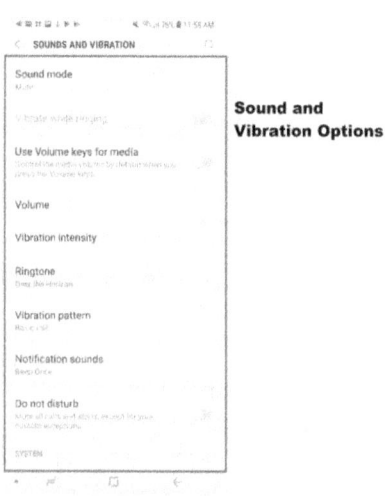

Adjusting the Volume of Your Phone

To adjust the volume of your phone, press the Volume key. The volume key is usually the long key located at the left side of many Android phones.

Adjusting the Brightness of the Display

- Swipe down from the top of the screen using your two fingers. Then drag the slider under the Quick action icons to adjust the brightness.

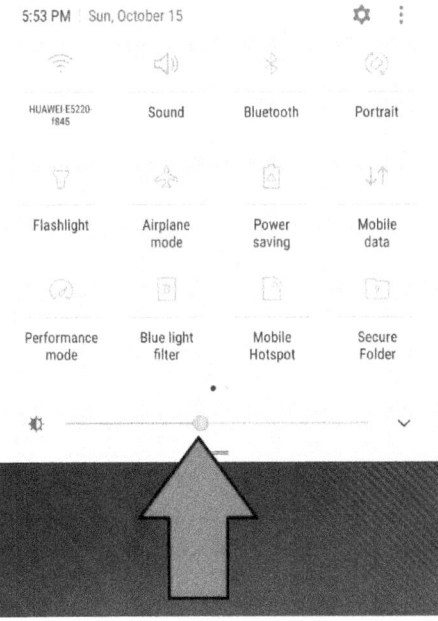

Hint: The brightness level of the display will affect how quickly the phone consumes battery power. I would advise that you turn it reasonably low if you are very concerned about saving your battery. In addition, using your phone on high brightness for a long time may strain your eye.

Setting a Lock Screen Password or PIN

You can lock your phone by activating the screen lock feature. *Note:* Once you set a screen lock, your phone will require an unlock code each time you turn it on or unlock the touch screen.

1. Swipe down from the top of the screen and tap settings icon .

2. Tap "Security & location", "Security & Privacy" or "Lock screen and security".

3. Tap "Screen lock", "Screen lock type" or "Screen lock & Passwords".

4. Tap a screen lock type you like.

5. If you choose **Password or PIN**, then enter the **password/PIN** you wish and follow the onscreen instructions to complete the setup. In addition, you may choose **Pattern** or **Swipe.** If you don't want a lock screen, tap **None**.

Tip: If supported on your Android phone, you may also use your fingerprint or iris to unlock your phone. More on this in the next section (see page 148)

Adjusting Text/Font Size on Your Android Phone

You can change the font on your Android phone to a bigger or smaller font by following the steps below:

1. Swipe down from the top of the screen and tap settings icon  .

2. Tap **Display**.

3. Tap **Advanced**.

4. Select **Font Size** and choose an option.

For some Android phones, the steps above may not work. If this is the case, try the following:

1. Swipe down from the top of the screen and tap settings icon  .

2. Tap **Accessibility**. If you are using LG Android phone, you may need to tap **General** tab, before you see "Accessibility".

3. Select **Font Size** and drag the slider as you want. If you don't see "Font size", tap **Vision** and then tap **Font and screen zoom**. Thereafter tap **Font size** and adjust the font as you like.

Changing the Display Size

You can change the display on your Android phone to a bigger or smaller display. When the display is bigger, the items on the screen should appear bigger. When the display is smaller, the item on the screen should appear smaller. To change the display size, follow the steps below:

1. Swipe down from the top of the screen and tap settings icon  .

2. Tap **Display**.
3. Tap **Advanced**.
4. Select **Display Size** and adjust the display as you like.

For some Android phones, the steps above may not work. If this is the case, try the following:

1. Swipe down from the top of the screen and tap settings icon  .

2. Tap **Accessibility**. If you are using LG Android phone, you may need to tap **General** tab, before you see "Accessibility."

3. Select **Display size** and drag the slider as you want. If you don't see "Display size," tap **Vision** and then tap **Font and screen zoom**. Thereafter, tap **Screen zoom** and adjust the display as you like.

Entering a Text

You can enter a text by selecting characters on the virtual keypad or by speaking words into the microphone using a voice command app.

To enter a text:

1. Enter a text by selecting the corresponding alphabets, symbols or numbers.
2. You can use any of the following keys:

Please note that the on-screen keyboard on your phone may be different from the one shown below. This is because the on-screen keyboard you see depends on the text input field you select and the type of Android phone you are using. Nevertheless, the icons usually represent similar functions on Android phones.

Below is the type of virtual keyboard found on many Android phones.

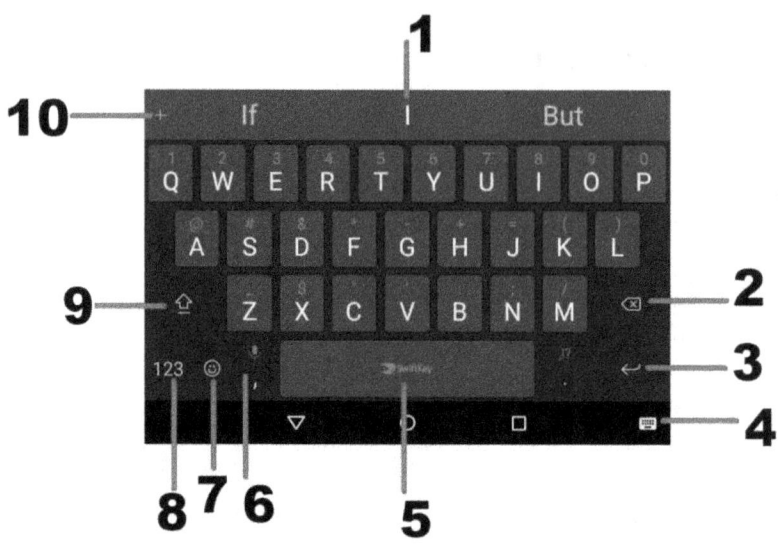

Number	Function
1.	**Predictive text bar** **Tip**: Android phone has an auto replace feature, and as you type, your phone will give you text suggestions, the most likely suggestions will appear colored or bold on the predictive text bar. To use the suggestion that appears colored, (the suggestion that appears at the center), tap the space bar. To use a different suggestion, tap on it. Please be informed that you can disable this auto replace feature, to do this, please see page 144-45.
2.	Clear input/backspace
3.	Start a new line.
4.	Tap this icon to select a new keyboard type

5.	Space bar: You can swipe right or left to switch between input languages. To add input language, please go to page 131.
6.	Tap and hold this icon to access the voice input feature
7.	Tap this to access emoticons
8.	Switch between Number/Symbol mode and ABC mode
9.	Change case
10.	Option tab: when you tap this button, you will gain an access to a list of icons/functions.

Furthermore, below is the type of virtual keyboard found on many Samsung Android phones.

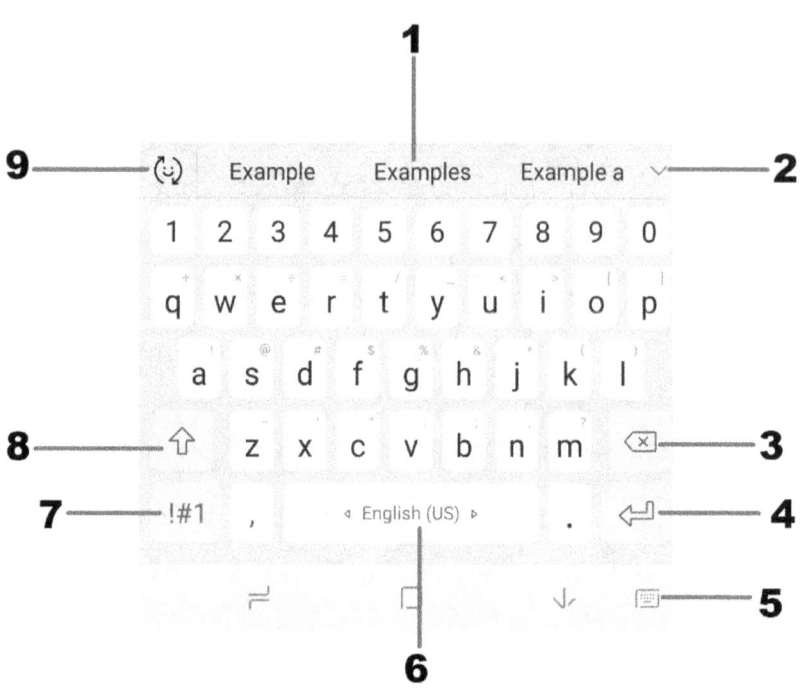

Number	Function
1.	**Predictive text bar** **Tip**: Android phone has an auto replace feature, and as you type, your phone will give you text suggestions, the most likely suggestions will appear in blue on the predictive text bar. To use the suggestion that appears in blue, (the suggestion that appears at the center), tap the space bar. To use a different suggestion, tap on it. Please be informed that you can disable this auto replace feature, to do this, please see page 144-45.
2.	Tap on this to see more predictive texts or more settings.

3.	Clear input/backspace
4.	Start a new line.
5.	Tap this icon to select a new keyboard type
6.	Space bar: You can swipe right or left to switch between input languages. To add input language, see page 131.
7.	Switch between Number/Symbol mode and ABC mode
8.	Change case
9.	Option tab: When you press and hold this button, you will gain an access to a list of icons/functions.

Hint: On Samsung Android phones, when you tap the option tab

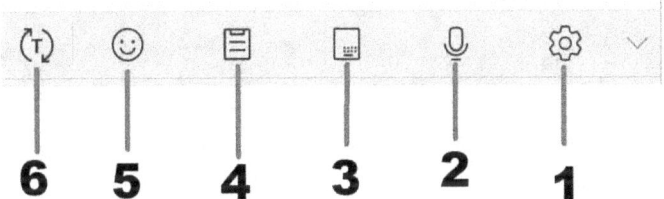 you will gain access to the following:

1. **Keyboard settings:** Tap this to access the keyboard settings.
2. **Voice input**: Enter text by voice.
3. **One-handed keyboard**: Tap this to be able to control the virtual keyboard using one hand. When you tap the **One-handed keyboard** button, you will see a keyboard that looks like the one below.

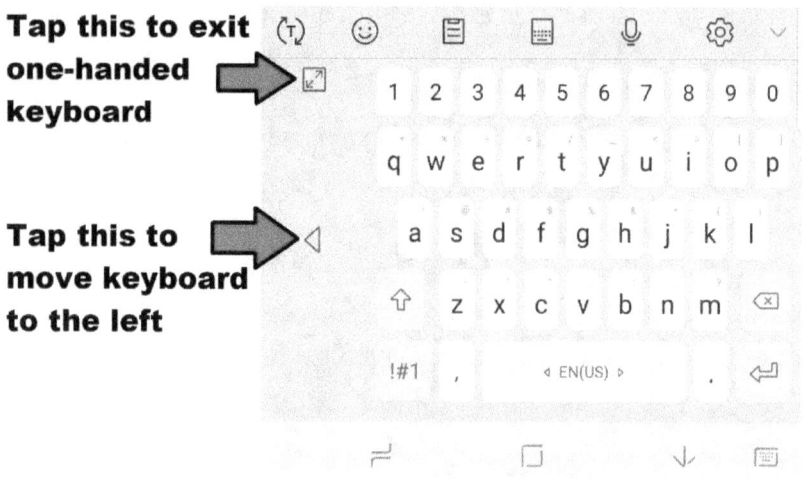

Tap this to exit one-handed keyboard

Tap this to move keyboard to the left

4. **Clipboard:** Tap this to add an item from the clipboard. After using an item on the clipboard, tap the arrow icon (located at the bottom of the screen) to exit.

5. **Emoticon:** Tap this to add emoticons to your texts.

6. **Option button:** Tap this to switch to predictive texts.

Tip: To learn how to manage the on-screen keyboard, go to page 130. On some Android phones, when you select two or more languages, you can switch between the input languages by swiping to the left or right on the space key.

Note: By default, you may notice that your Android phone automatically replaces typed word with another one (a corrected one) when you press the space bar. While this option is cool, it may be unwanted sometimes. To disable this function:

1. Access the virtual keyboard.

2. Tap the more option icon "+", ▣ or ☺ located at the top of the virtual keyboard.

3. Tap the settings icon ⚙ .

4. If available, tap "Smart typing".

5. Tap "Autocorrect" or "Auto replace" to disable it.

To Copy and Paste a Text

While entering or reading a text, you can use the copy and paste options. To do this:

1. Tap and hold a word to display copy options. The icons below will show up after selecting a text or texts.

| Cut | Copy | Clipboard | Share | Dictionary |

2. Drag ◖ or ◗ to select more texts.

3. Select **Copy** icon to copy or select **Cut** icon to cut the text onto the clipboard.

4. In another application or where you want to paste the text, tap and hold the text input field.

5. Select **Paste** icon to insert the text from the clipboard into the text input field. If available, you can also tap the clipboard

icon ▤ to access the clipboard for more paste options.

Using the Voice Typing

1. Tap the microphone icon  on the keyboard. If you can't see the microphone icon, tap the option tab , and then select .

2. Speak your text. Your device types as you speak.
3. To pause the voice typing, tap the screen.

4. To manage the voice typing option, swipe down from the top

of the screen, and tap **Settings** ⚙ > **System** and tap

Language and input. Tap **Virtual keyboard** and tap

Google voice typing.

If you are using a Samsung Android phone, do the following

instead:

Swipe down from the top of the screen and tap **Settings**

⚙ > **General management** and tap **Language and input**.

Tap **On-Screen keyboard** and select **Google voice typing** or

Samsung voice input.

5. To exit the voice typing, tap the arrow icon ↓ , ◁ or

▽ (located at the bottom of the screen).

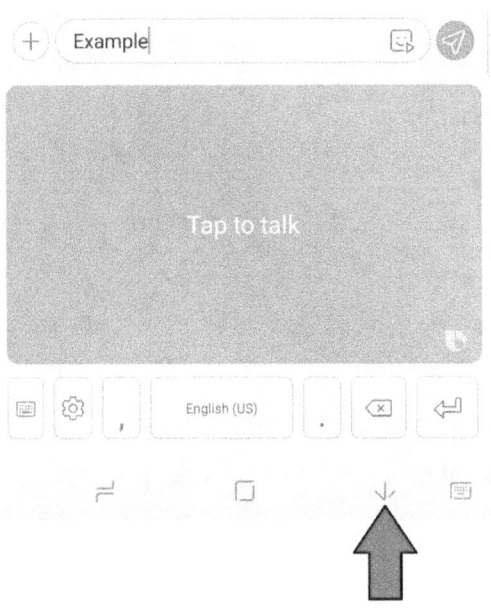

Using The Special Features

Some Android phones came with special features that make them distinct from others. I will now explain how to use these features.

Using the Fingerprint Feature

One of the cool features on an Android Phone is Fingerprint. This allows you to unlock applications without entering boring passwords.

Registering your fingerprint

Before you can start using your fingerprint on the device, you will need to first register your fingerprint. Depending on the type of Android phone you are using, you can register up to three (or more) fingerprints. In addition, you also have the option of registering a password as a backup.

To do this:

1. Swipe down from the top of the screen and select settings

   icon ⚙ .

2. Tap **Lock screen and security**, **Biometrics and security** or **Security & Location**.

3. Tap **Fingerprint scanner**, **Fingerprint Manager** or **Pixel/Nexus Imprint**.

4. Follow the onscreen instructions to complete the setup.

Renaming fingerprints

1. Swipe down from the top of the screen and select settings

    icon   .

2. Tap **Lock screen and security** or **Security & Location**.

3. Tap **Fingerprint scanner**, **Fingerprint Manager** or **Pixel/Nexus Imprint**.

4. If prompted, unlock the screen using the preset screen lock method and tap **NEXT**.

5. Tap the fingerprint you want to rename. For example, tap **Fingerprint 1**.

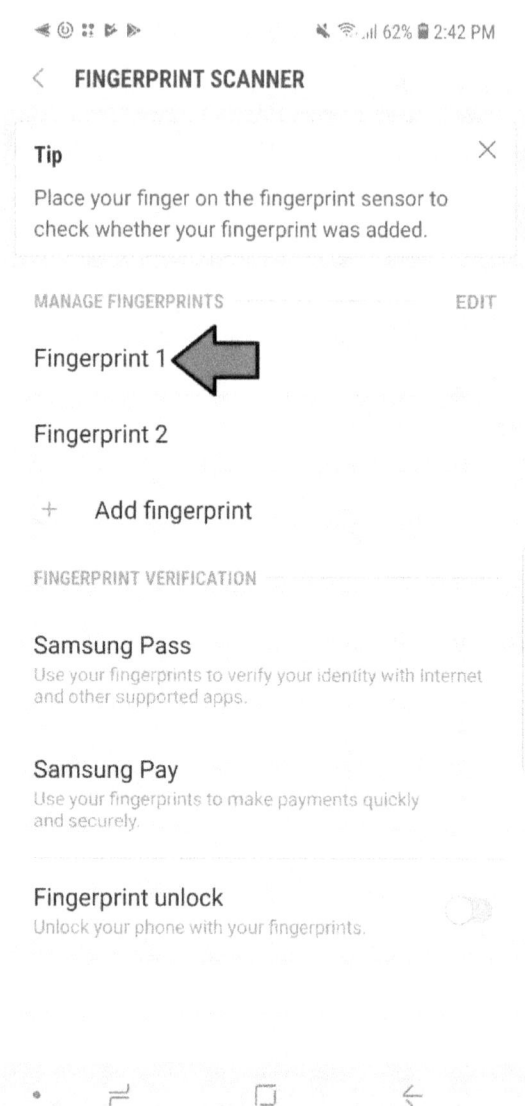

Tip   ✕

Place your finger on the fingerprint sensor to
check whether your fingerprint was added.

MANAGE FINGERPRINTS   EDIT

Fingerprint 1

Fingerprint 2

+   Add fingerprint

FINGERPRINT VERIFICATION

Samsung Pass
Use your fingerprints to verify your identity with internet
and other supported apps.

Samsung Pay
Use your fingerprints to make payments quickly
and securely.

Fingerprint unlock
Unlock your phone with your fingerprints.

6.   Enter a new name, and then tap **Rename/OK**.

Tip: When renaming your fingerprint, make sure you use the name
of the finger you registered. For example, you can use the name
Index finger or **Forefinger**. This prevents unnecessary confusions.

Deleting fingerprints

1. Swipe down from the top of the screen and select settings

   icon  .

2. Tap **Lock screen and security** or **Security & Location**.

3. Tap **Fingerprint scanner**, **Fingerprint Manager** or **Pixel/Nexus Imprint**.

4. If prompted, unlock the screen using the preset screen lock method and tap **NEXT**.

5. Tap the fingerprint you want to delete, and then tap **Delete**.

6. Alternatively, touch and hold the fingerprint you want to delete, and then tap **Remove**.

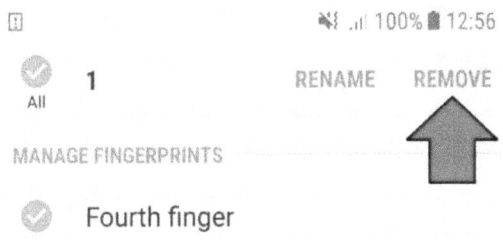

Setting a screen lock with fingerprint

You can lock the screen with your fingerprint instead of using a pattern, PIN, or password.

1. Swipe down from the top of the screen and select settings

   icon  .

2. Tap **Lock screen and security** or **Security & Location**.

3. Tap **Screen lock** or **Screen lock type**.

4. Unlock the screen using the preset screen lock method and tap **NEXT**.

5. Tap the status switch next to **Fingerprint**.

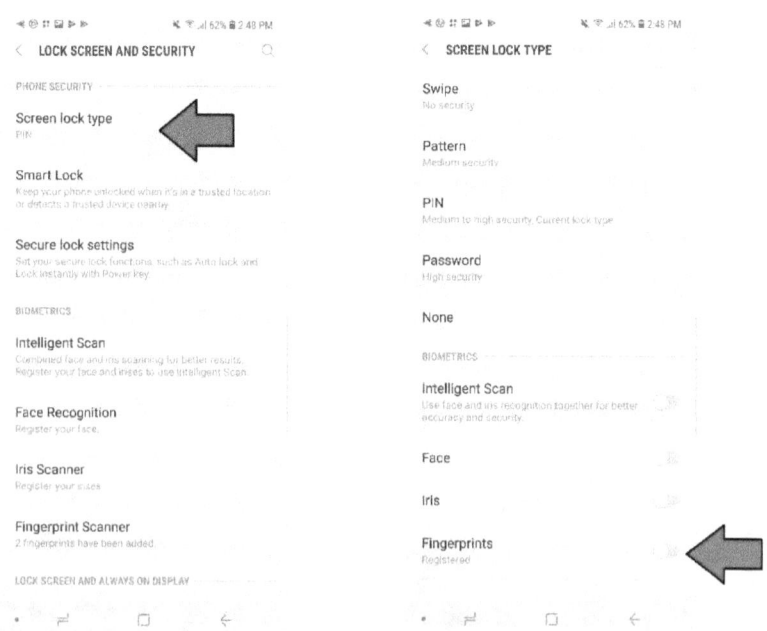

Using fingerprints to sign into accounts

Apart from using your fingerprint to unlock your device, some Android phones allow you to use fingerprint to access online features including making payments and unlocking apps. To check if your phone supports this feature

1. Swipe down from the top of the screen and select settings icon .

2. Tap **Lock screen and security** or **Security & Location**.

3. Tap **Fingerprint scanner**, **Fingerprint Manager** or **Pixel/Nexus Imprint**.

4. If necessary, unlock the screen using the preset screen lock method and then check if payment or app unlocking information is available. For example, if you are using a Samsung Android phone, you would see:

   a. **Samsung Pass**: Tap **Samsung Pass** to access your online accounts/apps using your fingerprint. To get started with this feature, just tap Samsung Pass and follow the prompts.

   b. **Samsung Pay**: Tap **Samsung Pay** to use your fingerprint for secured and fast payments with the Samsung Pay app. To get started with this feature, just tap Samsung Pay and follow the prompts. Samsung Pay may not be available in some locations in the world.

   c. **Fingerprint unlock:** Tap the switch next to **Fingerprint unlock** to enable or disable fingerprint security.

Troubleshooting the fingerprint scanner

If the fingerprint scanner is not responding, try any of the following:

1. Remove any phone case that may be covering the fingerprint reader.

2. Ensure that you are not using the tip of your fingerprint. Make sure to cover the entire fingerprint reader with your finger.

3. If your finger has scars, try using another finger, this is because your device may not recognize fingerprints that are affected by wrinkles or scars.

4. Ensure the finger you registered with is used.

5. Make sure that your finger and the surface of the fingerprint scanner are clean and dry.

Iris Scanner

Some Android phones allow you to unlock your phone using your iris.

To do this:

1. Swipe down from the top of the screen and select settings icon ⚙ .

2. Tap **Lock screen and security, Biometrics and security** or **Security & Location**.

3. Tap **Iris scanner**. You may need to setup an alternative lock screen method or enter your lock screen information if you have already setup a lock screen.

4. Follow the onscreen instructions to complete the setup. *Unless advised otherwise, please note that it is recommended that you keep the screen at least 8 inches away from your face to protect your eyes when using iris scanner.*

Deleting iris data:

1. Swipe down from the top of the screen and select settings

   icon .

2. Tap **Lock screen and security** or **Security & Location**.

3. Tap **Iris Scanner**.

4. Tap **Remove iris data** and tap **Remove**.

Troubleshooting the iris scanner

If the Iris scanner is not responding, try any of the following:

1. Remove any screen protector that may be covering the iris camera, LED sensor, or proximity sensor usually located above at the top of the screen of the supported Android phones.

2. Ensure that you are not wearing glasses.

3. Ensure that you are not trying to use the iris scanner under the direct sunlight.

4. Ensure you hold the phone to the level of your face/eyes.

5. If available, ensure that you follow the instructions provided by the manufacturer of your phone.

Water Resistance

Another cool feature present on some Android phones is the water resistance feature. You don't have to worry that your phone is going to get wet when you are drenched by the rain or inside a bathroom. To know more about water resistance, please go to page 35.

Smart Lock

Smart lock allows you to lock your device like a pro. This feature allows you to quickly lock and unlock your phone.

To use smart lock:

1. Swipe down from the top of the screen and select settings

   icon  .

2. Tap **Lock screen and security** or **Security & Location**.

3. If available, tap **Trust agents**.

4. Tap **Smart Lock.**

5. If necessary, unlock the screen using the preset screen lock method. You may need to setup a screen lock if you don't have any.

6. Pick an option on the screen (the options might include **On-body detection**, **Trusted places**, **Trusted devices** and **Trusted voice.**) Then follow the on-screen instructions to complete the setup.

To remove or deactivate a smart lock option:

1. Repeat steps 1 to 4 above.
2. Pick an option on the screen (the options might include **On-body detection**, **Trusted places**, **Trusted devices** and **Trusted voice.**) Then tap an option corresponding to what you want to do. For example, to remove "Trusted places," tap "Home" and then tap "Turn off this location". To clear your home address, tap "Edit" and then tap the delete icon

 . .. Thereafter, tap "Clear".

Note: However, please note that using smart lock may allow third party to easily access your phone. For example, if you set up "trusted places", your phone might unlock while in this place (or around it) even when you don't want it to unlock.

Tip: You can use **Trusted places** option to automatically unlock your phone while at home and automatically lock your phone while at work or outside the home. All you need to do to achieve this is to set up your home as a trusted place.

In addition, to use "Trusted places", you need to enable location (if you have not done so). To enable location:

To activate location services:

1. Swipe down from the top of the screen and select the settings

   icon  .

2. Tap **Connection** or **Security & Location**.

3. Tap **Location**.

4. Next to the switch under **Location**, select **on**.

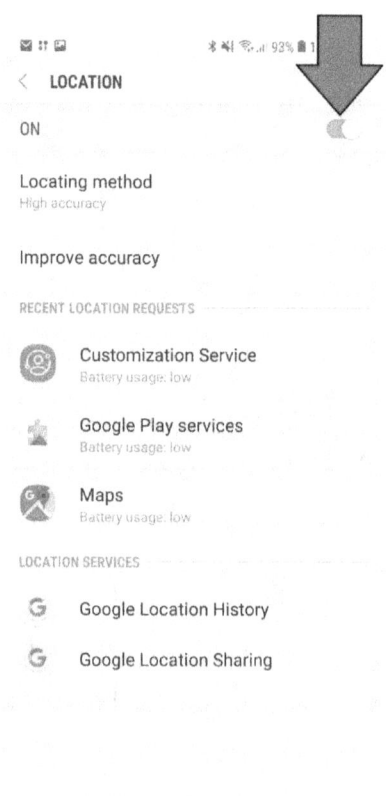

Using the Always On Display Feature

The Always On Display allows you to display information, such as a clock, notifications, or calendar on the screen when it is turned off. I personally love the fact that you can check the time with this feature even if the screen is off. *Please note that not all Android phones have the feature, if your phone doesn't have this feature, you can download an app called "Always On AMOLED" from Google Play store to have a similar experience.*

To access the Always on Display on Google Pixel 2 and some Android phones:

1. Swipe down from the top of the screen and select settings icon  .
2. Tap **Display**.
3. Tap **Advanced**.
4. Tap **Ambient display**.
5. Tap the status switch next to **Always on**.

To access the Always on Display on Samsung Android phones:

The Always on Display on Samsung Android phone appears to give you more robust experience than the one found on Google Pixel 2.

1. Swipe down from the top of the screen and select settings icon  .
2. Tap **Lock screen and security**.

3. Scroll down and tap **Always on Display**.

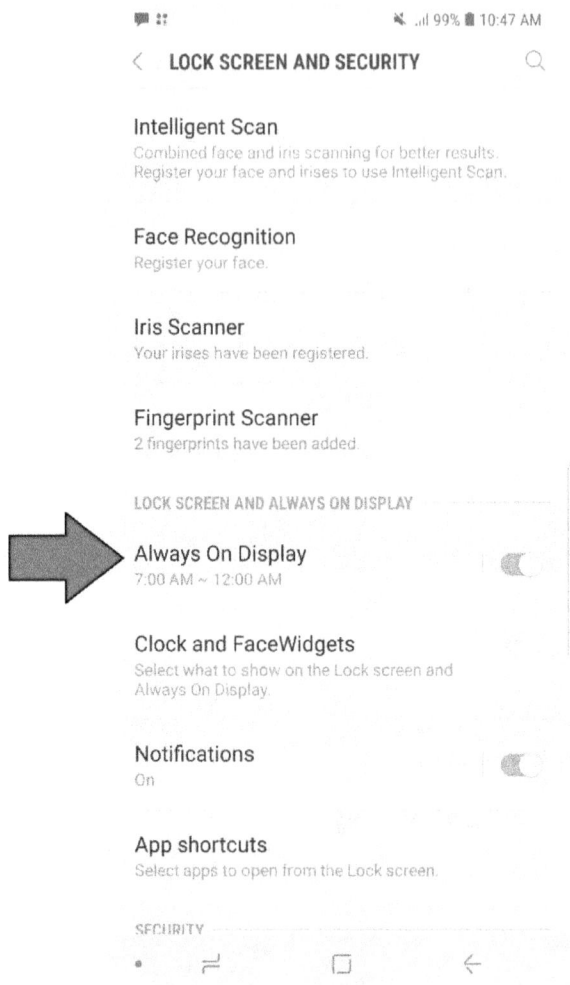

4. Tap On/Off switch to enable or disable Always on Display.

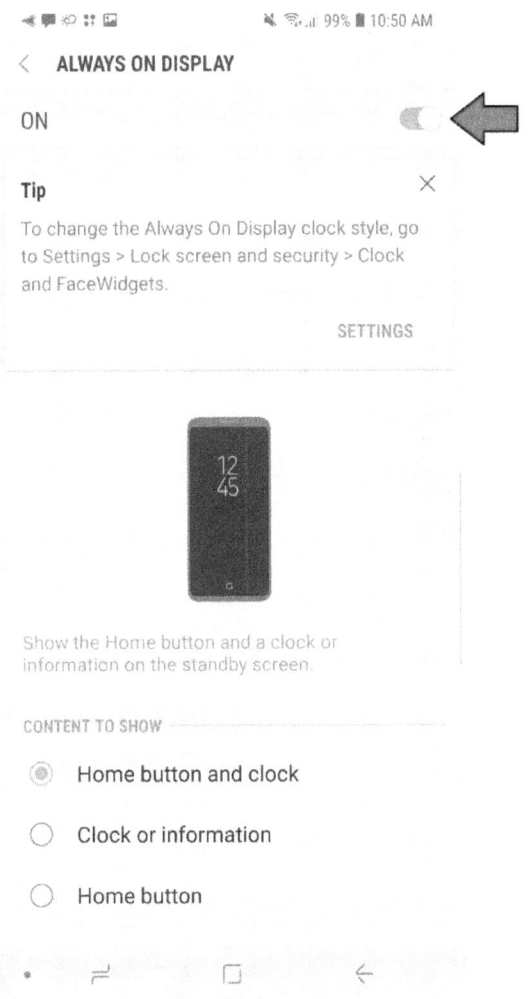

When you enable the **Always on Display** on Samsung Android phone, you can access the following:

a. **Content to show**: This feature allows you to choose the content to show when the screen is off. See the screenshot below.

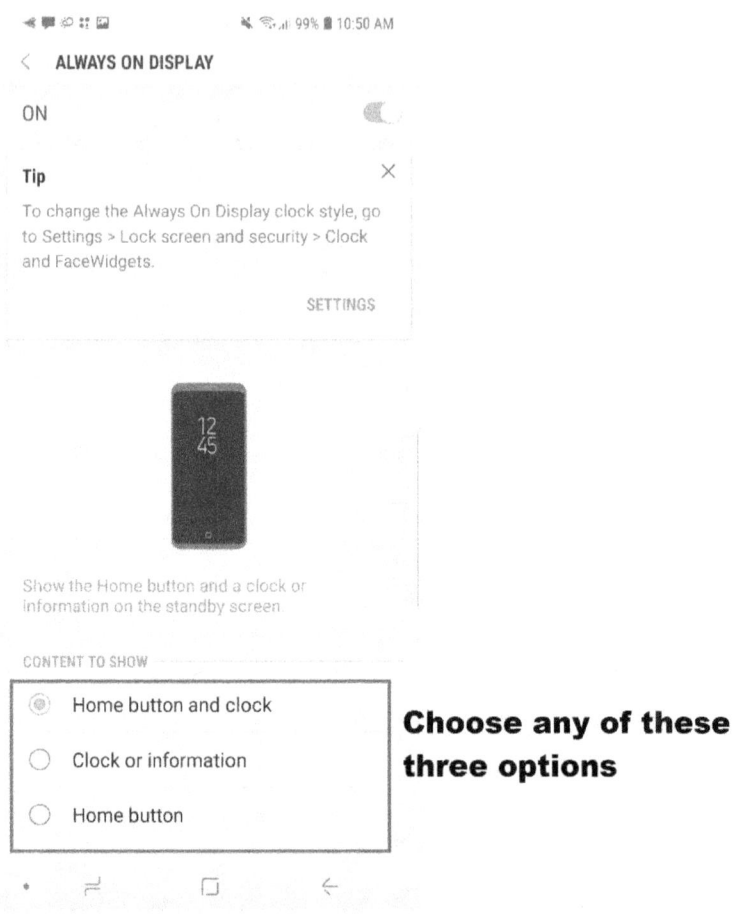

b. **Show Always**: When this is enabled, the Always on Display is active every time. To customize when the Always on Display will be active, tap the status switch next to **Show Always** and set a schedule.

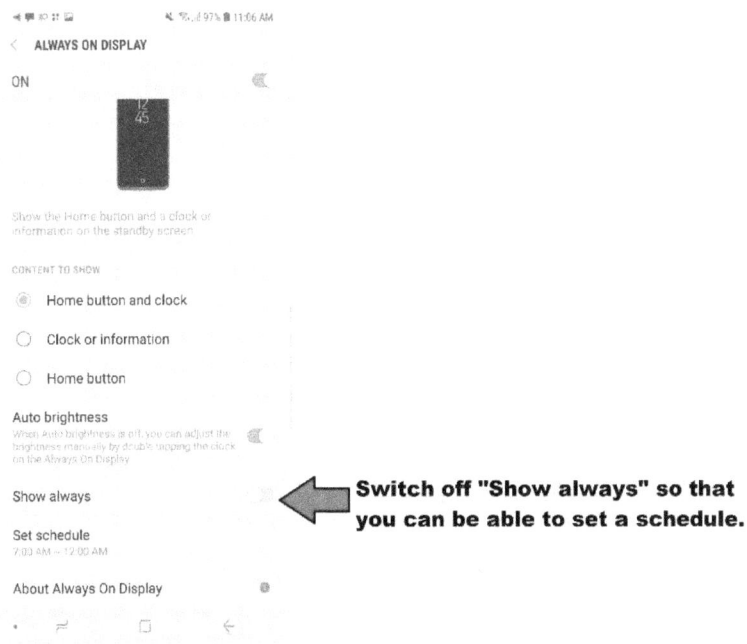

ALWAYS ON DISPLAY

ON

Show the Home button and a clock or information on the standby screen.

CONTENT TO SHOW

⦿ Home button and clock

○ Clock or information

○ Home button

Auto brightness
When Auto brightness is off, you can adjust the brightness manually by double tapping the clock on the Always On Display.

Show always

Set schedule
7:00 AM ~ 12:00 AM

About Always On Display

Switch off "Show always" so that you can be able to set a schedule.

c. **About Always on Display**: Tap this to view the current software version, update the app and check license information.

Good news: One interesting thing about the Always on Display option is that it consumes a very low amount of battery energy.

Changing the Clock style/Calendar style/Image on the "Always on Display" (on Samsung Android phone)

You can choose the clock style, calendar style, or image to be displayed when the Always on Display is active. To do this:

1. Swipe down from the top of the screen and select settings icon 🔧 .

2. Tap **Lock screen and security**.

3. Scroll down and tap **Clock and FaceWidgets**.

4. Tap **Clock style**.

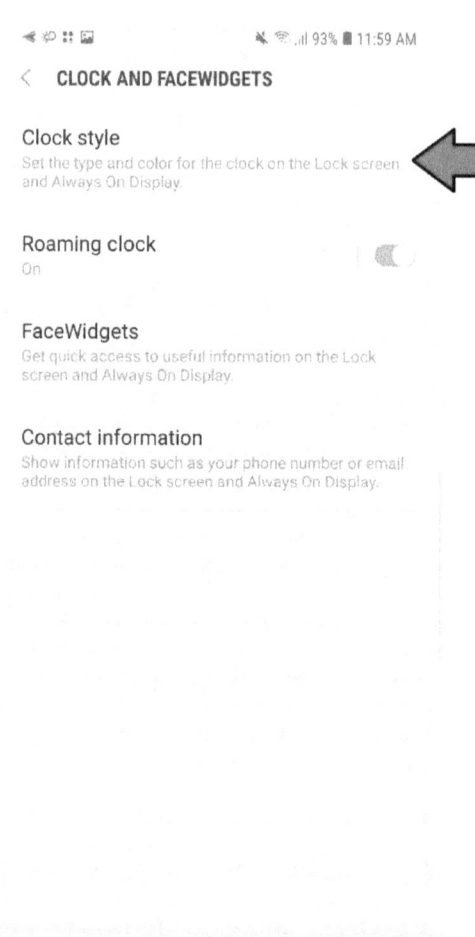

5. Scroll through the available clock styles/calendar styles/image thumbnails and choose one. If clock/calendar style thumbnails are not showing, tap **Type** (located at the bottom of the screen).

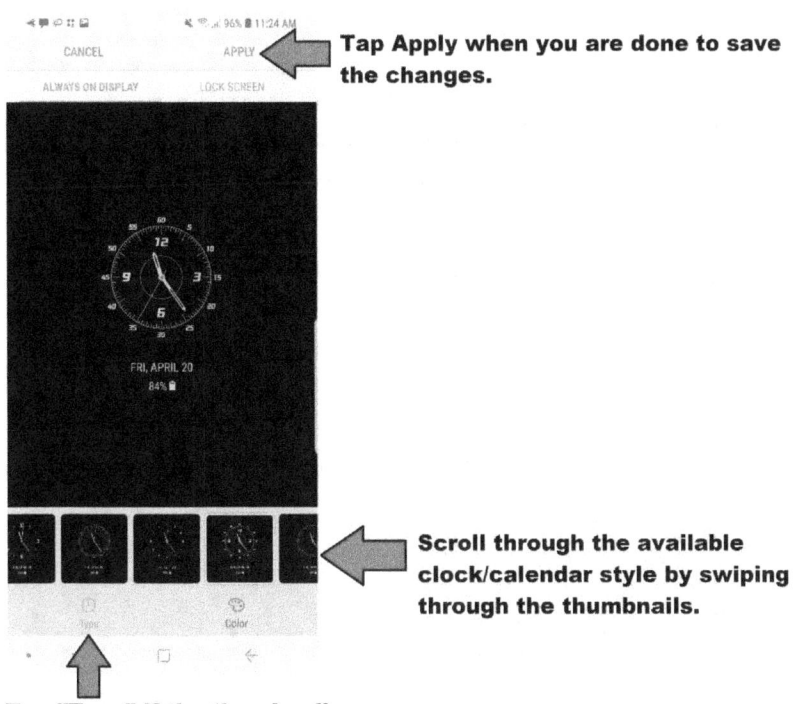

Tap Apply when you are done to save the changes.

Scroll through the available clock/calendar style by swiping through the thumbnails.

Tap "Type" if the thumbnails are not showing up

6. Tap **Color** 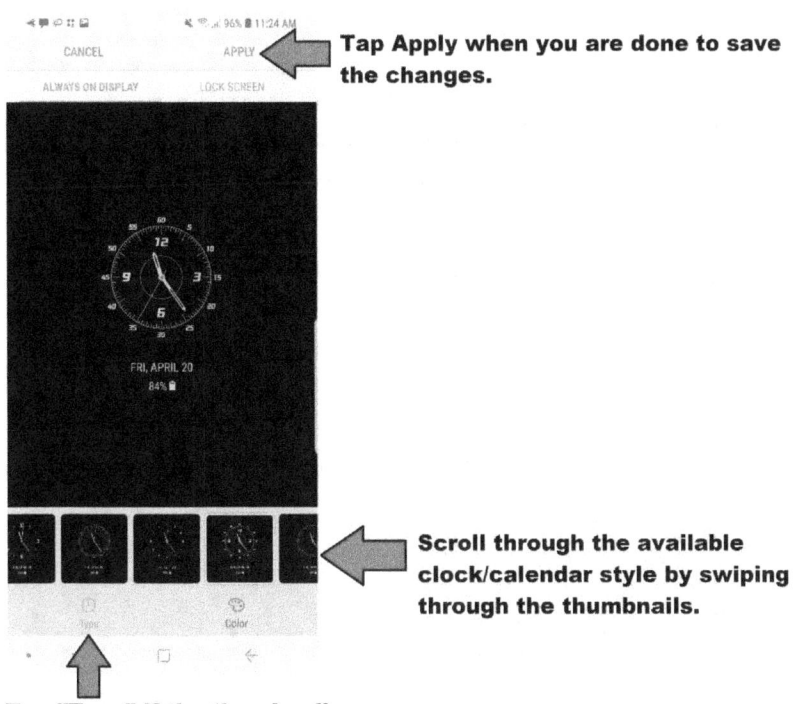 and select color of your choice.

7. Tap **Apply** located at the top of the screen to effect changes. Note that you may not be able to choose a clock, image or calendar to display if you choose **Home button** only under **Content to Show** (see page 161).

8. To change the clock style on the lock screen, tap **Lock Screen** (see the picture below) and choose a clock. Then tap **Apply** to save the changes.

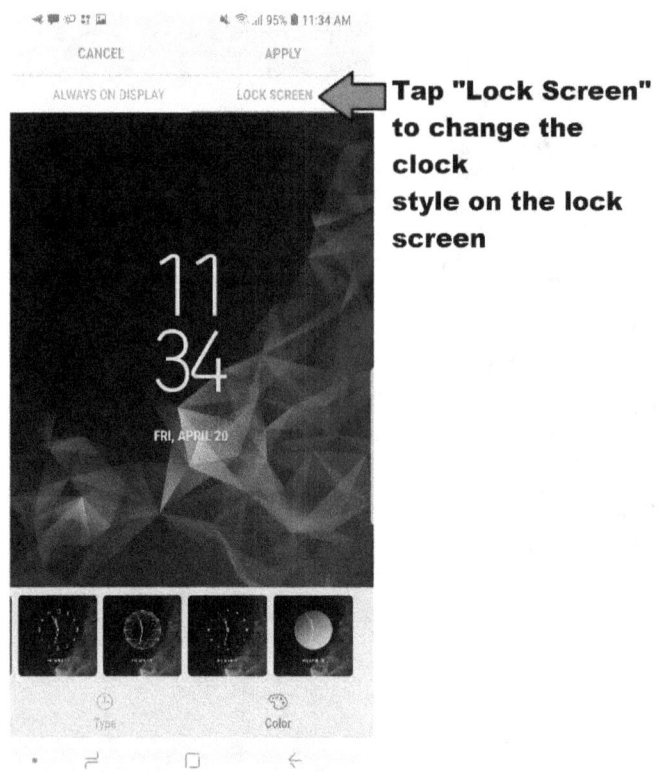

Tap "Lock Screen" to change the clock style on the lock screen

Tip: You can enable your Samsung Android phone to show you today's schedule and next alarm even when your screen is locked.

To do this, go to settings ⚙ > **Lock screen and security** > **Clock and FaceWidgets > FaceWidgets**. Then tap the status switches next to **Today's schedule** and **Next alarm**.

Fast Battery Charging

One of the cool features on some Android Phones is Fast Battery Charging. With this feature, you can charge your phone faster. You can learn how to use this feature by going to page 16.

Using the Edge Screen on Samsung Android Phones

The Edge screen transforms the way you handle Samsung Android phone. Edge panels can be used to access apps, tasks, contacts and more. To access the Edge panel, drag the Edge panel handle located at the Edge of the screen. To access more Edge items, swipe again from the edge of the screen.

Swipe this handle

To access Edge panel settings, tap the settings ⚙ icon located at the bottom of the screen (this setting icon appears while viewing the Edge options).

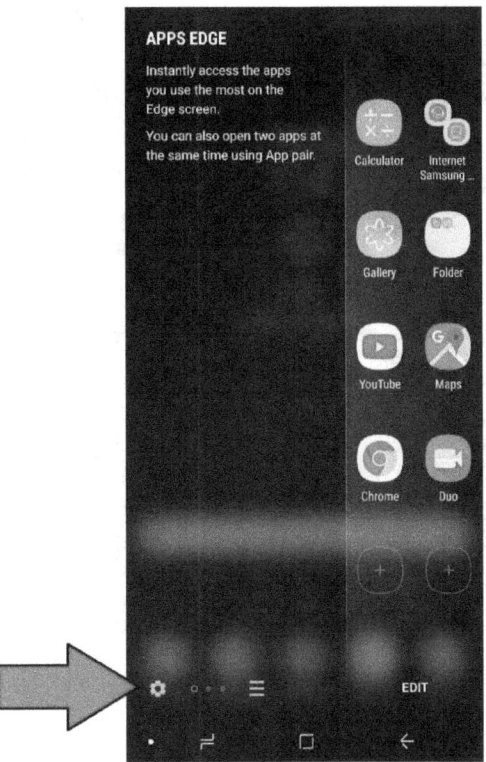

Tip: You can view all the Edge panels at once. To do this, drag the Edge panel handle located at the edge of the screen and then tap the menu icon. To access any of the panels displayed, simply tap it.

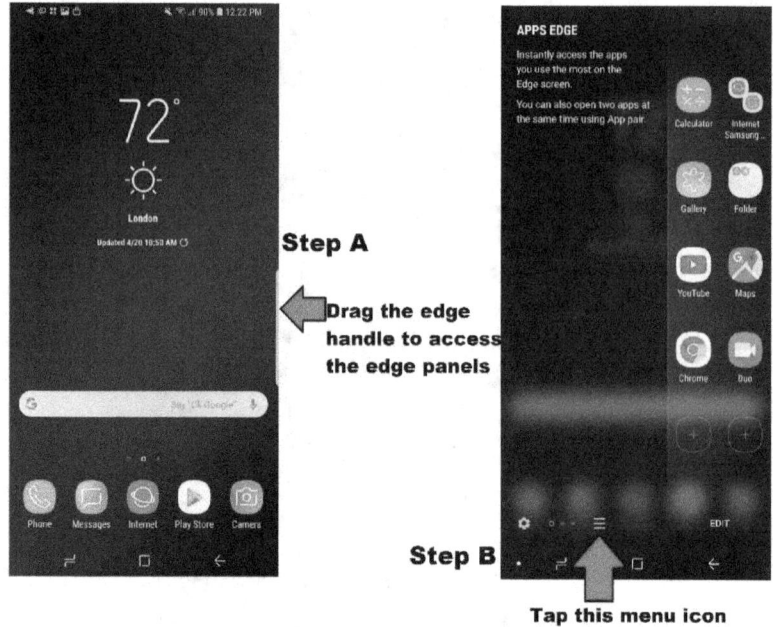

Step A

Drag the edge handle to access the edge panels

Step B

Tap this menu icon

Using the Edge Panel on Samsung Android Phones

The Edge panel allows you to use the Edge screen in a special way.
To manage the Edge panel:

1. Swipe down from the top of the screen and select the settings

   icon ⚙ . Then tap **Display** tab.

2. Scroll down and tap **Edge Screen**.

3. Tap **Edge Panels**.

4. To download helpful panels, tap **Download** located at the top
   of the screen and tap the Edge panel you want to download.

Then tap **Install** to download and install your chosen panel.
To go back to the Edge panel screen, tap the back button

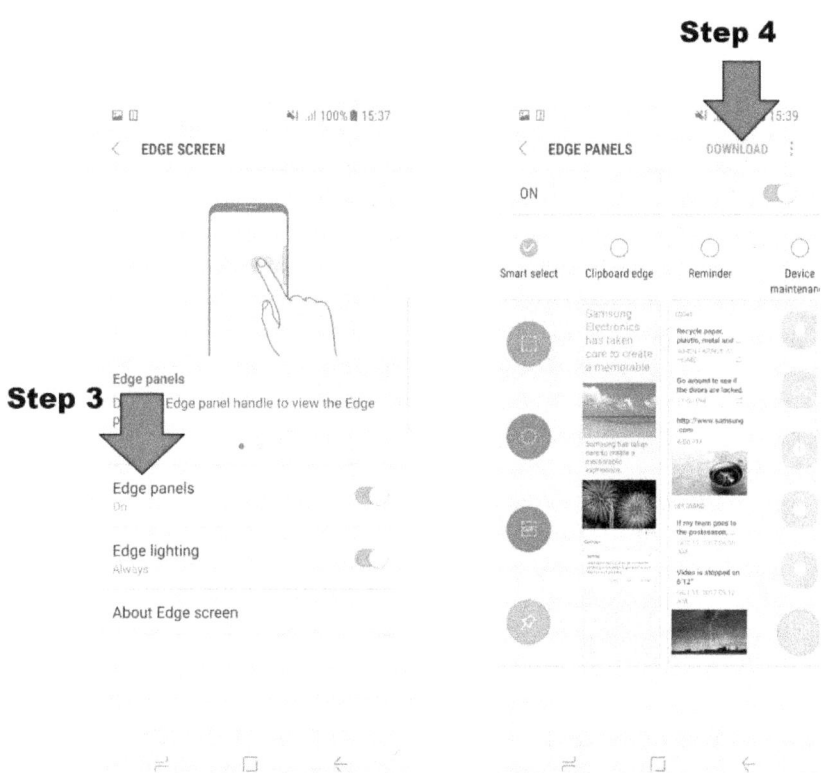

To see your newly installed panel, navigate to the **Edge panels** screen and swipe left.

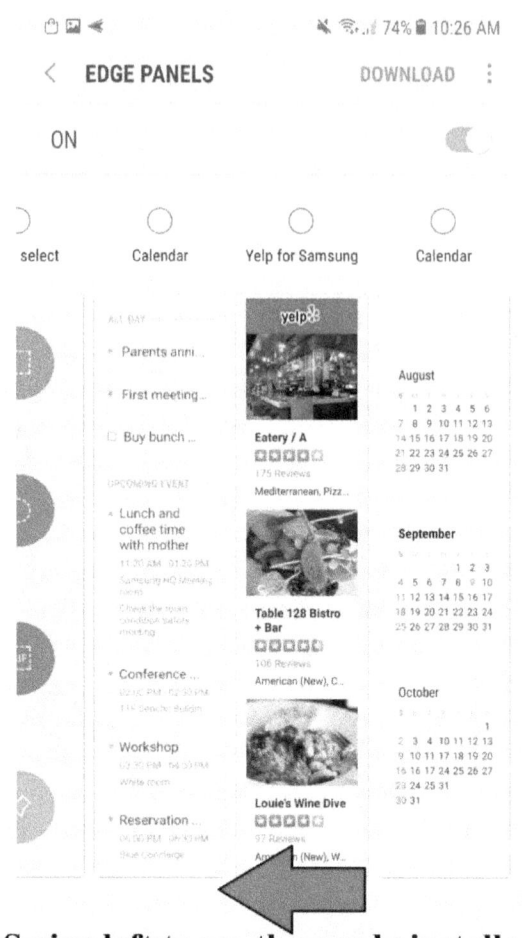

Swipe left to see the newly installed panel. In this case, calendar panel is the newly installed panel.

5. To uninstall an Edge panel that you don't like, tap the menu

    icon ⋮ located at the top of the Edge panel's screen and

    select **Uninstall**. Then select the minus icon (--) located at

    the top of the panel you want to uninstall. When prompted,

    tap **OK**. Please note that the uninstall button may not be available if you have not installed any Edge panel from the Edge panel store.

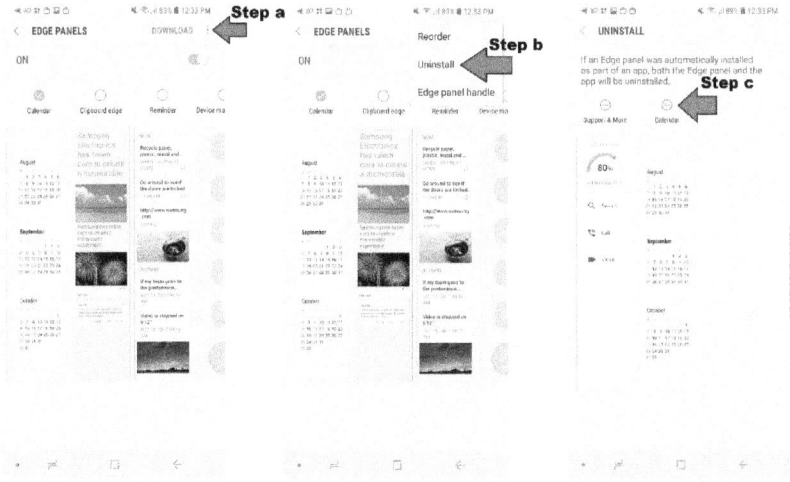

6. There are some Edge panels that allow you to edit them. To edit an editable panel, just tap **EDIT** next to the panel you want to edit. Please note that you may need to enable a panel before you can edit it. To learn how to enable a panel, please go to step 7.

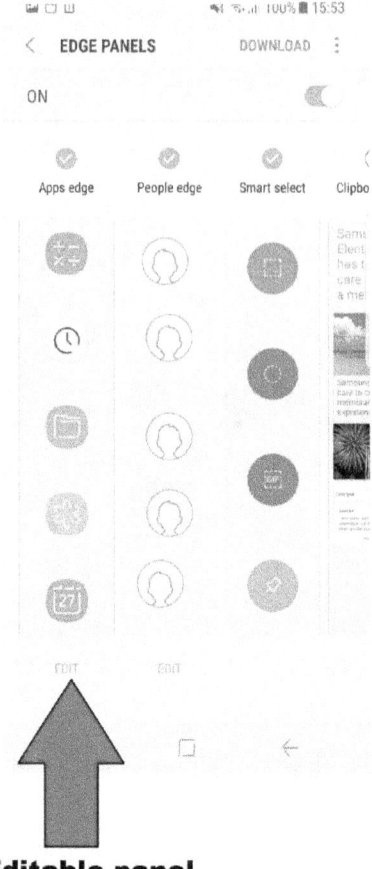

Editable panel

Then tap and hold an item and move it to the Edge screen. To remove an item, tap the minus icon. To rearrange the icons, tap and drag the icon(s) to a new location. See the picture below.

Tap and drag any of these icons to move it to another location

Tap, hold and drag an icon to right side of the screen to add it to the edge screen

Tap this minus icon to remove an app from the edge screen

Although, *Apps Edge* has been used in the example above, you can also manage People Edge in similar way. In addition, please note that there is a maximum number of items you can add to the Edge screen.

To create "app pair" on the edge screen, tap **Create App pair**, select the two apps you like, and tap **DONE** to save the changes. To move the bottom app to top and vice versa, tap **Switch**. To delete your selection and select another apps, tap **Clear**.

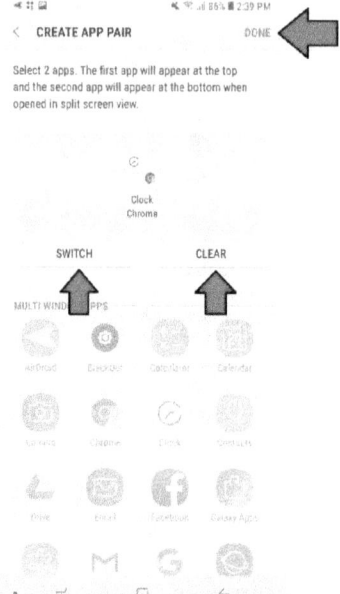

7. To enable an Edge panel or select the Edge panel that you want to see on the Edge screen, simply tap/tick the circle on top of the panel. To disable/remove a panel, simply unselect the circle.

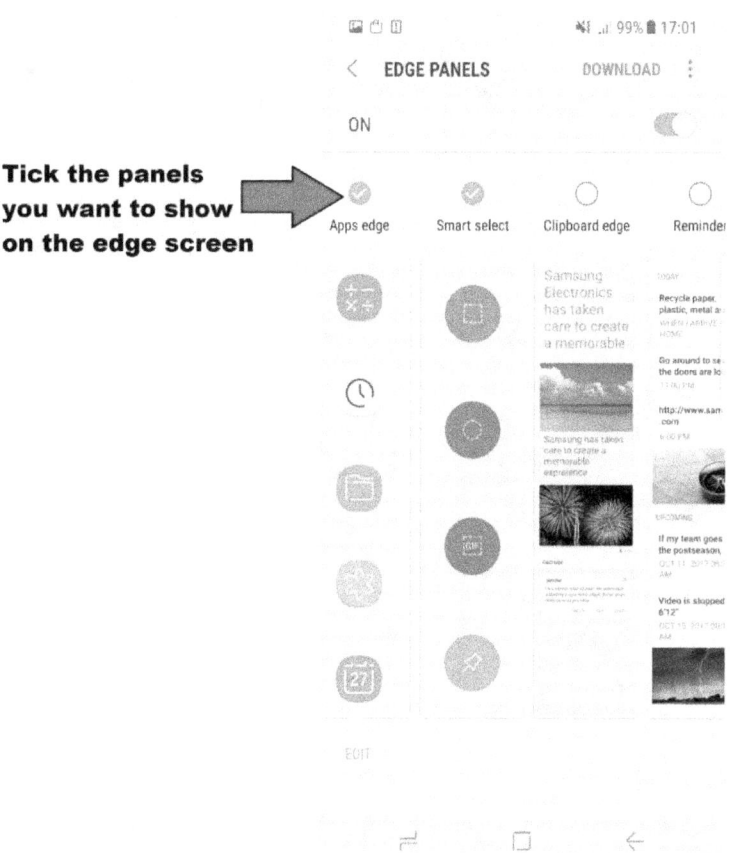

Tick the panels you want to show on the edge screen

8. To disable Edge panels, tap the status switch next to **ON**.
   Please note that when you disable Edge Panel, the Edge
   handle will disappear.

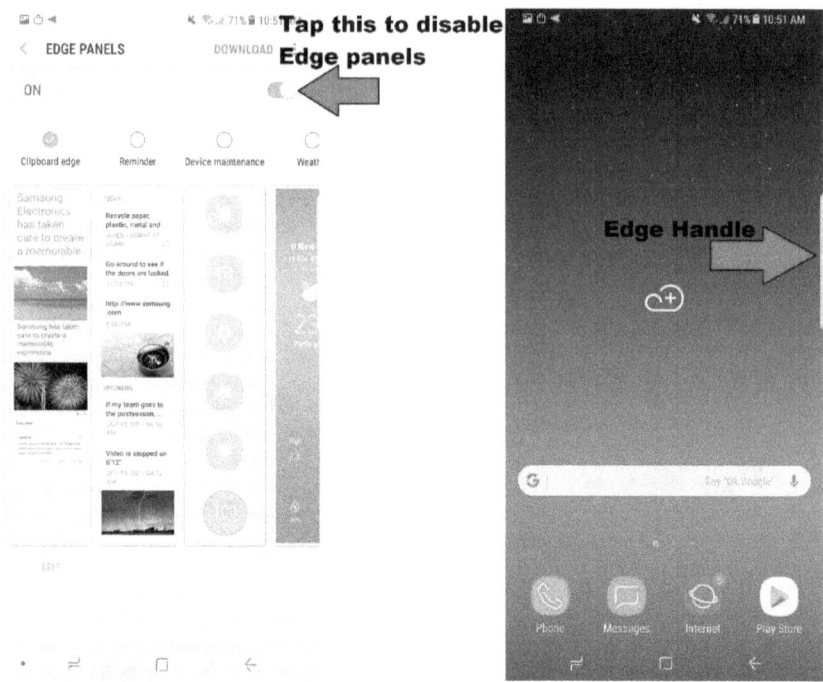

Note: If you download many Edge panels, you may not be able to access all these panels at once on your Edge screen. You may not be able to use more than nine Edge panels at once. To select the Edge panels that you want to access, simply follow the step 7 above.

Using the Edge Lighting on Samsung Android Phones

This feature allows you to set the Edge screen to light up when you receive calls or notifications.

1. Swipe down from the top of the screen and select the settings icon ⚙. Tap **Display** tab.

2. Scroll down and tap **Edge Screen**.

3. Tap **Edge Lighting**.

4. Tap the switch next to **ON**. The switch will appear bold when enabled.

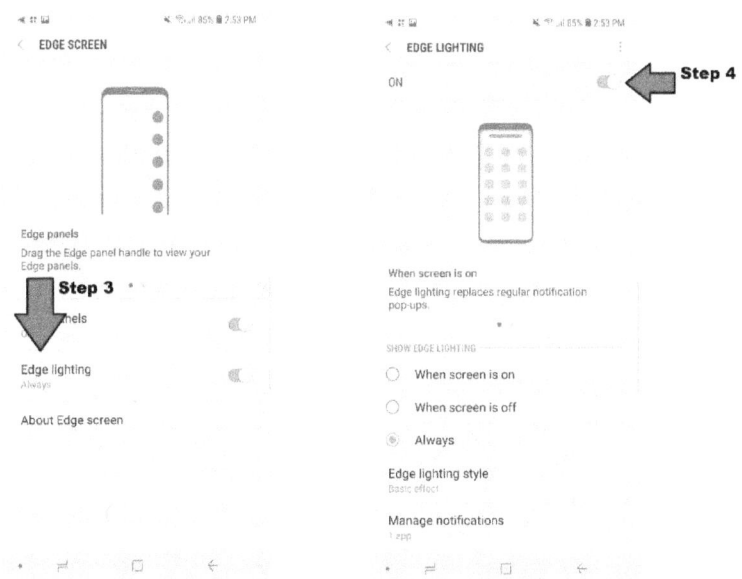

5. Select when to show the Edge lighting. If you want Edge Lighting to be active every time, then select **Always**.

6. Tap **Manage notifications** to select those apps that will work with Edge Lighting.

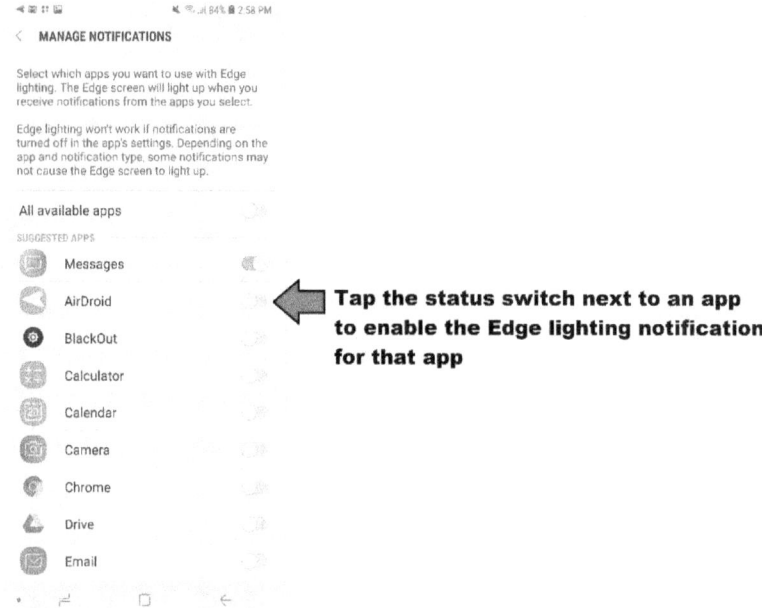

Tap the status switch next to an app to enable the Edge lighting notification for that app

Note: It appears that not all notifications may be received as Edge lighting.

Tip: To customize the color, size, or transparency of the Edge lighting, tap the **Edge lighting style** and use the onscreen buttons to customize edge lighting. Then tap **Apply** to save the changes.

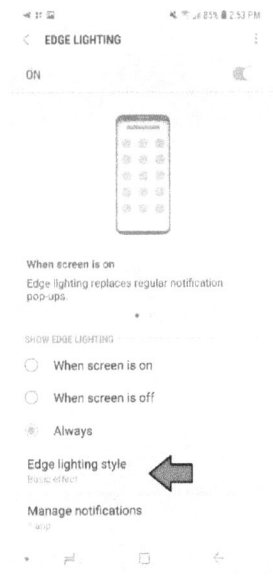

Tap this to save the changes

Use these icons to adjust the effect, color, transparency and width of the lighting

Reordering the Edge Screen Panel on Samsung Android Phones

1. Swipe down from the top of the screen and select the settings

   icon ⚙. Tap **Display** tab.

2. Scroll down and tap **Edge Screen**.

3. Tap **Edge Panels**.

4. Tap the menu ⋮ icon located at the top of the screen and tap **REORDER**.

5. Tap and hold the Re-order icon (<>) on an Edge screen panel and drag it to the desired position. Make sure that the panels you use most are in the first 3 or 4 panels so that you can access them faster.

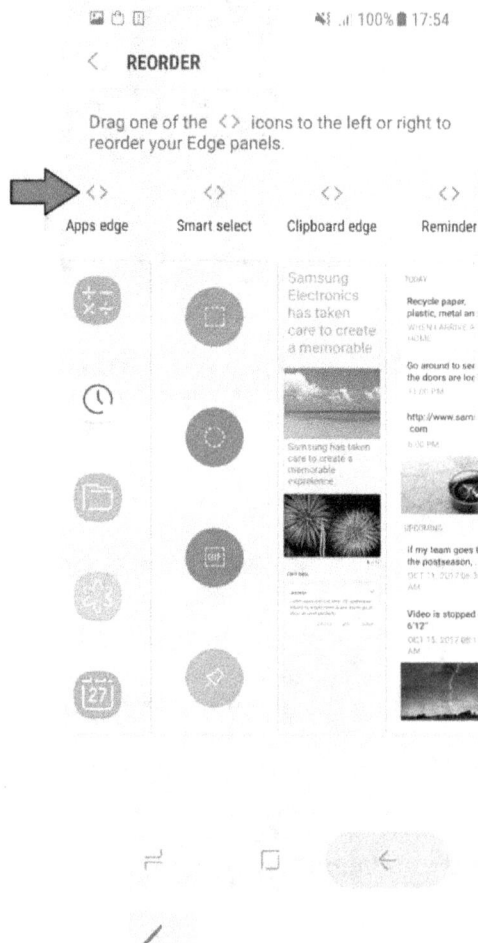

6. Tap the back icon to save the changes.

Managing the Edge Panel Handle Settings/Changing the Edge Panel Location on Samsung Android Phones

Edge panel handle settings allow you to change the position of Edge panel and more.

1. Swipe down from the top of the screen and select settings

   icon ⚙. Tap **Display** tab.

2. Scroll down and tap **Edge Screen**.

3. Tap **Edge Panels**.

4. Tap the menu icon ⋮ located at the top of the screen and select **Edge panel handle**.

5. Under **Position** tab, tap the side you would like the panel to appear on.

6. To change the size of Edge panel, drag the slider next to **SIZE**.

7. To change the transparency of Edge panel, drag the slider next to **Transparency.**

8. To move the Edge panel handle to another part of the screen, tap and drag the Edge handle anchor (the small V-shape icon).

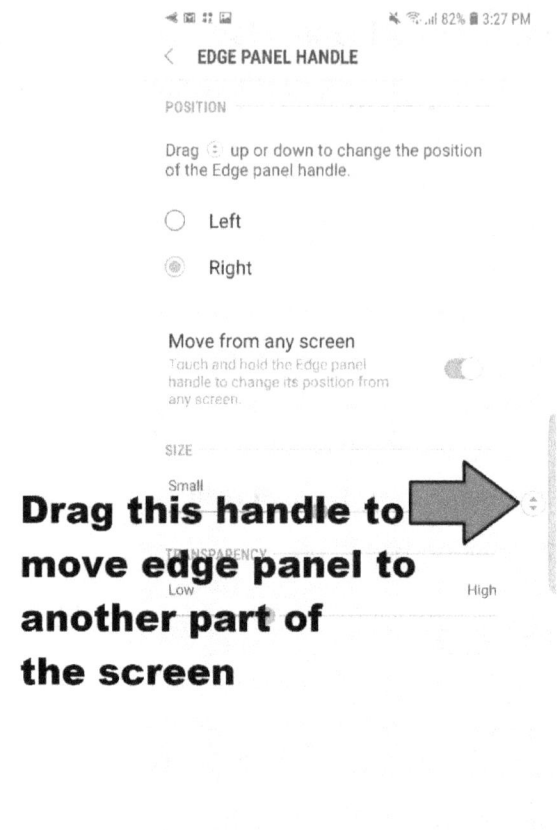

Drag this handle to move edge panel to another part of the screen

Using People Edge on Samsung Android Phones

People Edge gives you the opportunity to quickly access your favorite contacts from the Edge Panel.

To manage People Edge:

1. Swipe down from the top of the screen and select the settings

   icon  . Tap **Display** tab.

2. Scroll down and tap **Edge Screen**.

3. Tap **Edge Panels**.

4. Tap **EDIT** under **People Edge.** If you can't see the Edit button, then People Edge is disabled. To enable People Edge,

   simply tap/tick the small circle ◯ located on top of this panel.

5. Tap **SELECT CONTACT** and select all the contacts you want by tapping them. Please note that you may need to give access to People Edge before it can read your contacts. Tap **DONE** to save the changes. You should now be able to access the selected contacts when you access the Edge panel.

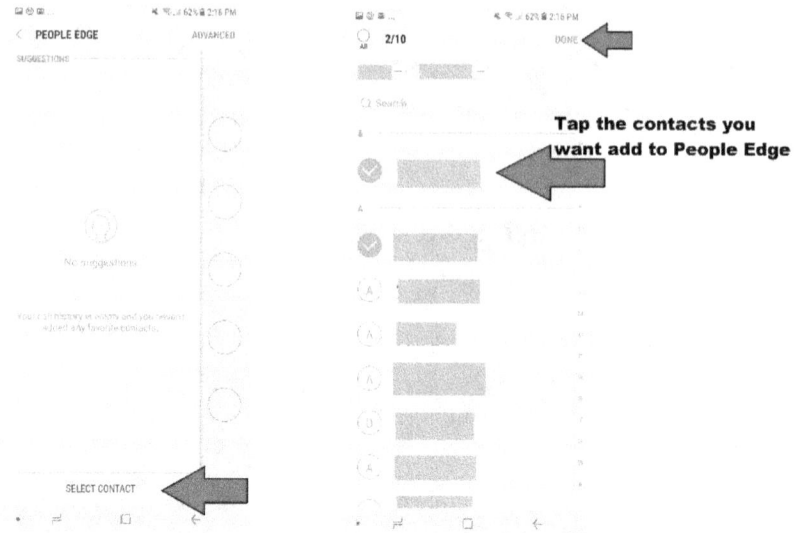

Tap the contacts you
want add to People Edge

6. To remove a contact from the People Edge, tap the minus
   icon next to the contact you want to remove.

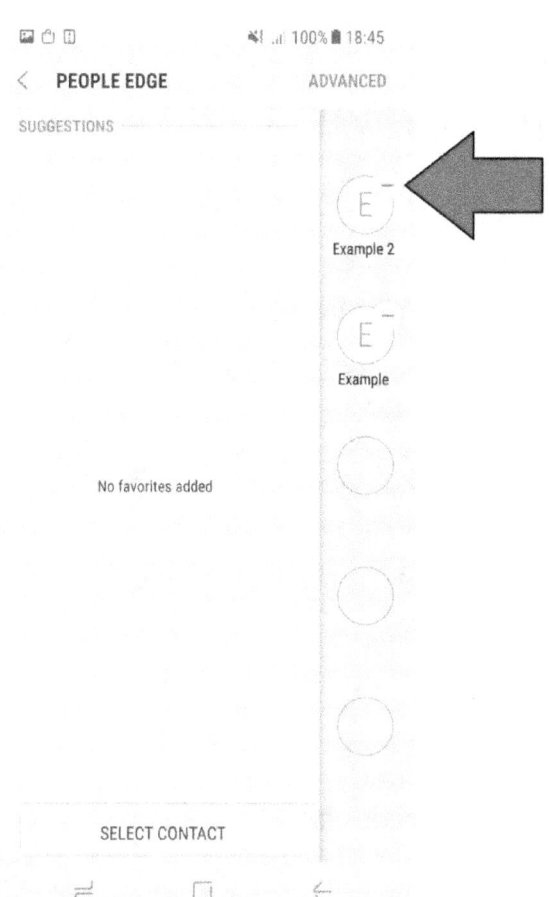

Using the Floating Bars on Supported LG Android Phones

Just like the Edge panel, floating bar allows you to quickly access options like contacts, screenshots, and shortcuts.

To disable or enable Floating bar:

1. Swipe down from the top of the screen and select the settings icon ⚙. If necessary, tap **General**.

2. Tap **Floating Bar**.

3. Tap the status switch next to **Floating Bar** to enable or disable this option.

Using the Floating Bar

After you enable the floating bar, you can use it by following the steps below:

Note: When enabled, the floating bar will appear as an arrow-like icon "<" or ">" on the edge of the screen.

1. To access the floating bar options, tap the floating bar icon "<" or ">" (located at the edge of the screen) and choose an option. To access more options, swipe left or right on the floating bar.

2. To close the floating bar, tap the arrow icon ">" or "<".

3. To move the floating bar to another part (edge) of the screen; tap, hold and drag the floating bar icon to where you would like it to be.

Customizing the Floating Bar Options

1. Swipe down from the top of the screen and select the settings

   icon ⚙ . If necessary, tap **General**.

2. Tap **Floating Bar**.

3. To change the position of Floating bars on supported phones, tap **Position** and choose an option and select **OK.**

4. To deactivate a floating bar option, tap status switch next to the option you want to deactivate. When an option is disabled/deactivated, the status switch should appear grey.

5. To customize an option, tap the option. For example, to customize **Shortcuts**, tap it and then tap the app icon(s) you want to set as shortcut(s).

Tip: To quickly disable floating bar, tap and hold the small arrow

icon ">" on the floating bar and then drag it to delete 🗑 located at the top of the screen. To re-enable it again, see "**To disable or enable Floating bar**" above.

Virtual Assistance

The popular virtual voice assistances on Android phones include Google Assistant, Bixby, and Alexa. In this section of the guide, I will be talking about Google Assistant and Bixby.

Google Assistant

Google Assistant is a trained virtual assistant that has been built to answer questions, and interestingly, you probably don't need any technical training to use this feature. If you need any, it will be some tweaks and how to ask questions and that is what this section of the guide is mainly for. This section of the guide will show you how to manage Google Assistant like a pro and how to ask questions and give commands that Google Assistant will understand.

Getting Started with Google Assistant

1. Tap the Google Assistant app icon and follow the prompts to set up this assistant.
2. To access the Google Assistant any other time after the setup, tap and hold the Home button (the middle button at the lower part of the phone) and then speak your command.

3. In addition, you can use "Ok Google" to activate Google Assistant. If you have not enabled this option during the setup, you can enable it afterwards by performing the following steps:

   a. Open the Google Assistant app and tap the telephone icon located at the top right of the screen.

   b. Tap the More icon ⋮ .

   c. Tap **Settings**.

   d. If necessary, select your phone under the "Devices" tab.

   e. Tap **Google Assistant**.

   f. Tap to turn on "**Ok Google**" **detection**.

Note: If you are using this app for the first time, you may need to accept some terms or read some instructions.

Speaking to Google Assistant

One of the ways you will interact with Google Assistant is by saying your questions. There are few things to know when talking to Google Assistant to get the best experience.

To get Google Assistant into action, you will need to get its attention. To do that, please follow the steps below:

1. Press and hold the Home button (the middle button at the lower part of the phone) and speak your question. If enabled, you may also say **Ok Google**.

2. To ask another question, simply tap the microphone button

   . Alternatively, say "Ok Google" followed by the question you want to ask.

3. In addition, you may notice that the question you ask Google Assistant is different from what it types into the search box (what Google Assistant types into the search box is what it thought you have said), I will advise that you always try to speak clearly.

Getting What You Want from Google Assistant

I will like to mention that interacting with Google Assistant is not an examination (so there is nothing like cheating) and you get help by saying **"What can you do."**

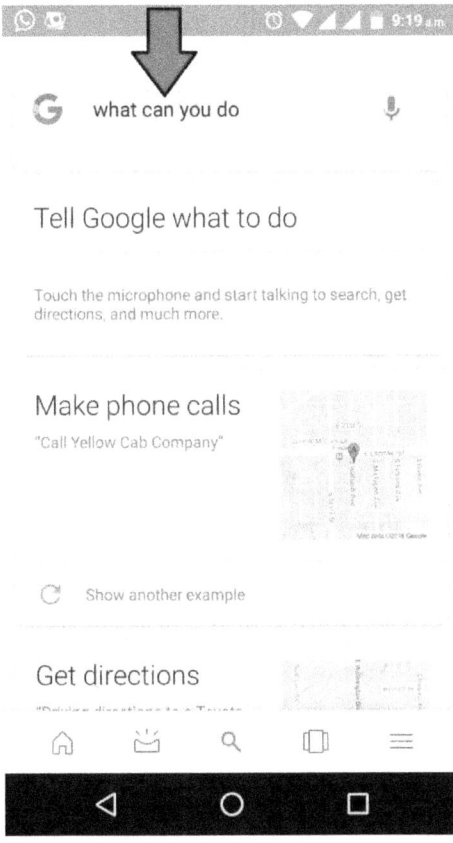

Using Google Assistant to Open Apps or Programs

One of those things you would want to use Google Assistant to do is accessing your apps. You can quickly open an app by

saying **Open** and then mentioning the name of the app. For example, to open Contacts, say or type **Open Contacts.** To open calculator,

say **Open calculator**.

You may also say **Launch** Calculator.

In addition, you may give a more specific command like **Open sound settings** to go to sound settings. Say **Launch Wi-Fi Settings** to open the Wi-Fi settings.

Using Google Assistant to Call

1. Press and hold the Home button (the middle button at the lower part of the phone). If enabled, you may also say **Ok Google**.

2. Then say **Call** followed by the name of the person that you want to call.

Using Google Assistant with Calendar

One of the fantastic features that Google Assistant can do for you is making an appointment. This personal assistant is compatible with your device's Calendar making it easy for it to make appointments for you.

With just few commands, you can get Google Assistant to put an event or appointment into your calendar. To do this:

1. Press and hold the Home button (the middle button at the lower part of the phone). If enabled, you may also say **Ok Google**.

2. Then say whatever you want to include in the Calendar. For example, you can say

- Appointment with Clinton for Monday at 1 p.m.

When it has gotten the information, it will let you know. You can then say **Yes** if you are Ok with the event. Or you can say **Cancel** or **Delete** to remove the event.

In addition, you can check how your calendar looks like today. To do this,

Tap the microphone button and say, "**Open my calendar app**" or say "**Let me see the events in my calendar**" or just any variant. Note that you can also ask Google Assistant about your calendar for a month. To do this, say "**what is my agenda for this month**".

Note: Note: In case, Google Assistant sets a wrong appointment, you can edit it by simply saying another command with a correct information. You probably don't need to say "Cancel" before you say another appointment with the correct information.

Tip: You can set Google Assistant to give you a customized briefing when you ask "What does my day look like?" or "Tell me about my day". To do this:

- Tap the Google Assistant app icon .

- Tap the menu icon ⋮ located at the top of the screen.

- Select **Settings**.

- Tap **My Day**.

- Check all the information you want to receive in your daily briefing. To customize those news you want to hear, tap the settings icon ⚙ next to **News** and select the news category you will like to receive. To customize other options like "Work commute," tap the settings icon ⚙ next to it.

Using Google Assistant with IFTTT

IFTTT (If This Then That) is an online service that allows you to automate different actions. Although Google Assistant can perform a lot of tasks, but it can't do everything. Connecting your Google Assistant device to IFTTT allows you to perform some actions that may not be possible with Google Assistant alone. With the help of IFTTT, Google Assistant can be used with third-party control devices that are not officially supported.

To connect Google Assistant to IFTTT:

1. From your web browser go to ifttt.com

2. Click on **Sign in**, if you don't have an account click on **Sign up**.
3. Enter the necessary information and click Sign in or Sign up.
4. Click on search button located at the top of the screen.

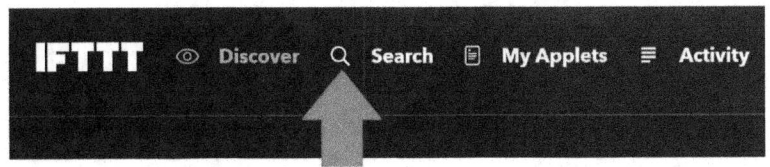

5. Search for **Google Assistant.** The list filters as you type. Click on **Google Assistant.**
6. Click on **Connect** and follow the prompts.

Using IFTTT

After you have connected Google Assistant and IFTTT, you would need to choose some applets. Applets are simple conditional statements/actions which are triggered based on what you tell Google Assistant to do.

For example, you may choose an applet that allows you to add a task to Todoist by voice when you ask Google Assistant to add a task...

To do this, while on Google Assistant channel page, just scroll down, tap on the **Add a task to Todoist by voice**.

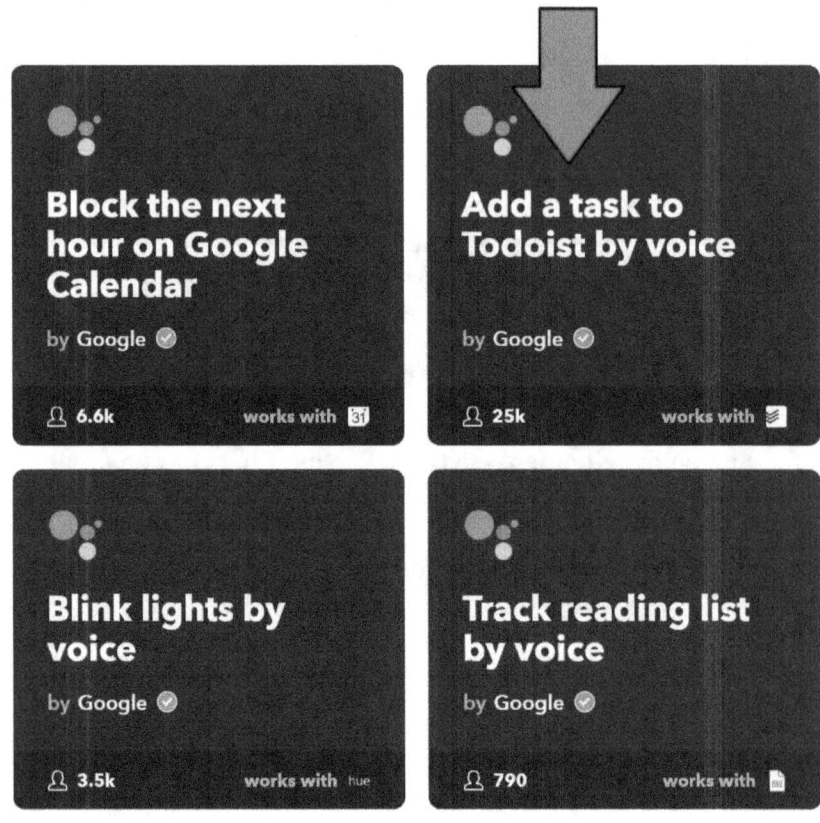

Tap on **Turn on** and follow the onscreen instructions.

Tip: After activating this recipe/applet, you get your task added to Todoist when you say **Ok Google, add a task…**

Using Google Assistant to Set Reminders

There are probably many things going through your mind and it will be quite interesting if you can get a personal assistant to assist in remembering some of your duties. Fortunately, Google Assistant can help you in this regard.

To set a reminder using Google Assistant:

1. Press and hold the Home button (the middle button at the lower part of the phone). If enabled, you may also say **Ok Google**.

2. Then say whatever you want to include in the Calendar. For example, you can say the following:

   - Remind me to fix the car by 3 p.m.

   - Remind me to drop the cake at the restaurant at 4 p.m. today.

   - Remind me to pick my daughter at 4 p.m.

   - Remind me to call Ibrahim at 1 p.m.

3. When it has gotten the information, the reminder will appear. You can then say **Yes** if you are Ok with the reminder. Or you can say **Cancel** or **Delete** to remove the reminder.

Please note that it is not compulsory that you put remind in every statement as I did above, but I would advise that you do this whenever you can. This is because it will help Google Assistant to easily get what you are saying and avoid any confusion.

Note: In case, Google Assistant set a wrong reminder, you can edit it by simply saying another command with a correct information. You probably don't need to say "Cancel" before you say another reminder with the correct information.

Using Google Assistant to Remember Things

If you have problem remembering where you keep things, you can ask Google Assistant to help you with remembering these things. This is cool if you have many things going through your mind and you easily forget where you keep things.

To use this cool feature:

1. Press and hold the Home button (the middle button at the lower part of the phone). If enabled, you may also say **Ok Google**.
2. Then say whatever you want Google Assistant to remember. For example, you can say:
    *   Remember that my car key is on the shelf.
    *   Remember that my pen is on the drawer.

To get where you put your things. Simply say "where is my key?" or "what did I ask you to remember?".

Using Google Assistant with Alarm

You can also set an alarm using this personal assistant. To do this:

1. Press and hold the Home button (the middle button at the lower part of the phone). If enabled, you may also say **Ok Google**.

2. Say the time for alarm. For example, you can say: "**set an alarm for 1 p.m. tomorrow**" or "**alarm for 3 p.m. today**". You may not be able to set an alarm more than 24 hours in advance.

3. When it has gotten the information, the alarm will appear, and it will tell you that it has set the alarm.

Using Google Assistant with Clock

You can ask Google Assistant what your local time is. In addition, it can also tell you the time in a specific place.

1. Press and hold the Home button (the middle button at the lower part of the phone). If enabled, you may also say **Ok Google**.

2. Then say, "**What is the time?**" or say "**what is the time in the New York?**".

Using Google Assistant to Get a Flight Information

You can also use this virtual assistant to get information about a flight. This is a smarter way to know when an airplane will take off.

For example, you can say **What is the flight status of Delta 400** to get the flight information about this flight.

Using Google Assistant with a Weather App

To know about your weather, just say "**What's the weather going to be today?**". You may also know about the weather condition of a place by asking "**What is the weather of the New York today?**".

Using Google Assistant with a Message App

You can instruct Google Assistant to compose a text message for you. You may also ask this assistant to read your text message to you. To do this:

1. Press and hold the Home button (the middle button at the lower part of the phone). If enabled, you may also say **Ok Google**.

2. Then say the subject and the person you want to text message. For example, you can say:

- Send a text message to Pharm Ibrahim.
- Send a text message to Clinton.

Google assistant will then ask you for the body of the message. If you want to cancel the message, simply say **Cancel**.

3. You may also tell Google Assistant to show you your messages.

- Say, "show me my messages". To manage your messages, simply follow the Google Assistant reply prompts.

Using Google Assistant with a Mail App

You can instruct Google Assistant to compose an email for you. To do this:

1. Press and hold the Home button (the middle button at the lower part of the phone). If enabled, you may also say **Ok Google**.

2. Then say the subject and the person you want to email. For example, you can say:

- Send an email to Pharm about the class.

- Email Clinton about the meeting.

- Email Clinton and Steve about the budget.

- Send Urgent email to Steve about the ball.

Please note that you will usually have to include one or more information before you send the email. For example, you will need to say or type the body of the email before you send the email. In addition, you need to have in your contact the email address of the person you are sending an email to.

3. You may also tell Google Assistant to show you your email.

- Say, "show me my email". To manage your email, simply follow the Google Assistant reply prompts.

Using Google Assistant with a Map App

You can also use the Google Assistant to search the map. To get how the map of a place looks like:

1. Press and hold the Home button (the middle button at the lower part of the phone). If enabled, you may also say **Ok Google**.

2. Then say the map of an area you want to get. For example, you may say:

- Show me the New York map.

- Show me the map of Seattle.

What about Math?

Google Assistant can also help you with some mathematics and conversions. For example, you can tell Google Assistant "**What is the square root of four?**". You may also say "**convert one foot to centimeter**" or "**What is the exchange rate between dollars and pounds?**" and so on. As I have said before, the most important thing is to make sure Google Assistant gets the message you are trying to pass across.

Using Google Assistant to Get Definitions

You can quickly check for a meaning of a word by asking Google Assistant. For example, you may say "**What is the meaning of flabbergasted?**".

Using Google Assistant to Get Translations

You can use Google Assistant to translate words, phrases or sentences from one language to another. This is cool when you are in a foreign country or you are learning a new language.

To do this:

1. Press and hold the Home button (the middle button at the lower part of the phone). If enabled, you may also say **Ok Google**.
2. Say what you want to translate. For example, you may say:
   a. Translate "you are welcome" to Spanish.
   b. Translate "good morning" to German.

Clearing Your Information from Google Assistant Memory

You can delete your conversation or information from Google. To do this:

1. Open **https://myactivity.google.com**
2. Tap **Filter by Date & Product**.
3. Uncheck **All Products**.
4. Tap the checkbox next to all the information you want to delete. In this case, select "Assistant", and "Voice & Audio".

If you want to delete all the stored information, select "All products".

5. Tap the search icon  .

6. At the top right corner of the information you want to delete, select the menu icon ⋮ and then select **Delete**. Tap **Delete** to confirm.

Google Assistant's Settings

To access these settings, follow the instructions below:

1. Open the Google app  .

2. Tap the menu icon ☰ .

3. Tap **Settings** and choose an option.

Tip: To block offensive words from voice results, repeat steps 1 to 3 above and then tap **Voice**. Tap the status switch next to **Block offensive words**. When this feature is enabled, the switch will appear bold.

Troubleshooting Google Assistant

Although much efforts have been put into making this virtual assistant, I am quite sure that Google Assistant will misbehave at one time or the other. When this happens, there are few things to do.

- **Ensure that you are connected to a strong network**: If you have a bad or no internet connection, Google Assistant may not work properly. Therefore, the first thing to check when Google Assistant starts to misbehave is the internet connection.

- **Speak clearly in a silent place**: Make sure you are speaking clearly and try to avoid background noise.

- **Tap the microphone button**: Tap the microphone button 🎤, if the device does not hear you, or when you want to give it another command.

- **Clear the cache of the Google Assistant app:** You can clear the cache data to clear errors. To do this:

  1. Swipe down from the top of the screen and tap settings icon ⚙.
  2. Swipe up and tap "Apps".
     If you don't see "Apps", tap "Apps & Notifications" and then "App info" or "Apps".

Please note that if you are using an LG Android phone, you may need to tap **General** tab, before you see "Apps & notifications".

3. Tap the app you want to manage. In this case, tap **Assistant** or **Google**.

4. Tap **Clear Cache**. If you can't see "Clear Cache", tap "Storage & Memory" and then select "Clear Cache".

- **Try to Restart Your smartphone**: If you find out that all what I have mentioned above does not work, you may try restarting your device because it may be that it is your device that is confused and not Google Assistant.

The Bixby

Bixby is a trained virtual assistant that has been built to answer questions, and let you interact with your phone in a special way. Bixby is divided into three parts:

1. Bixby Home
2. Bixby Vision
3. Bixby Voice

This section of the guide will show you how to manage Bixby like a pro.

Please note that Bixby is majorly common with Samsung Android phones using Android 7 version or later.

Getting Started with Bixby

You would need to setup Bixby when you first start using your device and you will learn how to do that in this section of the guide. To setup this voice assistant:

1. Press the Bixby button (the button next to the volume button at the side of the supported Samsung Android phone).

2. If you see a screen telling you to update Bixby, simply tap **UPDATE**.

3. Tap **Next**.

A new way to interact

Press and hold the Bixby key to call Bixby. Bixby responds to commands you say or type.

NEXT >

4. Choose a language for Bixby Voice and tap **Confirm**.

5. Read the terms and conditions. If you agree to all the terms and conditions, tap **I have read and agreed to all** and then tap **NEXT**.

6. Follow the onscreen instructions to setup and register your voice so that Bixby can recognize your voice.

7. To manage a card, swipe in from the left edge of the screen and tap the menu icon ⋮ next to the card you want to manage. Then tap an option.

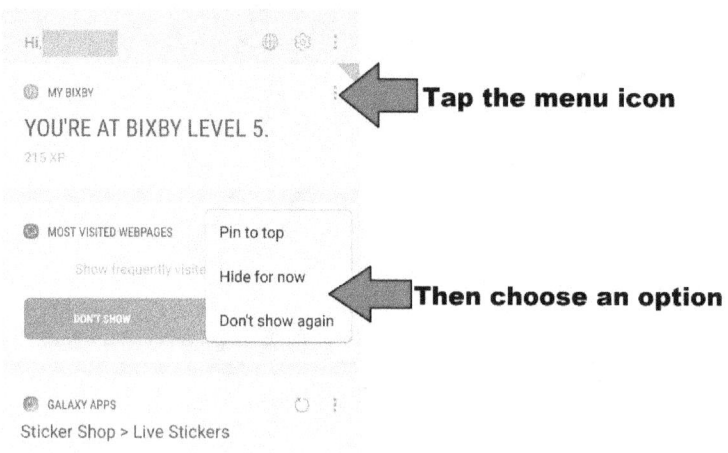

8. To adjust Bixby settings, tap the menu icon ⋮ located at top of the screen and tap **Settings**. Then choose an option.

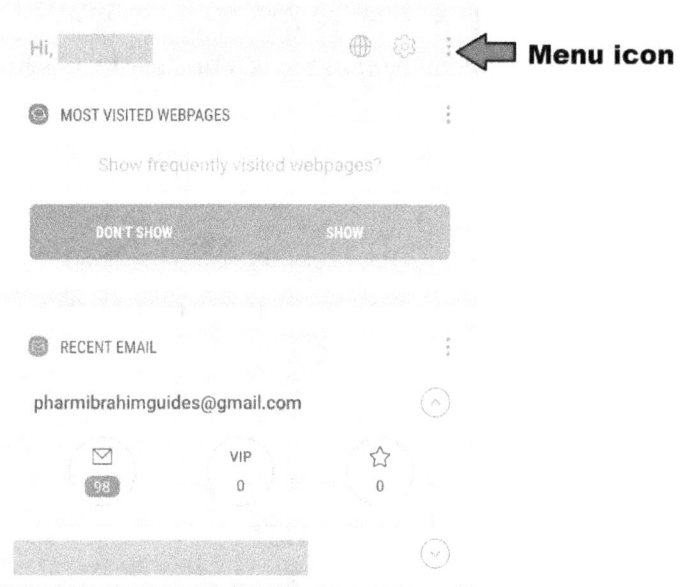

To choose which card is displayed to you on the Bixby home page; while on settings page, tap **Cards**, scroll down and use the status switch to turn off/on a card.

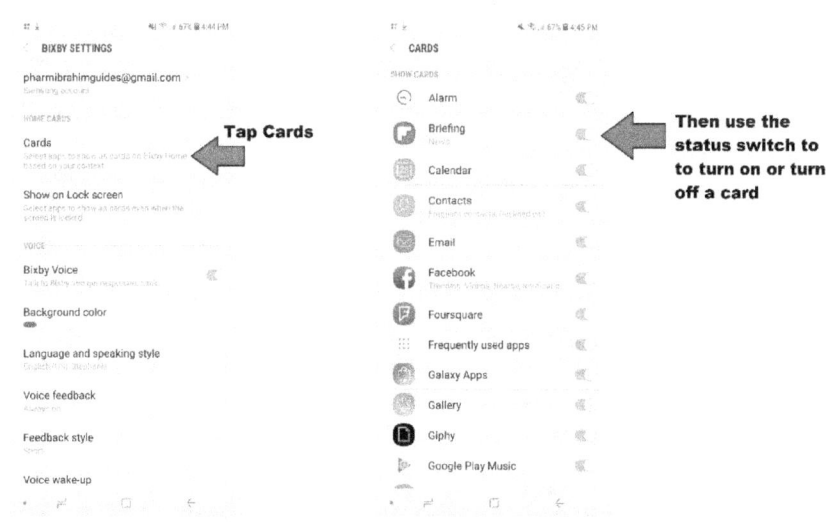

Tip: To customize the type of briefing you receive on the Bixby home page, tap the menu icon next to the briefing card and select **Customize content**.

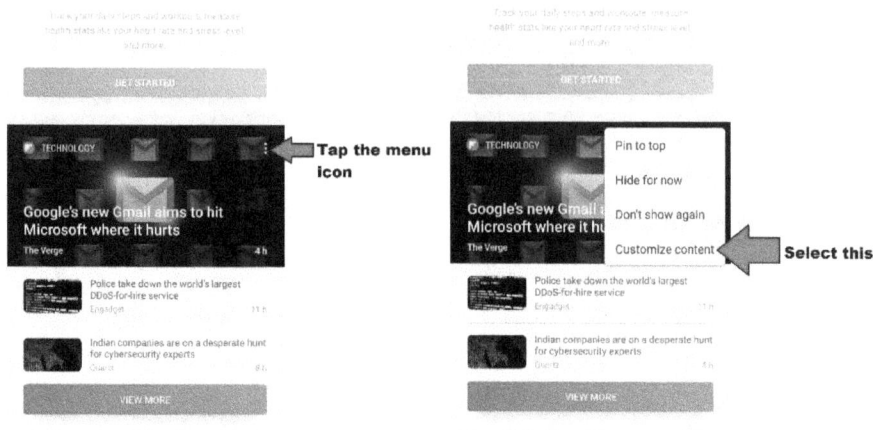

Then choose the categories you want to receive information about.

Tap the back icon ⬅ to save the changes.

Bixby Home

After the initial setup discussed above, you can access the Bixby Home by pressing the Bixby button (the button next to the volume button at the side of the supported Samsung Android phone). Alternatively, swipe right while on the home screen to access Bixby Home.

Bixby Voice

Bixby voice allows you to interact with Bixby using your voice.

Speaking to Bixby

One of the ways you will interact with Bixby is by speaking to it. The other way would be to type a command into the search bar and hit **Go**.

To get Bixby into action, you would need to get its attention. To do that, perform any of the actions below:

1. Press the Bixby button located next to the volume button at the side of your Samsung Android phone and speak your command while still pressing it.

2. Alternatively, you can get Bixby's attention by saying **Hi Bixby!** However, you may need to enable this feature before you can put it to use. To enable **Hi Bixby** function:

    -   Press the dedicated Bixby button once.

    -   Tap the menu icon ⋮ located at top of the screen and tap **Settings**.

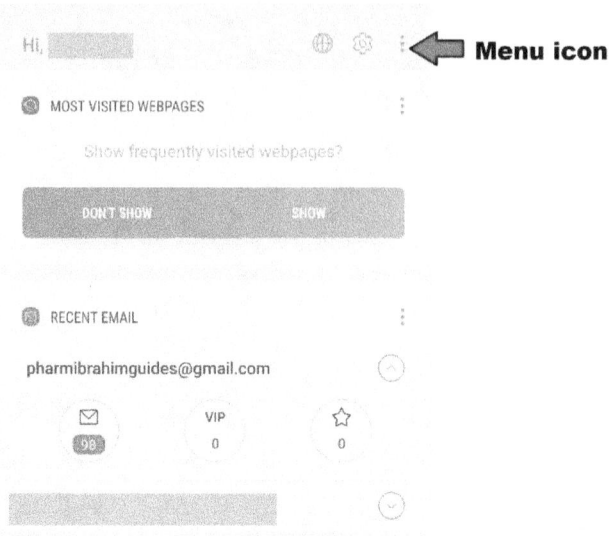

Hi, ⬜⬜⬜   ⊕ ⚙ ⋮ **⬅ Menu icon**

🌐 MOST VISITED WEBPAGES   ⋮

Show frequently visited webpages?

DON'T SHOW   SHOW

📧 RECENT EMAIL   ⋮

pharmibrahimguides@gmail.com   ⌃

✉   VIP   ☆
98   0   0

⌄

- Scroll down and tap **Voice wake-up**. Make sure the indicator switch under Voice Wake-Up is **ON** (see the picture below).

- If you want to increase the sensitivity of Bixby to the wake word, drag the slider under **Wake-up sensitivity** to medium or high position.

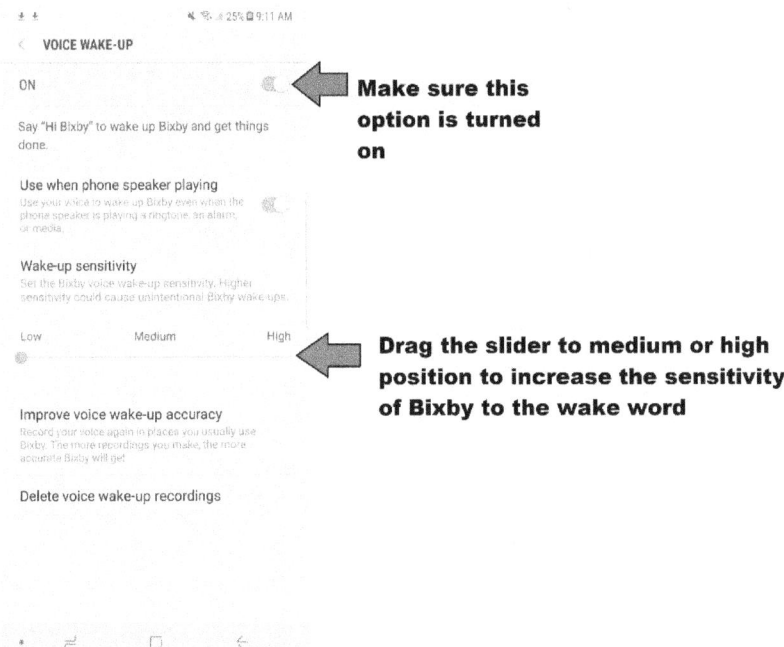

When Bixby is activated, it will respond by displaying a small action box on the screen. Bixby will then give you an answer to your request.

In addition, occasionally, you may notice that the question you asked Bixby is different from what it types into the action box. What Bixby types into the action box is what it thought you have said.

Tip: You can train Bixby to better recognize your voice, to do this:

- Press the dedicated Bixby button once (the button located next to the volume button at the side of the supported Samsung Android phone).

- Tap the menu icon located at top of the screen and tap **Settings**.

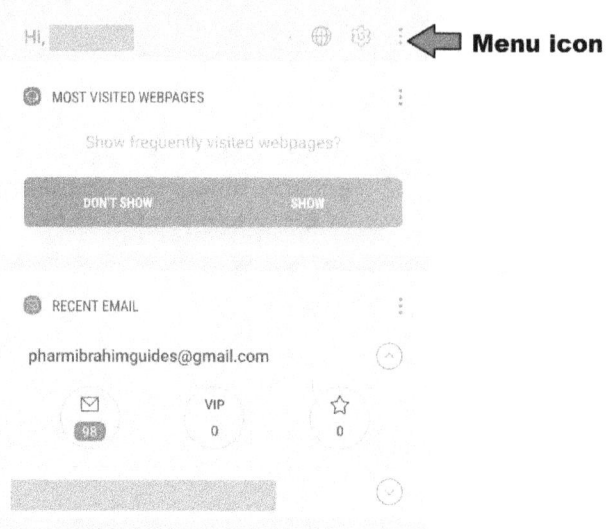

- Scroll down, tap **Enhanced voice recognition** and follow the onscreen instructions.

What about Typing?

The interesting thing is that Bixby can also listen when you command it using your onscreen keyboard. You can type in commands and get a similar result just as you will get by speaking to it. This is a great feature especially if you can't speak to Bixby for one reason or the other e.g. if you are in a noisy place or your microphone is not working properly.

To use the Bixby typing feature:

- Press the Bixby button (located next to the volume button of the supported Samsung Android phone) for two to four seconds or say, "**Hi Bixby**".
- Tap **Full Screen**.
- Tap the search bar located at the top of the screen and type your command.

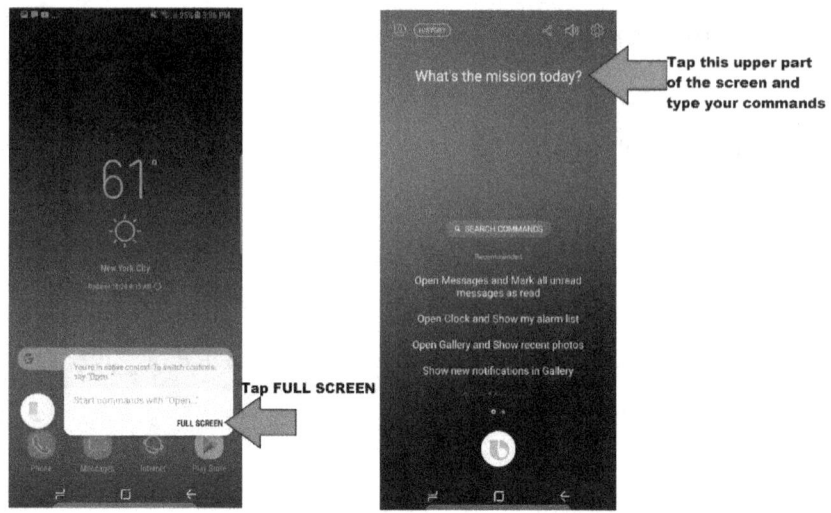

Tap this upper part of the screen and type your commands

Tap FULL SCREEN

- Tap the send icon and wait for a reply.

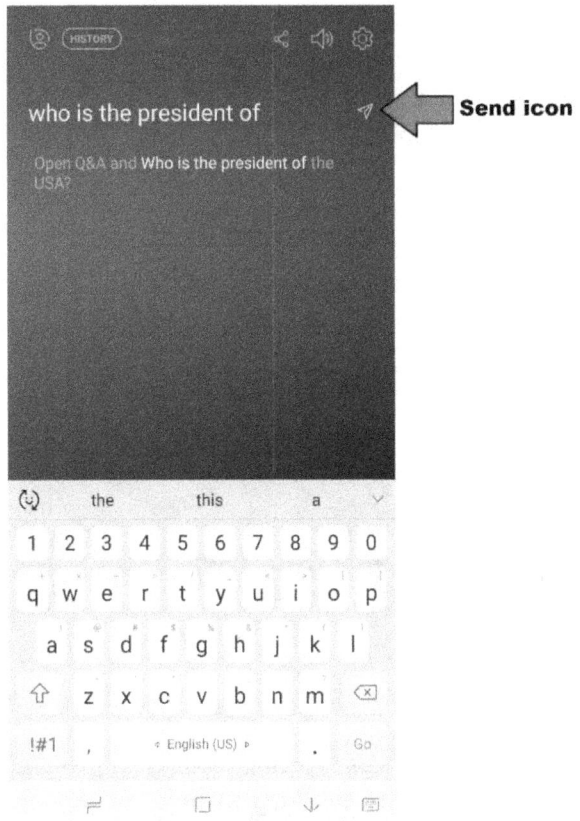

Send icon

Tip: If you are stuck, and you don't know what to ask Bixby, you can use the typing menu to get some ideas. To do this, simply type a keyword into the search menu and scroll through the suggestions. For example, if you are searching for ideas on how to use Bixby with the Email app, just tap the text menu and key in **email**. Then scroll through the search results to see example commands.

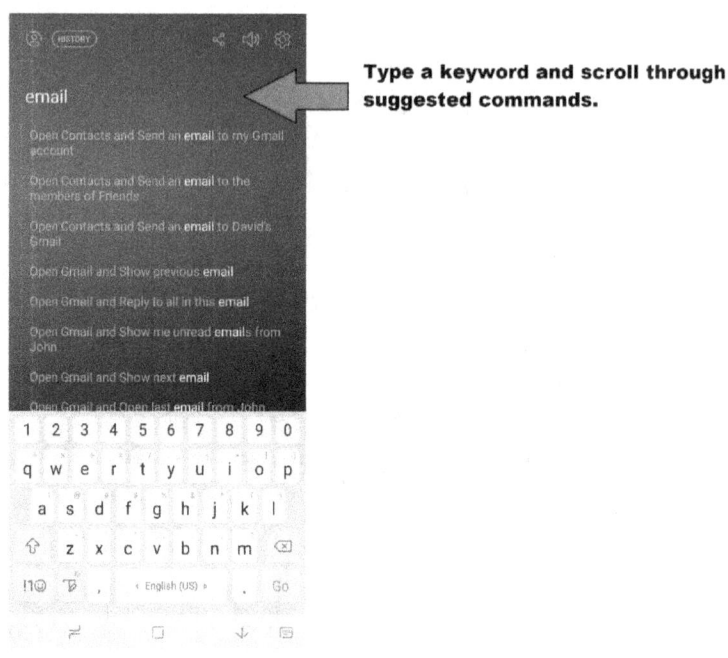

Type a keyword and scroll through suggested commands.

Using Bixby to Open Apps or Programs

One of those things you might want to use Bixby to do is accessing your apps. You can quickly open an app by saying **Open** and then mention the name of the app. For example, to open settings, say or type **Open settings**. To open calculator, say **Open calculator**.

You may also say **Launch settings** instead of **Open settings**.

In addition, you may give a more specific command like **Open notification settings** to go to notification settings. Say **Launch Wi-Fi Settings** to open the Wi-Fi settings. To turn off airplane mode, say **Turn off airplane mode** and so on.

Using Bixby with Calendar

One of the fantastic features that Bixby can do for you is making an appointment. This personal assistant is built to work with your device Calendar making it easy for it to make appointments.

With just few commands, you can get Bixby to put an event or appointment into your Calendar. **To do this**:

1. Press the Bixby button located next to the volume button at the side of your Samsung Android phone and speak your command while still pressing it. Alternatively, say **Hi Bixby!**

2. Say whatever you want to include in the Calendar. For example, you can say any of the following:

   - Appointment with Clinton for Monday at 1 p.m.

   - Add meeting with Ibrahim at 10 a.m. on Sunday to my calendar.

   - Remind me to fix my car at 9 p.m. tonight.

Please note that you can also say all the examples given above in other ways, the most important thing is to get Bixby to understand what you are saying. When it has gotten the information, the Calendar/Reminder app will appear. You can then make any adjustment using the virtual keyboard.

Please note that when Do Not Disturb is running, you may not get a voice feedback from Bixby instead you may only get a text feedback.

In addition, you can check how your calendar looks like. To do this, click the microphone button and say, "**What is on my calendar today?**" or say, "**Any appointment today**?" or just any variant. Note that you can also ask Bixby about your calendar for a day in the future. To do this, say "**Any appointment tomorrow?**" or say, "**Any appointment on November 1st?**".

Note: In case, Bixby sets a wrong appointment, you can edit it using your on-screen keyboard instead of trying to speak another word to it. Editing any misinformation with keyboard appears smarter and faster.

In addition, instead of speaking, you may type any of the commands mentioned above into the search box to get a similar result.

Using Bixby to Set Reminders

There are probably many things going through your mind, and it will be quite interesting if you can get a personal assistant to assist in remembering some of your duties. Fortunately, Bixby can help you in this regard.

To set a reminder using Bixby:

1. Press the Bixby button and speak your command while still pressing it. Alternatively, say **Hi Bixby!**

2. Say whatever you want to set a reminder for. For example, you can say the following:

   - Remind me to fix the car by 3 p.m.

   - Remind me to drop the meat pie at the restaurant.

   - Remind me to pick my daughter by 4 p.m.

   - Remind me to call Clinton at 1 p.m., and so on.

Please note that it is probably not compulsory that you put **remind** in every statement as I did above. But I would advise that you do so whenever you can. This is because it will help Bixby to easily get what you are saying and avoid any confusion.

Note: In case, Bixby sets a wrong reminder, you can edit it using your on-screen keyboard instead of trying to speak another word to it. Editing any misinformation with keyboard appears smarter and faster.

Using Bixby with Alarm

You can also set an alarm using this personal assistant.

To do this:

1. Repeat the first step mentioned above.

2. Say the time for alarm. For example, you can say: "**set an alarm for 1 p.m. every Monday**" or "**alarm for 1 p.m. every Wednesday**" or "**set an everyday alarm for 2 p.m.**" or "**set an alarm for 1 p.m. on 24th of October**".

3. When it has grabbed the information, the alarm would appear, and it will tell you that it has set the alarm.

Using Bixby with Clock

You can ask Bixby what your local time is. In addition, it can also tell you the time in a specific place.

1. Press the Bixby button and speak your command while still pressing it. Alternatively, say **Hi Bixby!**

2. Then say, "**What is the time?**" or say, "**What is the time in the New York?**".

Using Bixby to Get Flight Information

You can also use this virtual assistant to get information about a flight. This is a smarter way to know when an airplane will take off.

For example, you can say **Flight status of Delta 400** to get the information about this flight.

Using Bixby with a Weather App

To know about the weather condition of a place, just say "**What's the weather going to be like today?**". You may also know about the weather condition of a place by asking "**What is the weather of the New York today?**".

Using Bixby with a Mail App

You can instruct Bixby to compose an email for you. To do this:

1. Press the Bixby button located next to the volume button at the side of your Samsung Android phone and speak your command while still pressing it. Alternatively, say **Hi Bixby!**

2. Then give the command. For example, you can say:

   - Send an email to Clinton.

   - Send an email to Clinton and Steve.

   - Search for emails from Clinton.

   - Search for emails from Steve and mark them all as important.

Please note that you will usually have to include one or more information before you send the email. Simply follow the voice prompts to add subject and email's body.

Tip: You can get example commands to help you use the email app like a pro. To do this, please refer to the "Tip" on page 221.

Using Bixby with a Map App

You can also use the Bixby to search the map. This virtual assistant is built to work with the Map app on your device. **To get how the map of a place looks like**:

1. Repeat the first step above.
2. Then say the map of an area you want to get. For example, you may say:

   - Map of Seattle.

   - Show me the map of London.

What about Math?

Bixby can also help you with some mathematical calculations and conversions. For example, you can tell Bixby **What is the square root of four?** You can also say **convert one meter to centimeter**.

Using Bixby to Get Definitions

Also, you can ask Bixby for the meaning of words. For example, you may say **what is the meaning of flabbergasted.**

Bixby's Settings

The settings tab allows you to manage Bixby's functions. To access Bixby's settings:

1. Press the dedicated Bixby button once (the button located next to the volume button at the side of your Samsung Android phone).

2. Tap the menu icon ⋮ located at top of the screen and tap **Settings**.

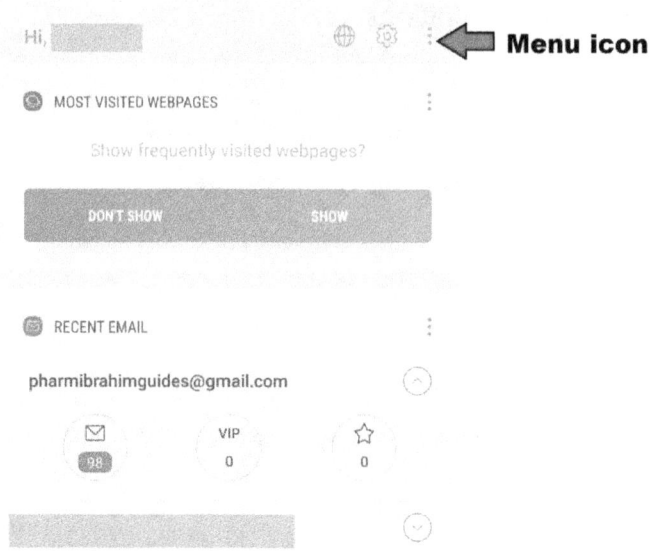

Hi, ▓▓▓▓▓▓ ⊕ ⚙ ⋮ ⬅ **Menu icon**

⊙ MOST VISITED WEBPAGES ⋮

Show frequently visited webpages?

| DON'T SHOW | SHOW |

✉ RECENT EMAIL ⋮

pharmibrahimguides@gmail.com ⌃

✉   VIP   ☆
98   0   0

⌄

3. Tap an option.

The settings menu allows you to manage Bixby like a maven. I would advise that you take time to go through the various settings options on the settings page.

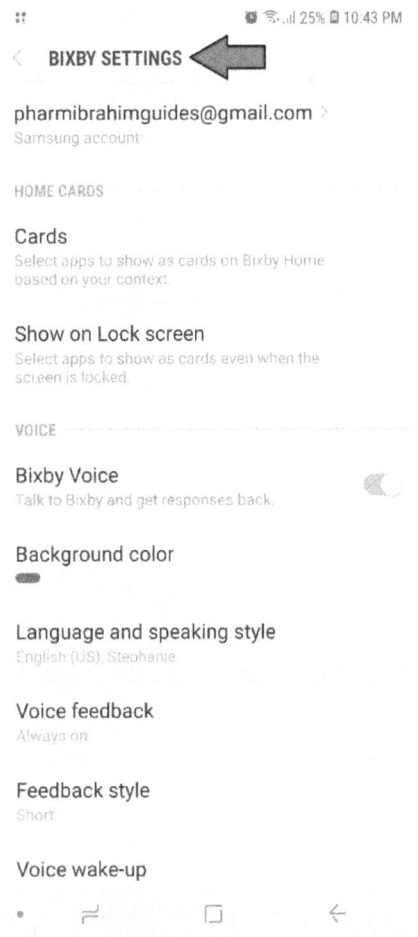

How to Clear Bixby's Voice Interaction Data

To erase whatever voice interaction Bixby has stored:

1. Press the dedicated Bixby button once.

2. Tap the menu icon located at the topmost part of the screen and tap **Settings**.

3. Scroll down and tap **Privacy.**

4. Tap **Erase Bixby Voice interaction data**.

Troubleshooting Bixby

Although much efforts have been put into making this virtual assistant, I am quite sure that Bixby will misbehave at one time or the other. When this happens, there are few things to do.

- **Ensure that you are connected to a strong network**: If you have a bad or no internet connection, Bixby may not work properly. Therefore, the first thing to check when Bixby starts to misbehave is the internet connection.

- **Use the Virtual Keyboard**: You may need to use the keyboard to pass your message to Bixby if you find out that it is not getting your speech. Many of what you say (If not all) can also be typed into the Bixby's search bar. Please go to page 219 to learn more.

- **Try to Restart Your Phone**: If you find out that what I have mentioned above do not work, try restarting your phone.

Conclusion

Bixby is like a learning machine and it is being improved upon. If you are having difficulty passing your message across to it, you may try typing (see page 219) some of your commands into the command box. I believe you should know how to use it more as time goes on.

Bixby Vision

Bixby allows you to interact with images in an educating manner. It also gives you more understanding of what you are looking at. When first using Bixby Vision, you may need to agree to some terms and conditions.

To Use Bixby Vision:

1. Launch the camera app of your Samsung Android phone.
2. Aim the lens of the camera at what you want to capture.
3. Tap the Bixby button. You can use the Bixby Vision to extract texts, translate a language, scan Barcodes, shop etc.

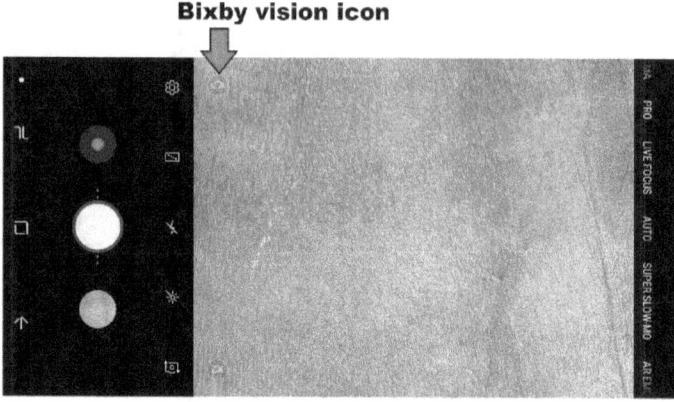

4. Choose an option. For example, if you are trying to extract a text, scroll right or left and tap **Text**. Then tap **Text** again to extract the texts.

5. To exit, tap the back button ←.

You can also access Bixby vision while using the Gallery app. Simply launch the **Gallery** app, tap an image and tap the Bixby button. Please note that some pictures may not have Bixby button.

Using the Web

In this section of the guide, I will be explaining two popular browsers on Android phones. These browsers are Google Chrome and Samsung Internet. Please note that you may need to download and install these browsers form the Google Play store before you can access them.

Google Chrome Browser

Opening the Chrome Browser

This can be done by simply tapping the **Chrome** icon on the home screen.

1. From the home screen, tap the **Chrome** icon .

2. If you are using Chrome browser for the first time on your phone, you may be prompted to accept terms and conditions, tap **Accept & Continue** if you agree.

3. If necessary, sign in using your Google account information and tap **Continue**.

4. Google will then inform you that it will import all your bookmarks and other Web preferences for use on your phone. Tap **Ok, Got It** to import all these data.

Get to Know the Chrome Browser Interface

The following screenshot will introduce you to various features found on Chrome browser:

Depending on the version of Chrome you are using, please note that the chrome browser on your device may be slightly different from the one shown below.

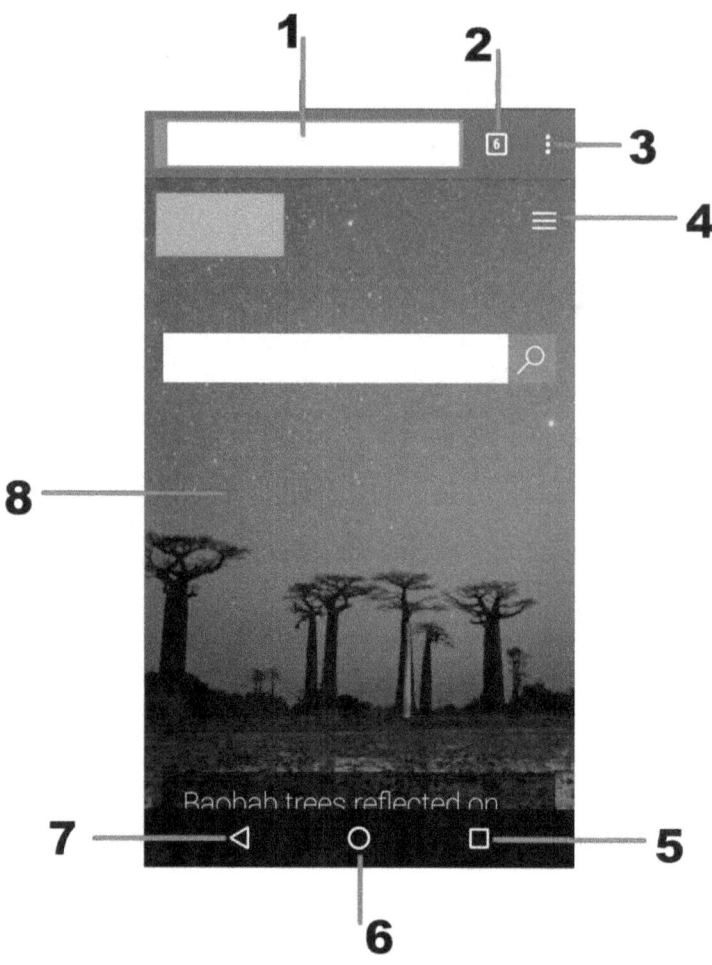

Baobab trees reflected on

1	**Address bar**: Tapping this bar lets you enter the web address of a page. You may also type in search phrase into the address bar.
2	**Tabs:** Tap this to navigate between different webpages. The number inside the small square indicates the number of tabs presently opened.
3	**More/Menu Options:** Tap this icon to access additional options such as **Share** and **Bookmarks.**
4	**Webpage menu**: If available, you can use this button to navigate between different categories on a website.
5	**Recent Key:** Tap this to navigate between different apps.
6	**Home button:** Tap this icon to go to the home screen.
7	**Back:** Tap this icon to revisit the page you just visited.
8	**Webpage view**: Webpage information is shown here.

Hint: If you mistakenly tap a wrong button, don't panic, just keep holding your finger on the wrong button and then stylishly move away your finger (just as if you are dragging the wrong icon) to stop the command from executing. Generally, commands don't get executed until you release you finger.

In addition, you can quickly refresh a webpage. To do this, while on the webpage, swipe from the top/middle of the webpage towards the middle/bottom.

Add Your Favorite Webpage to the Home Screen

You can make your favorite webpage a shortcut on the home screen. This allows you to easily access the webpage directly from your home screen. To do this:

- While the Chrome browser is opened, tap the menu button

  ⋮ .

- Tap **Add to Home screen**, edit the name of the website if you like and then tap **Add**.
- Then tap the Home key [O] located at the bottom of the screen to view this newly added webpage.

Using the Address/Search Bar

Every web browser must have an address bar and Chrome browser has one. This bar serves the function of URL address bar and search bar. The address/search bar is usually located at the upper part of the screen. But It can also be located at the middle part of the screen where you see **Search or type URL**. By default, the searches done on this bar are executed by Google. To learn how to change the search engine to another one, go to page 244.

You choose whether to launch a webpage or search for a term based on what you type into the address bar. For example, if you type **Freedom to** into the address bar and tap **Go**, Google search results for that phrase is displayed. On the other hand, if you type **Freedom.to** and tap **Go**, you will be taken to the website bearing the name.

Chrome browser makes website suggestions to you based on the sites you have recently visited, to choose any of the suggested sites, tap it.

When you begin to type inside the address bar, Chrome browser automatically makes suggestions beneath your typing. You can choose one of these suggestions to make things faster, provided that the suggestions truly read your mind.

Hint: To view detail security information of a website, open the website and tap the menu icon ⋮ . Then tap the punctuation mark ⓘ located at the top of the screen.

Using Tabs on Chrome Browser

The tabs allow you to open different webpages at once. You can open many tabs at once on Chrome browser. Please see the screenshot under **Get to know the Chrome browser Interface** to have a pictorial view of the Chrome browser tab icon.

To manage browsing tabs:

1. Tap the tab icon **1** located at the top of the screen.
2. To open a new tab, tap + icon located at the top of the screen.

   You may also tap the menu ⋮ icon and select **New tab**.
3. To open a tab, tap the tab icon **1** and then tap the desired tab.
4. To close a tab, tap the tab icon **1** and then tap the **X** icon at the top right corner of the thumbnail of the tab you want to close.

5. To close all tabs, while on the tabs' screen, tap ⋮ and then select **Close all tabs**.

Favorites (Bookmarks)

With several billions of webpages in the internet world, you may need to select your favorites. Just like other modern-day browsers, Chrome browser gives you the opportunity to select a favorite or bookmark a page. This makes it easier to visit the website or webpage in the future.

To bookmark a webpage:

1. Open the website you want to bookmark.

2. Tap the menu icon and then tap the star icon located at the top of the screen.

3. To enter a new name, repeat steps 1 and 2 above and tap the star icon again. Enter a name for your bookmark. Tap the back icon (located at the top of the screen) to save the changes.

Please note that when a webpage is bookmarked, the star icon will appear bold.

Accessing Your Bookmarks/Favorites

After you have added a webpage to your favorites list, you would need to access this list sooner or later. To access your bookmarks, tap the menu icon (the three dots icon) and then tap **Bookmarks**.

While on the bookmark page, you may select the three dots icon next to a bookmark to manage/edit it.

Changing the Search Engine

The default search engine on Chrome browser is Google. Some people may love to change this to another search engine.

You can change the Chrome browser search engine by following the steps highlighted below:

1. While the browser is opened, tap ⋮ (next to address bar) and select **Settings**.

2. Tap on **Search engine** and select a search engine. Tap the back button ◁ when you are done.

Making Chrome Browser Your Default Browser

If you have multiple web browsers on your device, you can select Chrome browser to be the default browser. To do this:

1. Swipe down from the top of the screen, select the settings icon ⚙ .

2. Tap **General** tab (if needed).

3. Tap **Apps & notifications** or **Apps**.

4. Tap the **Advanced**. If you can't see "Advanced," tap the menu icon ⋮ .

5. Tap **Default apps**.

6. Tap **Browser app** and choose Chrome app. You can use this method to make other app(s) your default app. For example, if you have two email apps on your device, you might be able to use this method to select the default app.

Tip: For some Android phones, you can quickly access "Default apps" page by doing the following. Open the settings page and tap the search icon (lens icon) located at the top of the screen. Key "Default apps" and choose Default apps from the result.

Managing the History List

If the secret mode is not enabled, Chrome browser collects the history of the webpages you visit and stores it.

To access your history:

1. Tap ⋮ .

2. Tap **History**.

Hint: To clear the browsing data, tap ⋮ > **Settings** > **Privacy** > scroll down and tap **Clear browsing data.** Check all the necessary boxes and tap **Clear data.**

Tip: If you delete history from Google Chrome, Google may stay still have your history in the cloud. To completely clear your history from the cloud, do the following:

1. **Open https://myactivity.google.com**

2. Tap **Filter by Date & Product**.

3. Unselect **All Products**.

4. Tap the checkbox next to all the information you want to delete. In this case, select "Chrome". If you want to delete all the stored information, select "All products".

5. Tap the search icon [Q].

6. At the top right corner of the information you want to delete, select the menu icon ⋮ and then select **Delete**. Tap **Delete** to confirm.

Sharing a Webpage with Friends

To share your webpage with friends, open the Chrome browser and tap ⋮ . Tap on **Share...** and then choose a sharing option from the list.

Printing Web Pages on Chrome Browser

Printing on Chrome browser is quite fantastic. Please note that printing may require a Wi-Fi connection.

1. Tap on ⋮ and then tap **Share...**
2. Select **Print**.
3. Tap the dropdown menu ▼ (next to "Save as PDF") and tap "All printer...".
4. Follow the onscreen instructions to complete the printing process.

You can customize the printing options by tapping on the dropdown menu below **Paper size**.

Saving a Web Page as PDF

1. Tap ⋮ located at the top of the screen and then tap **Share...**
2. Select **Print**.
3. Tap the dropdown menu (if necessary) and tap **Save as PDF**.
4. Tap the download icon located at the upper right side of the screen.

5. If available, select the folder where you want to save it to and then tap **Save**.

Secret Mode

There are times when you will not want your browser to save any information about your visit to a webpage. For instance, if you don't want a website to save cookies on your device or you don't want your children to know you are browsing about favorite gifts to buy for them.

In addition, Secret mode browsing allows for multiple sessions. For example, you may access your Yahoo mail account (or another web account) on a normal window and use the Secret mode tab to open the Yahoo mail account of that of your friend or family member without logging out of your account. Pages viewed in a secret mode are not listed in your browser history or search history and leave no traces (such as cookies) on your device.

To activate secret mode, tap ⋮ and then tap **New incognito tab**.

To close the incognito tab, tap the tab icon 1 next to the address bar and then tap **X** on the thumbnail of the incognito tab you want to close.

More on Chrome Browser Settings

Many options under Settings have already been discussed, but there are still some that I would like to mention.

1. **Auto fill and payments:** Use this option to enable Chrome browser to save your form entries whenever you fill in information into an online form so that it can be used when you are filling similar forms in the future. In addition, you can use this option to manage your payment information.

2. **Passwords:** Tap this option to manage your saved passwords.

3. **Privacy**: Use this option to access settings such as cookies, personal data and so on. You can use the privacy tab to delete history information on your browser. To do this, tap **Clear browsing data**.

4. **Accessibility**: Use this tab to manage settings like font/text size and "force zoom" option.

5. **Site settings**: Use this option to access advanced options such as **JavaScript**, **Location**, **Pop-ups**, **Notifications**, among others.

6. **Languages**: Tap this to manage language options for Chrome browser. To rearrange languages, tap and hold the two-line

icon (=) next to a language and drag it up or down. To

remove a language, tap the menu icon ⋮ and select **Remove**.

7. **Data Saver:** Use this option to manage data saving option.

8. **About Chrome:** Use this option to get information about the Chrome browser.

More on the More ⋮ tab

Many options under the **More** tab have already been discussed, but I would still like to point out few things.

1. **Download:** Use this option to access your downloaded files.
2. **Recent tabs:** Use this tab to access recently closed tab on your phone.

3. **Find in page:** Use this option to search for a word or a phrase on a webpage.

4. **Desktop site:** Use this option to request the desktop version of a webpage.

Troubleshooting Chrome Browser

Chrome browser may sometimes refuse to work properly, or it may hang. If this happens, just close the browser and open it again. To close the Chrome browser, tap the recent app icon or to view all the opened apps and then tap **X** next to the Chrome browser thumbnail. If the browser refuses to close, try this:

1. Swipe down from the top of the screen and tap settings icon .

2. Swipe up and tap "Apps".
    If you don't see "Apps", tap "Apps & Notifications" and then "App info" or "Apps".

3. Tap the app you want to manage, in this case "Chrome".

4. To force-stop an app, tap **FORCE STOP**. Force-stopping an app is useful when an app is misbehaving or when it refuses to close.

To access a force-stopped app again, just relaunch the app from the application screen. If this does not solve the problem, try restarting your phone.

In addition, if you see that a website/webpage is misbehaving, you can try deleting the *cache, cookies and site data* and see if this would solve the problem. To do this:

- On the Chrome browser's screen tap .

- Tap **Settings**.

- Tap **Privacy**.

- Scroll down and tap **Clear browsing data**.

- Check **"Cookies and site date"** and **"Cached images and files"** and then tap **Clear data**.

Troubleshooting Internet Connection when Using Chrome Browser

Chrome browser may sometimes refuse to browse the internet. When this happens, you may try any of the suggestions below:

1. Check if you are connected to a wireless network. When Wi-Fi is on, is displayed in the Status bar.

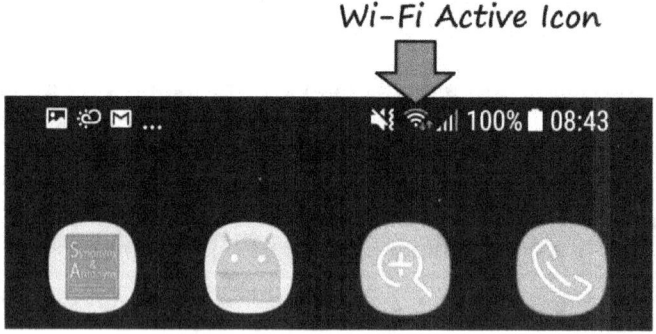

If your phone is not connected to a network, from the home screen, tap **Settings** > **Networks** or **Networks & Internet**. Tap **Wi-Fi**, and then tap On/Off switch to turn Wi-Fi on. If the method above does work for you, try this. Swipe down from the top of the screen and tap **settings icon** ⚙ > **Connections**. Tap **Wi-Fi**, and then tap On/Off switch to turn Wi-Fi on.

2. If you are trying to use a cellular connection and not a Wi-Fi connection, then check your cellular data connection. Swipe down from the top of the screen, tap **Settings** > **Networks** or **Networks & Internet** > **Mobile data**.
Alternatively, if you are using a Samsung Android phone, swipe down from the top of the screen, tap the **settings icon** ⚙ > **Connections** >**Data Usage**. Then make sure the switch next to **Mobile data** is turned on.

3. If you are trying to roam while abroad, check that you have allowed roaming. Swipe down from the top of the screen and tap the **settings icon** ⚙ > **Network & Internet** or **Connections** > **Mobile networks** > **Data Roaming**. Then make sure the switch next to **Data Roaming** is switched on. Please note that when roaming, international roaming charges may apply.

If after trying all the options above, and you can't still browse, then make sure that you have not mistakenly/knowingly installed a new browsing setting on your phone. If you have installed new settings from a text message, then uninstall the new settings. To do this, swipe down from the top of the screen and tap the **settings icon**

⚙ > **Apps** or **Apps & Notifications**. Look for the new settings. Tap the new settings and tap **Uninstall**.

If you can't still browse after following all these pieces of advice, then I would advise you contact your network service provider.

Samsung Internet App

Samsung Internet app allows you to surf the internet. You can download Samsung Internet from Google Play store.

Please note that the version of the Samsung browser discussed in this guide is the one that comes preloaded on Samsung Android phone. It is therefore possible that it might be slightly different from the one available on Google Play store.

Opening the Internet Browser

The first thing you would need to do to use the Internet app is to open it. To do this:

1. From the home screen or the app screen, tap **Internet** .
2. Alternatively, go to the app screen and tap **Samsung** folder. Tap **Internet** .
3. If you are using the Internet app for the first time, follow the prompts to get started.

Get to Know the Internet Browser Interface

When you open the Internet app, you should see the following buttons/icons:

Depending on the version of Samsung Internet you are using, please note that the internet browser on your device may be slightly different from the one shown below.

1	**Favorite:** Tap this icon to bookmark a webpage.
2	**Refresh:** Tapping this icon reloads a webpage.
3	**Menu icon:** Tap this icon to access additional options such as **Find on page** and **save webpage** etc.
4	**Tabs:** Tap this to navigate between different webpages. Tap and hold the tab icon to quickly open your browser's home page.
5	**Bookmarks:** Tap this icon to access bookmark pages, saved

	pages and history.
6	**Home:** Tap this icon to go to the browser's home page. To quickly change the default Homepage, tap and hold the Home icon and then select **Other**. Then enter the website of your choice (e.g. freedom.to) and tap **OK**.
7	**Forward**: Tap this icon to return to the page you just left.
8	**Back:** Tap this icon to revisit the page you just visited. To quickly access browsing history, tap and hold the back button
9	**Quick Menu:** Tap this button to access the quick menu. Quick menu allows you to quickly share a webpage, increase webpage font, or open a new tab. To move this icon to another location, simply tap, hold and drag the icon to the new location. To remove the icon; tap, hold and drag it to the top of the screen (where Remove icon is located).

Customizing the Home Page

The Home page is the page that opens when you open your Internet browser. Fortunately, you can choose what appears on your home page.

To do this:

- While the Internet browser is opened, tap menu icon and then scroll down and tap on **Settings**.

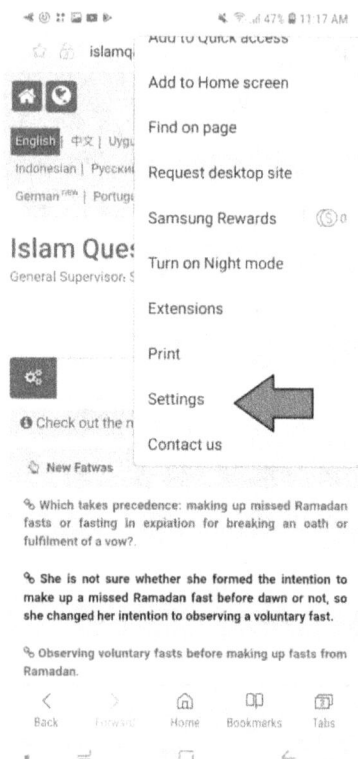

- Tap **Home page** and then choose an option.

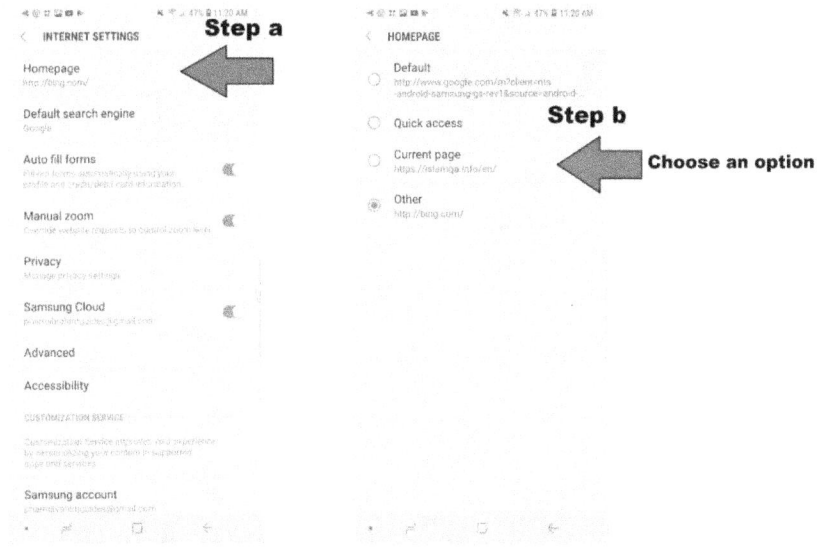

- To go to the Home page while using your internet browser, tap the internet browser Home button 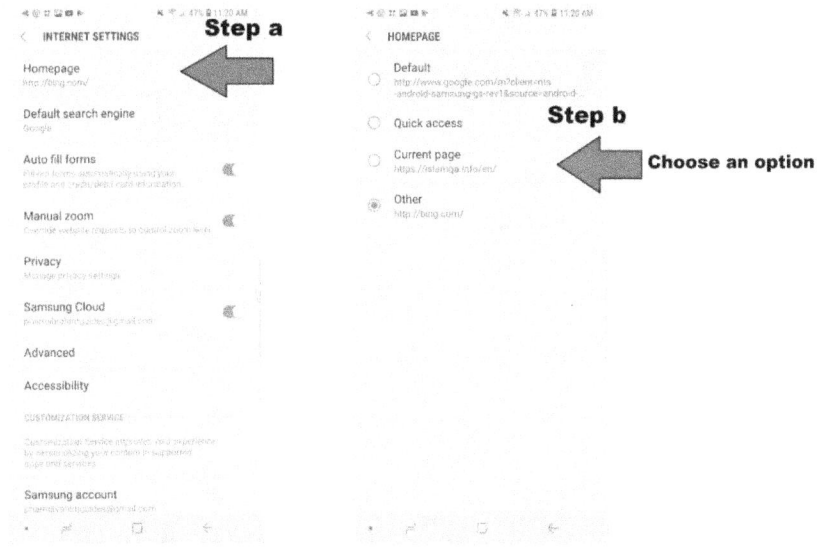 .

Tip: To quickly change the default Homepage, tap and hold the Home icon and then select an option.

Using the Address/Search Bar

Every web browser must have an address bar and Internet browser also has one. This bar serves the function of URL address bar and search bar. By default, the searches done on this bar are executed by Google. To learn how to change the search engine to another one, go to page 268.

You choose whether to launch a webpage or search for a term based on what you type into the address bar. For example, if you type **Freedom to** into the address bar and tap **Go**, Google search results for that phrase is displayed. On the other hand, if you type **Freedom.to** and tap **Go**, you will be taken to the website bearing the name.

Internet browser makes website suggestions to you based on the sites you have recently visited, to choose any of the suggested sites, tap it.

When you begin to type inside the address bar, Internet browser automatically makes suggestions beneath your typing. You can choose any of these suggestions to make things faster.

Zooming a Webpage in Internet Browser

To zoom in a webpage in Internet browser, place two fingers on the webpage and spread them apart. To zoom out, place two fingers on the webpage and move them closer together. To force zoom a webpage that doesn't readily respond to a zoom request, turn on the **Manual zoom**. To do this, while the Internet browser is opened, tap

menu icon ⋮ located at the top of the screen and then scroll down and tap on **Settings**. Tap the status switch next to **Manual Zoom**.

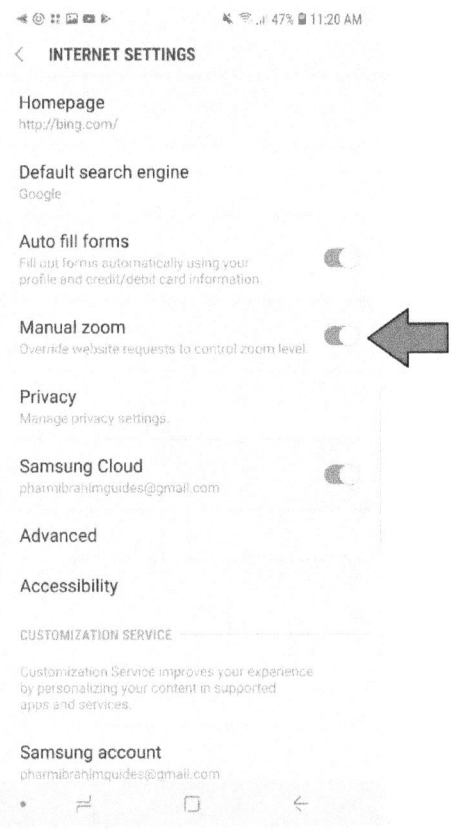

Using Tabs on Internet Browser

The tabs allow you to open different webpages at once. You can open many tabs at once on Internet browser.

To manage browsing tabs:

1. Tap the tab icon located at the bottom of the screen.

2. To open a new tab, tap **New Tab**.

3. To access a tab you have opened before, tap the tab icon

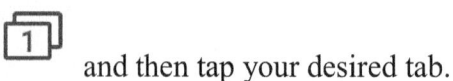 and then tap your desired tab.

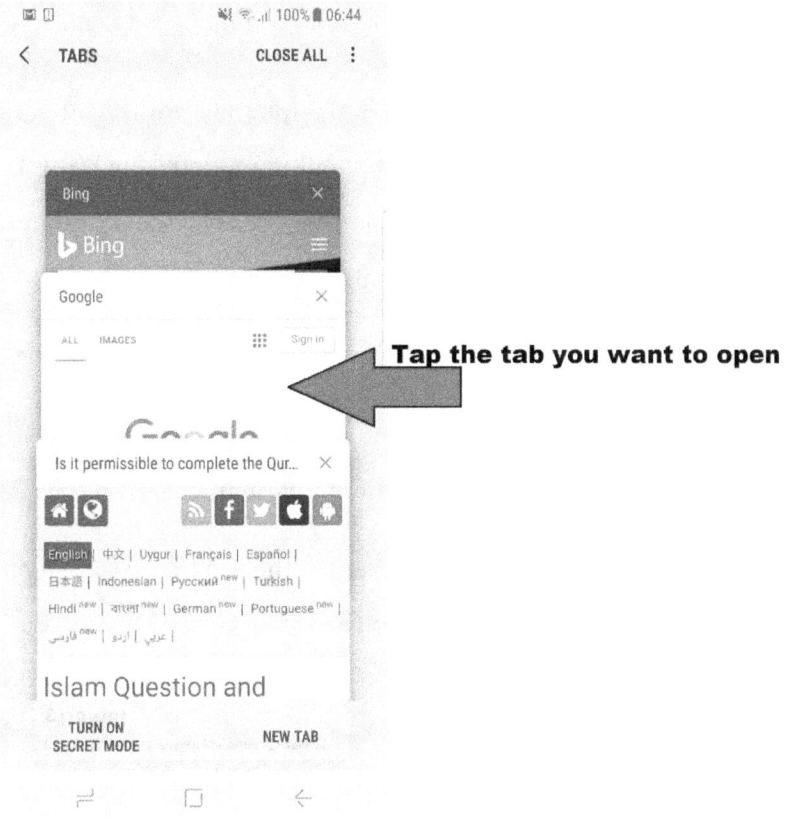

Tap the tab you want to open

4. To close a tab, tap the **X** icon at the top right corner of the thumbnail of the tab you want to close.

5. To close all tabs, while on the tabs' screen, tap **CLOSE ALL** located at the top of the screen.

Favorites (Bookmarks)

With several billions of webpages in the internet world, you may need to select your favorites. Just like other modern-day browsers, Internet browser gives you the opportunity to select a favorite or bookmark a page. This makes it easier to visit the website or webpage in the future.

To bookmark a webpage:

1. Open the website you want to bookmark.

2. Tap the menu icon ⋮ located at the top of the screen and then select **Add to Bookmarks**.

3. Key in the **Title** you want.

4. Tap **Save**.

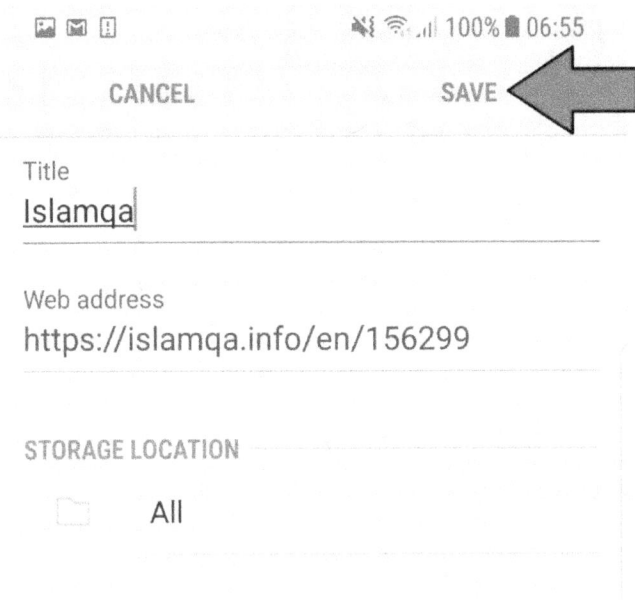

Tip: To quickly add a bookmark, just open the webpage and tap

favorite icon 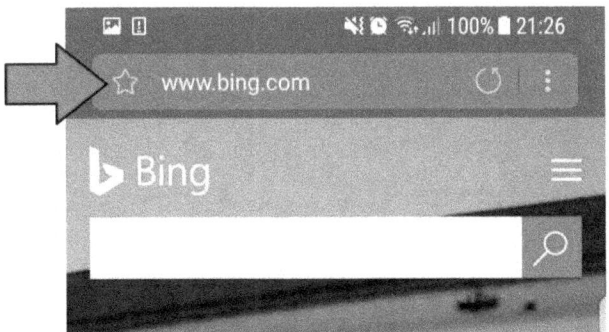 next to the address bar.

Accessing Your Bookmarks/Favorites

After you have added a webpage to your favorites list, you might need to access this list sooner or later. To access your bookmarks, tap the Bookmark icon (located at the bottom of the screen).

Saving a Webpage

Webpages contain a lot of information and you would probably need to schedule some webpages for later reading. Saving a webpage is a great way to do this. When you find an interesting information online and you don't have the time to read it, you can save it for a later reading.

To save a webpage, open the webpage and tap ⋮ (next to address bar) and then select **Save webpage**.

Accessing Your Saved Pages

After you have saved a page, you would need to access this page sooner or later. To do this, tap the **Bookmarks** icon (located at the bottom of the screen) and then tap **Saved Pages** located at the top of the screen.

Changing the Search Engine

The default search engine on Internet browser is Google. Some people may love to change this to another search engine.

You can change the Internet browser Search Engine by following the steps highlighted below:

1. While the browser is opened, tap menu icon ⋮ (next to address bar) and select **Settings**.

2. Tap on **Default search engine** and select a search engine.

Making Internet App Your Default Browser

If you have multiple browsers on your device, you can select internet app to be the default browser. To do this:

1. Swipe down from the top of the screen, select the settings icon ⚙ .

2. Tap **General** tab (if needed).

3. Tap **Apps & notifications** or **Apps**.

4. Tap the **Advanced**. If you can't see "Advanced," tap the menu icon ⋮ .

5. Tap **Default apps**.

7. Tap **Browser app** and choose **Samsung Internet**.

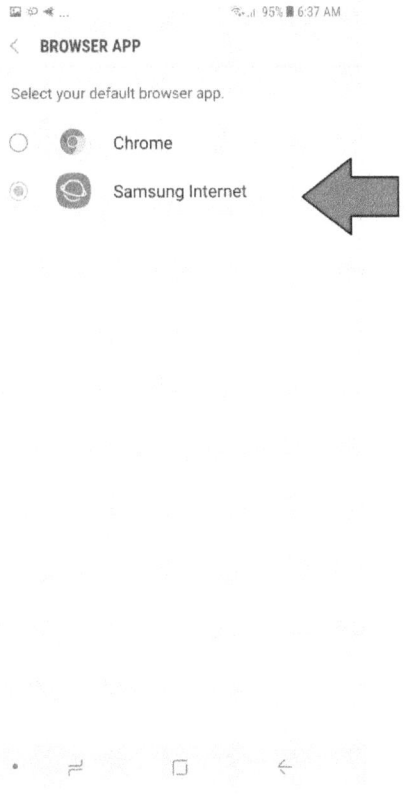

Hint: You can use the method mentioned above to set other favorite app(s) as default app(s). For example, if you have many Contact apps on your device, you can select a default Contact app using this method.

Managing the History List

If the secret mode is not enabled, Internet browser collects the history of the webpages you visit and stores it.

To access your history:

1. Tap the **Bookmarks** ⬜⬜ (located at the bottom of the screen).

2. Tap **History**.

Hint: To clear the browsing data, tap ⋮ (located at the top of the screen) > **Settings** > **Privacy** > **Delete personal data.** Select what you would like to delete, and tap **Delete.**

In addition, if you see that a website/webpage is misbehaving, you can try deleting the *cache, cookies and site data,* and see if this would solve the problem. To do this, tap ⋮ (located at the top of the screen) > **Settings** > **Privacy** > **Delete personal data.** Select **Cache, Cookies and site data** and then tap **Delete.**

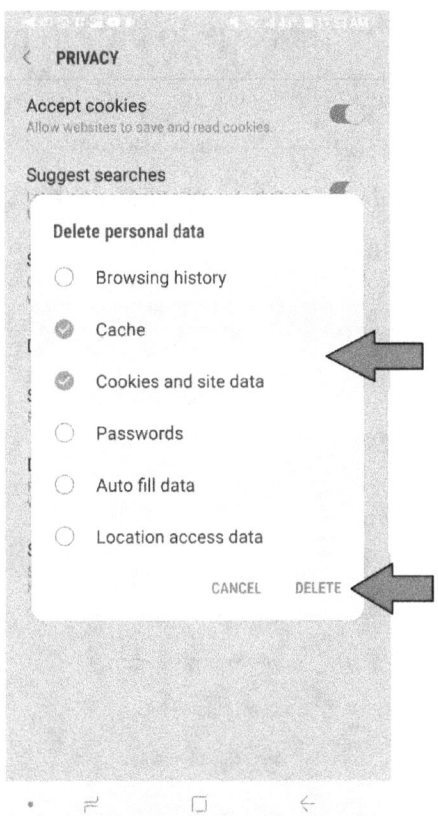

Sharing a Webpage with Friends

To share a webpage with friends, open the Internet app and tap the

menu icon ⋮ next to the address bar. Then tap on **Share**. Then

choose an app and follow the prompts.

Add Your Favorite Webpage to the Home Screen

You can make your favorite webpage a shortcut on the home screen. This allows you to easily access the webpage directly from your home screen. To do this:

1. Open a webpage and tap on the menu icon ⋮ (next to the address bar).

2. Tap **Add shortcut on Home screen**.

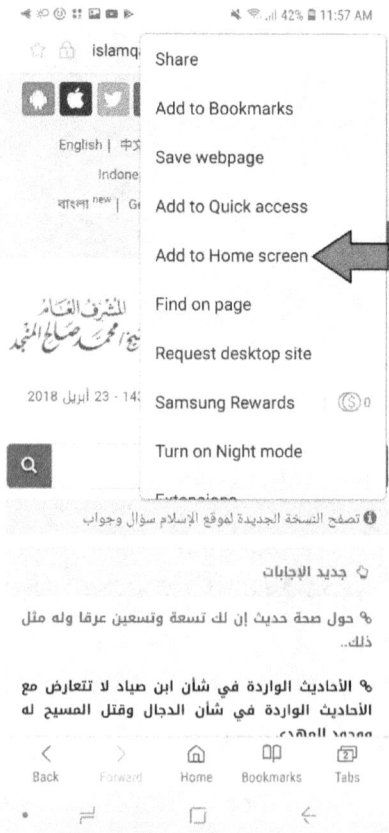

3. Tap **Add**.

4. To see the newly added webpage, tap the home button
   or (located at the bottom of the screen). If you can't see
   it on the first home screen, swipe left to check another home
   screen.

Printing Web Pages on the Internet Browser

Printing on the Internet browser is quite fantastic. You can initiate
the printing process by tapping on the menu icon (the three dots icon
located next to the address bar). Then tap **Print**. Tap the **dropdown
arrow** to select a printer. To adjust the printing options, tap **Copies**.

To save the webpage as a pdf, tap the dropdown arrow and select

Save as PDF. Thereafter, tap the yellow **PDF** icon and
choose a folder. Then tap **Done** to download.

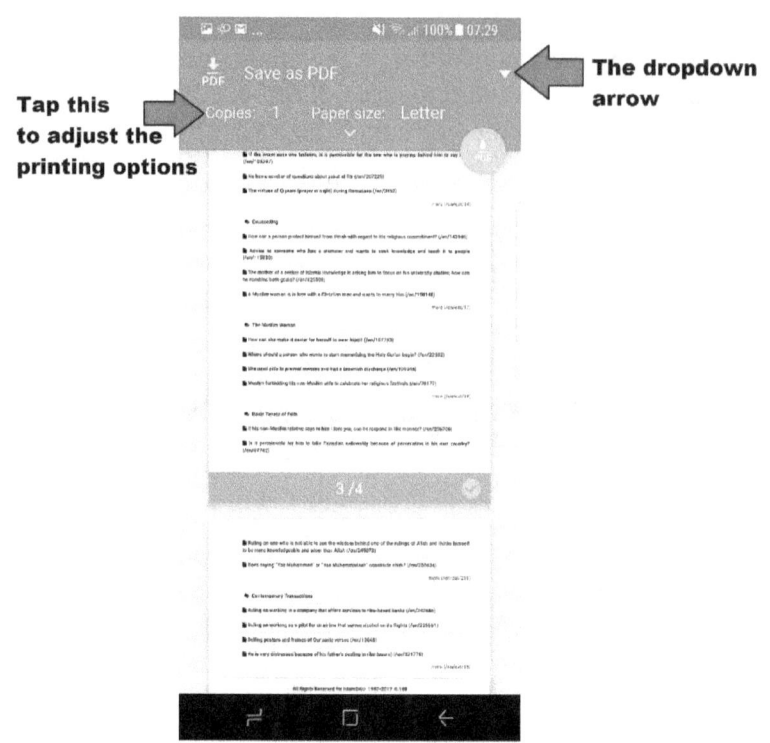

Secret Mode

There are times when you will not want your browser to save any information about your visit to a webpage. For instance, if you don't want a website to save cookies on your device or you don't want your children to know you are browsing about favorite gifts to buy for them.

In addition, Secret mode browsing allows for multiple sessions. For example, you may access your Gmail account (or another web account) on a normal window and use the Secret mode tab to open the Gmail account of that of your friend or family member without logging out of your account. Pages viewed in secret mode are not listed in your browser history or search history and leave no traces (such as cookies) on your device.

To activate the Secret mode, in the toolbar at the bottom of the screen, tap **Tabs** 🔲 → **Turn on Secret mode**.
Then tap **Set password** to protect your Secret mode data with a password. You may also tap **Do not use password** if you don't want to use a password.

To deactivate the Secret mode, close the Internet app. Alternatively, tap the tab button 🔲 , tap **Close All** (located at the top of the screen), tap the menu icon ⋮ (if needed) and then select **Turn off Secret Mode**.

More on Internet Browser Settings

Many options under settings have already been discussed, but there are still some that I would like to mention.

1. **Auto fill profile:** Use this option to enable Internet browser to save your form entries whenever you fill in information into an online form so that it can be used when you are filling similar forms in the future.

2. **Privacy**: Use this option to access settings such as **cookies**, **personal data** and so on. You can use the privacy tab to delete history information on your browser. To do this, tap **Delete personal data**.

3. **Advanced**: Use this option to access advanced options like **JavaScript**, **Pop-up blocker**, **Status bar**, **Manage website data** and **Web notifications**.

4. **Accessibility**: You can manage *high contrast mode* under this tab.

5. **Samsung account**: This tab displays the Samsung account address on your mobile phone.

6. **Personal information**: Use this tab to manage those information that can be sent to Samsung to provide you a customized experience.

7. **About Samsung Internet:** Use this option to get software information about the Internet app.

More on the Menu Icon

Many options under the **menu** tab ⋮ have already been discussed, but I would like to point out few more things.

1. **Add to Quick access**: Use this option to add a webpage to your quick access list so that you can access it easily in the future from the internet app homepage. To make sure you go to Quick access page when you tap the Internet browser home button 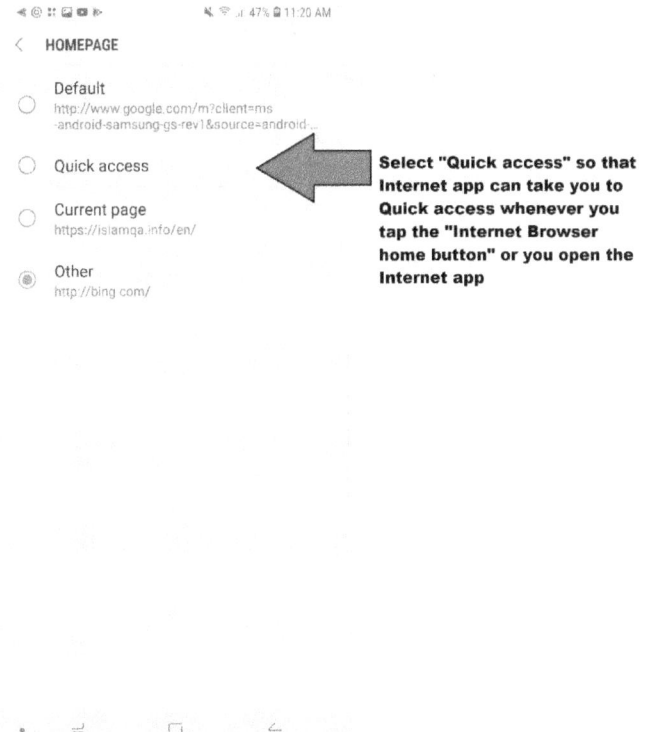 , tap and hold Internet browser home button and select Quick access.

HOMEPAGE

Default
http://www.google.com/m?client=ms
-android-samsung-gs-rev1&source=android-...

Quick access

Current page
https://islamqa.info/en/

Other
http://bing.com/

Select "Quick access" so that Internet app can take you to Quick access whenever you tap the "Internet Browser home button" or you open the Internet app

2. **Add to Home screen:** Use this option to make a webpage a shortcut on your home screen.

3. **Find on page:** Use this option to search for a word or a phrase on a webpage.

4. **Request desktop site:** Use this option to request the desktop version of a webpage.

5. **Turn on Night mode:** Use this option to give a webpage a darkish background.

6. **Extensions:** Internet app browser's extensions allow you to do more when using the Internet app. To see which extensions are available on Internet app, tap **Extensions**.

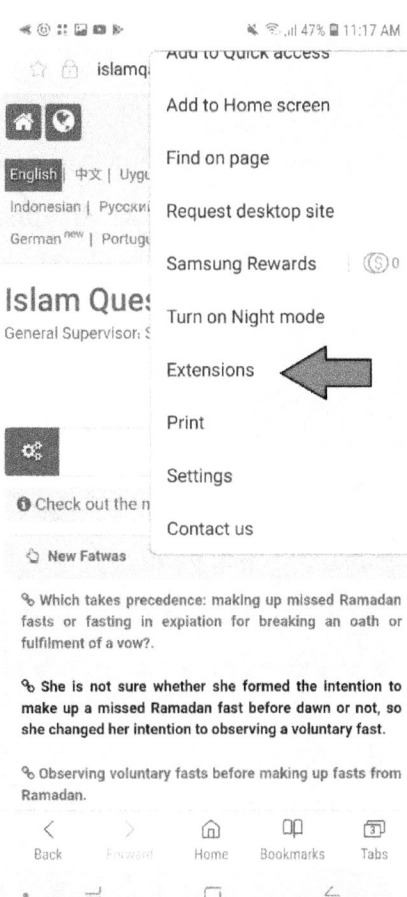

Troubleshooting the Internet browser

Internet browser may sometimes refuse to work properly, or it may hang. If this happens, just close the browser and open it again. To close the Internet app, tap the recent app button (located at the bottom of the screen) to view all the opened apps and then tap **X** next to the Internet app thumbnail. If this doesn't work, "force stop" the Internet app. To learn how to force stop an app, go to page 420. Alternatively, try restarting your phone.

In addition, if you see that a website/webpage is misbehaving, you can try deleting the *cache, cookies and site data* and see if this would solve the problem. To do this, tap Internet app menu icon

⋮ (located at the top of the screen) > **Settings** > **Privacy** > **Delete personal data**. Select **Cache** and **Cookies and site data** and then tap **Delete**.

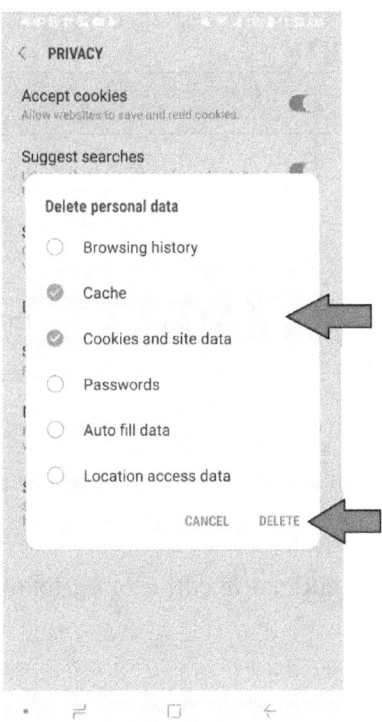

Troubleshooting Internet Connection when Using the Internet Browser

Internet browser may sometimes refuse to browse the internet.

Please refer to page 252 to know what to do such in such a situation.

Communication

Calling

The Phone apps found on Andriod phones vary from one phone manufacturer to another. In this guide, I would be talking about what is common with the Phone apps on many/most Android phones. In this section of the guide, you will learn how to use the calling functions, such as making and answering calls, using options available during a call, and using call-related features.

Making, Answering, Rejecting and Silencing a Call

To make a call or silence a call:

1. From the home screen, tap **Phone** (telephone icon) and enter a phone number. If the keypad does not appear on the screen, tap the keypad button to show the keypad. To call a number on your contact, tap the **Contact** button on the Phone app screen.

2. To make a call from the Recents or Call log tab, tap the **Recents** tab or **Call log** icon located at the top of the screen.

3. To make a phone call, tap a contact and then tap the phone

   icon 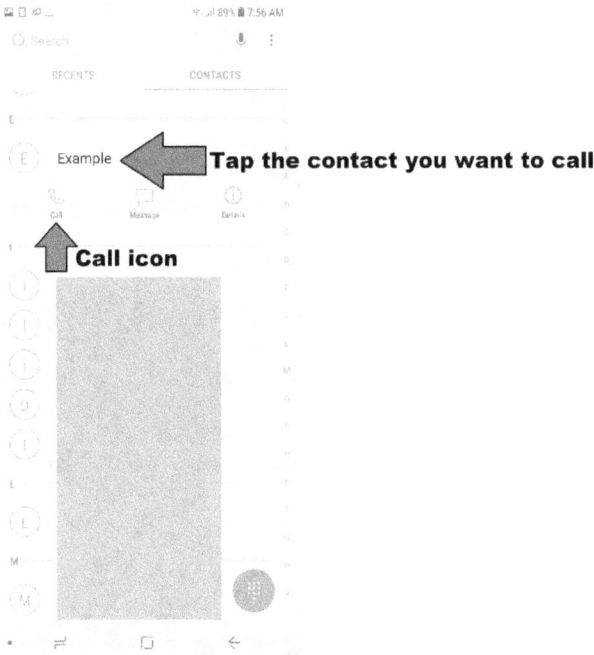 .

Tap the contact you want to call

Call icon

4. On supported Android phones, to silence or reduce the
   volume of an incoming call, press the volume down button
   (usually located at the side of the phone).

Hint: You can access apps/items on your phone while receiving a

call. To do this, tap the home key [O] or [ ] located at the lower

side of the screen and tap the item/app you want to access.

Tip: On Samsung Android phone, to call the contact whose message or contact details are currently on the screen, bring the phone close to your ear. However, please note that you may need to enable this option. To do this, swipe down from the top of the screen and tap the

settings icon ⚙ > **Advanced features.** Then tap the status switch next to **Direct call**.

To answer a call or reject an incoming call:
1. To receive an incoming call, tap or drag the **Green phone**

   icon 📞 .
2. To decline an incoming call, tap or drag the **Red phone icon**

   📞 .

3. To reply with a text, tap **Send Message** or tap the **Message** icon. For some Android phones, swipe up the message icon to reply with a message.
4. Then tap one of the pre-written messages. Alternatively, tap **Compose new message** or **Write new message** and write your message.

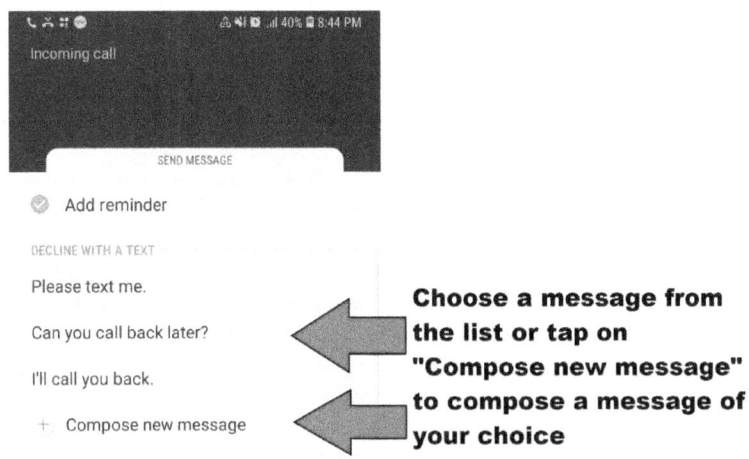

Choose a message from the list or tap on "Compose new message" to compose a message of your choice

Hint: If you are using an app, a pop-up screen is displayed for the incoming call, just tap the corresponding icon to accept, decline the call or reply with a message.

In addition, you can create rejection messages of your own. To do this:

1. From the home screen, tap **Phone**.

2. Tap **Menu icon** ⋮ .

3. Select **Settings**.

4. For Dual SIM users, tap "Calling accounts", and select a SIM.

5. Tap **Calls** (if needed).

6. Tap **Quick decline message** or **Reject call with message**.

7. Tap the message you want to edit and enter a message. Then tap the **Plus icon** + or tap **OK**. On supported phones, to delete a message, tap the minus icon next to it.

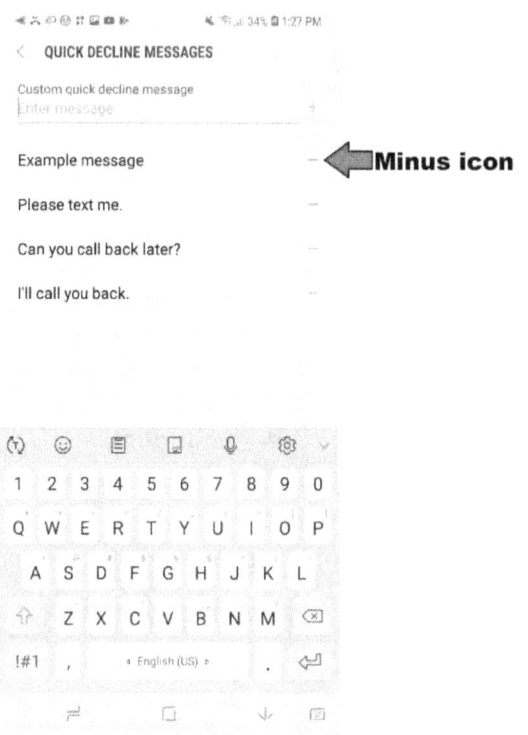

If you are using Google Pixel, simply repeat steps 1 to 3 above and tap Quick responses. Tap the message you want to edit and make necessary adjustments. Tap **Ok** to save.

Tip: On supported phones, if a phone number calls you or you call a number and you don't have it on your contact, you can easily add it to your contact. To do this, tap **Phone** app and tap **Recents** or **Call log** icon located at the top of the screen. Tap the phone number involved and then tap **Create new contact**. If "Create new contact" is not avalaible, tap **Details** and then tap **Create Contact** and follow the prompts.

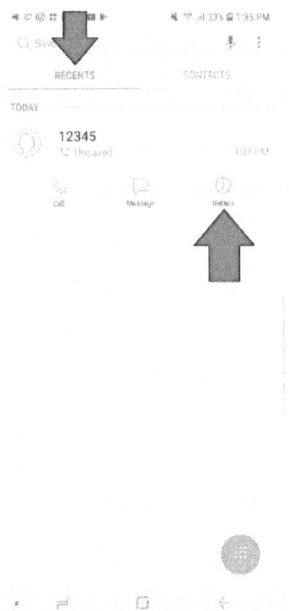

Tip: On Supported Samsung Android phones, to quickly reject an incoming call with a preset rejection message, place your finger on the heart rate monitor for two seconds while the phone screen is facing down. The heart rate monitor is located under the flash light at the back of supported Samsung Android phones. *Please note that this option may only work when your device is turned over and the screen is off.*

You can edit the preset rejection message on supported Samsung Android phones. To do this:

1. Swipe down from the top of the screen and select settings icon ⚙. Tap **Display** tab.

2. Scroll down and tap **Edge Screen**.

3. Tap **Edge Lighting**.

4. Tap the menu icon ⋮ located at the top of the screen.

5. Tap **Quick reply**.

6. Type in a **Quick Reply Message** and tap the back icon next to QUICK REPLY to save the changes.

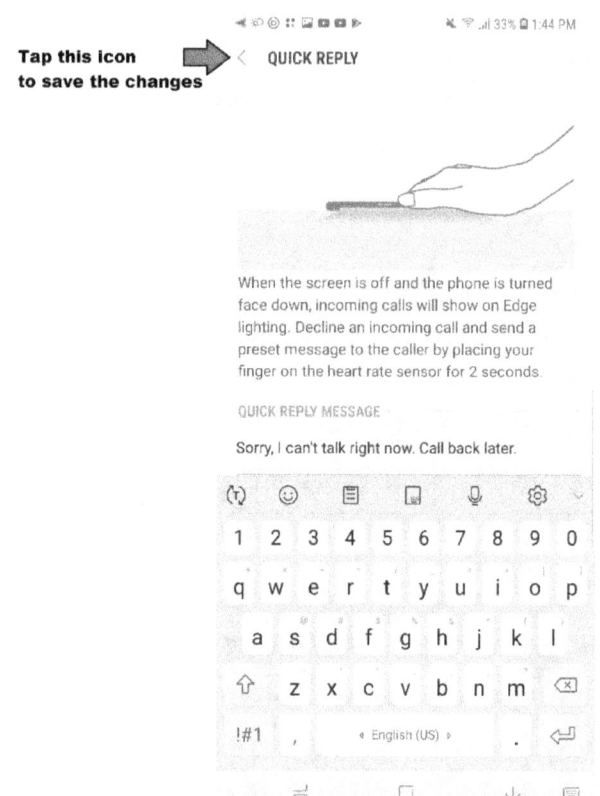

Learn How to Use Your Phone During a Call

You can perform any of these tasks when on a call:

Please note that the call screen on your phone might be different from the one shown below. However, the onscreen icons (shown on the screenshot below) are similar to what is avalaible on many Android phones.

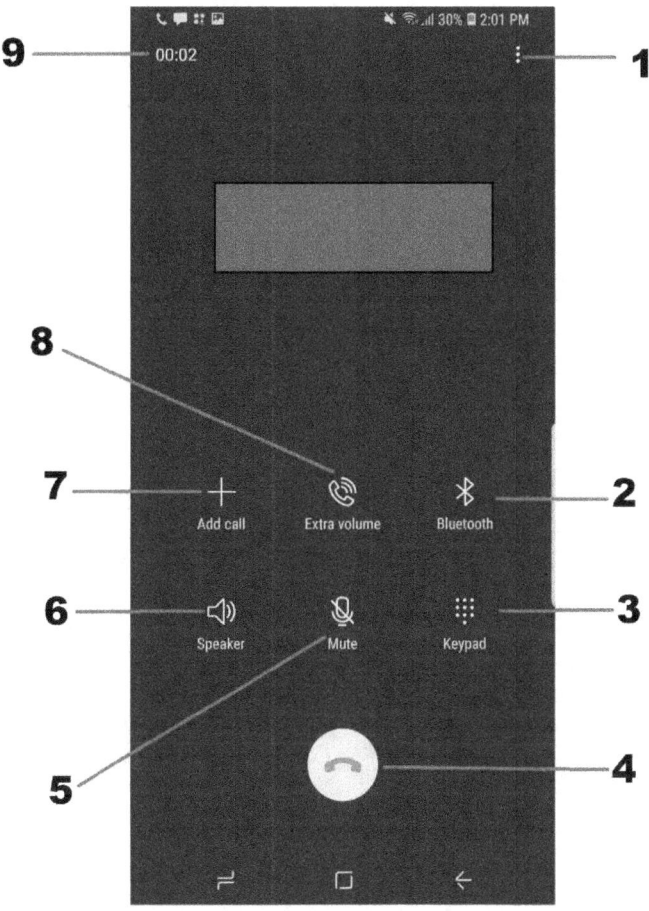

Number	Function
1.	Tap the **Menu icon** to hold a current call, view a contact or add a number to your contacts list, or send a message.

2.	Tap the Bluetooth icon to connect to a Bluetooth headset while on a call.
3.	Tap the keypad icon to access the keypad. To hide the keypad, tap the **Hide** icon.
4.	Tap the red phone icon to **end a call**.
5.	Tap this icon to mute the microphone.
6.	To turn Speakerphone on or off, tap the speaker icon.
7.	Tap the plus icon to add another contact to a call or start another call.
8.	Tap extra volume icon to add extra volume to a call.
9.	Call time

Tip: To access the application screen while on a call, tap the home button. If you want to return to the call screen, swipe down from the top of the screen and tap the current call. For some Android phones, you simply need to tap the phone icon at the top of the screen to return to your call.

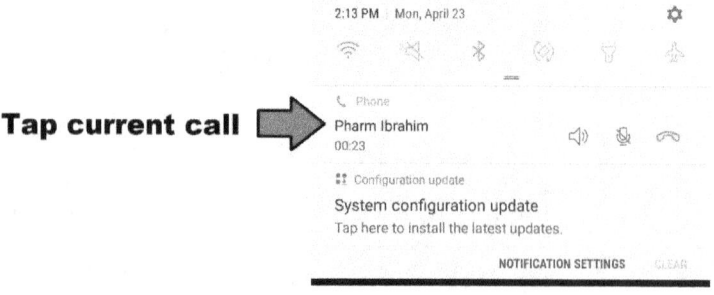

Place a New Call While on a Call (Conference Calling)

If your network service provider supports this feature, you can make another call while a call is in progress.

1. From the active call screen, tap + **Add call**.

2. Dial the new number and tap **Dial**. When the call is answered:

   i. Tap **Swap** to switch between the two calls.

   ii. Tap or **Merge** to turn the call to a conference call.

3. To end a call while on a conference call mode, tap the dropdown arrow (a v-like icon next to **Conference call**) and then select **Drop** next to the call you want to end. If this is not available on your phone, tap the manage icon and then tap the phone icon next to the call you want to end. To split the call, tap the "**Y**" icon.

Emergency Calling

You can use Android Phone to make an emergency call. From the home screen, tap **Phone** icon and enter the emergency telephone number. Note that if you dial 911 in the U.S, your location details may be provided to an emergency service provider even if your settings does not support this.

Please note that an emergency number can be dialed even if the phone is locked.

Using Call Waiting

Call waiting allows you to get another call while you're already in one.

1. To answer the new call, tap the phone icon or drag **Answer** to the right direction and then choose an option:

    i.   **Put ...on hold** or **Hold and Answer Voice** to place the previous caller on hold while you answer the new call.

    ii.   **End call with...** to end the previous call and answer the new call.

    iii. **Ignore** to reject the call.

2. Once the other call is answered, tap the contact/number or tap the swap icon next to the contact or phone number

you wish to continue talking to. The other(s) would be put on

hold. To merge the calls, tap merge icon ◁ or ⋀.

Please note that call waiting may be disabled by default. To enable

this feature, tap **Phone** > **Menu icon** ⋮ > **Settings** > **Calls** (if

needed) > **More settings** or **Additional settings** (if needed) , and

then tap the switch next to **Call waiting**.

Using the Speed Dial Options

The speed dial allows you to quickly access a number in your

contact. To set up speed dial:

1. Tap the phone icon ☏.
2. Tap **Contacts** located at the top of the screen.

3. Tap **menu icon** ⋮ located at the top (or bottom) of the
   screen.
4. Tap **Speed dial**.
5. To add a contact to the speed dial, tap the contact icon

   .

6. To change the speed dial number, tap the dropdown arrow
   and pick a number. Number one is reserved for voicemail.

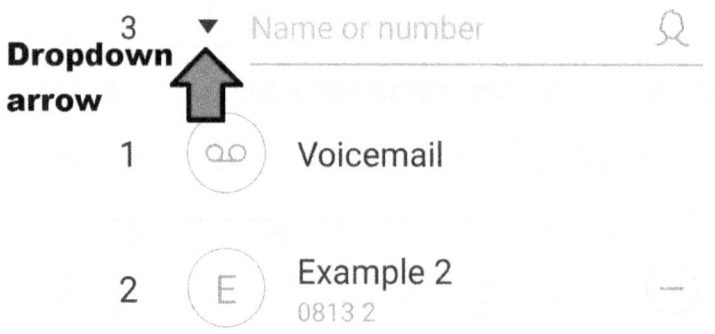

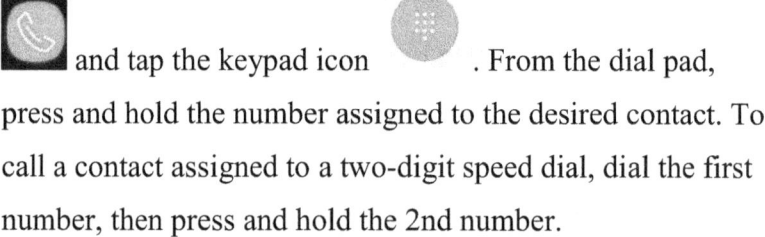

7. To call a contact you have added, tap the phone app icon

   ![phone icon] and tap the keypad icon ![keypad icon] . From the dial pad, press and hold the number assigned to the desired contact. To call a contact assigned to a two-digit speed dial, dial the first number, then press and hold the 2nd number.

8. On supported phones, to delete a speed dial number, tap the **Minus (-)** icon next to the assigned contact. Removing a contact from a speed dial list will not delete it from your phone.

If the instruction above does not work for you, try this. From the

home screen, tap **PHONE app icon** . Tap **menu icon** ⋮ . Tap

Settings. Tap **Speed Dial** and follow the prompts.

Using the Fixed Dialing Option

If you want to select the numbers your mobile phone can call, you need to turn on the fixed dialing. Once done, you can only call the selected numbers and emergency numbers.

1. From the home screen, tap **PHONE app icon** .

2. Tap **menu icon** ⋮ .

3. Tap **Settings**.

4. Scroll down and tap **More settings**, **Additional settings** or **Calls**.

5. Tap **Fixed Dialing Numbers**.

6. To turn the fixed dialing on, tap **Turn on FDN** or **Enable FDN**, type in your **PIN2** and tap **OK**. Please contact your local network service provider for your PIN2.

7. To turn the fixed dialing off, tap **Turn off FDN** or **Disable FDN**, enter your **PIN2** and tap OK.

Note: I am not sure if all network providers support this feature. If you notice that this feature is not available on your phone, you may need to contact your service provider to know if you can use it.

Adding Fixed Dialing Numbers

1. Repeat the steps 1 to 5 above.
2. Tap **FDN List**.
3. Tap **+ Add**.
4. Tap **Name** and enter the required name.
5. Tap **Number** and enter the required phone number.
6. Tap **Save** (if needed).
7. Tap **PIN2** and enter the PIN2. Please contact your local network service provider for your PIN2.
8. Tap **Save** or **Ok**.

Please note that when FDN is enabled, you may not be able to call any other numbers, apart from the numbers on the FDN list and the emergency numbers.

Call Forwarding (Diverting Calls to Another Number)

When you are busy, you can forward incoming calls to another phone number. Please note that your network provider would need to support this feature for it to be available.

1. From the home screen, tap **PHONE app icon** .

2. Tap **menu icon** located at the top of the screen.

3. Tap **Settings**.

4. If needed, scroll down and tap **More settings** or tap **Calls**.

5. Tap **Call forwarding**.

6. Tap the required divert type and follow the onscreen instructions. For example, to forward all your calls, tap **Always forward**.

7. To turn off call forwarding, select a divert type and select **turn off** or **disable**.

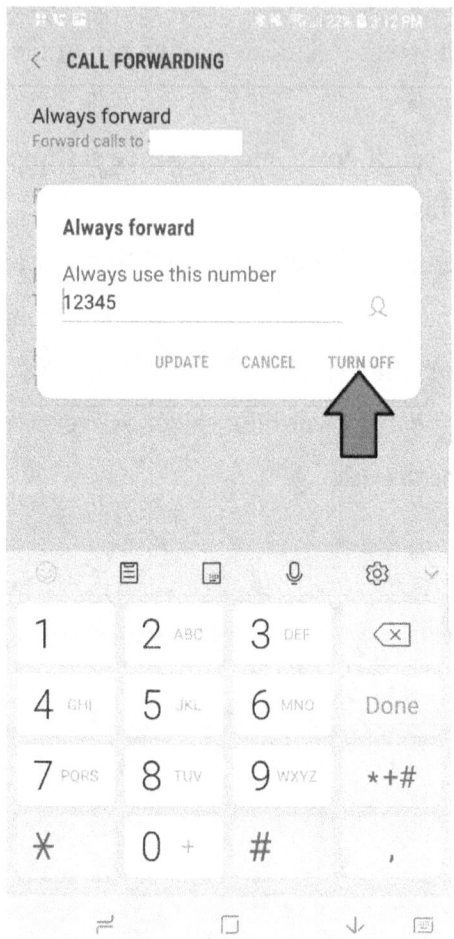

Note: When the call forwarding option is enabled, you should see the call forwarding icon (see the picture below) on the notification bar at the top of the screen.

In addition, depending on your network provider, you may be able to forward calls to your voicemail and listen to them later. Please contact your network service provider to know how to do this.

Block Calls

If your service provider supports this feature, you may be able to avoid receiving calls from certain numbers. Please note that the call blocking feature may not affect phone calls made or received via apps (e.g. Skype) installed on your device.

Please note that features available under Call blocking may differ from one service provider to another.

1. From the home screen, tap **PHONE app icon** .
2. Tap **menu icon** ⋮ located at the top of the screen.
3. Tap **Settings**.
4. Tap **Block numbers**.
5. To add a number to your block list, enter the desired phone number in the **Add phone number** field, then tap the + icon. To add a number from your contacts, tap Contacts icon

   (if available) and tap **Done** after adding a contact.
6. To remove a number from your block list, tap the Minus (-) icon or "**X**" icon next to a name or number on your block list.

7. On supported Android phones, to make sure that only the numbers that you have their contacts can call you, tap the status switch next to **Block unknown callers**.

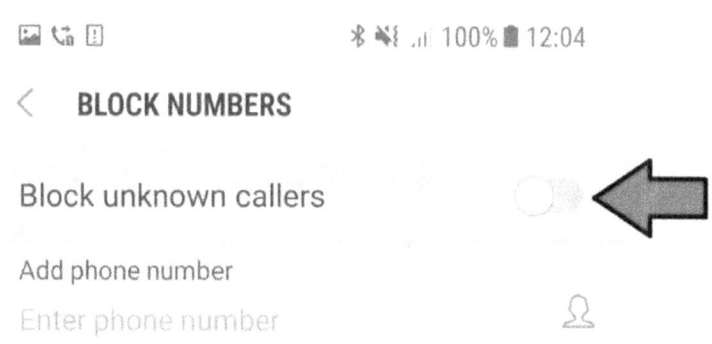

Note: In certain instances, blocking anonymous call may be unbeneficial and even dangerous. For example, blocking anonymous call may prevent you from accepting calls from those who have something important to tell you (unless you have their contacts). *In addition, if you are not able to use call blocking option after following the instructions above, please contact your network service provider.*

Tip: To block a contact from call log, follow these steps:

1. From the home screen, tap **PHONE app icon** 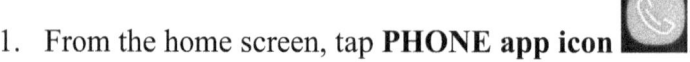.

2. Tap **Recents** or **Call log** icon located at the top of the screen.

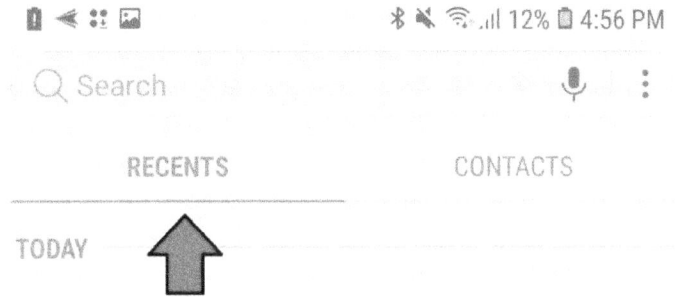

3. Tap and hold the contact you want to block and select "Block number". Then tap "Block".

4. Alternatively, tap the contact you want to block and tap details icon ⓘ. Tap menu icon ⋮ located at the top of the screen. Tap "Block contact".

If you don't have the number that you want to block on your contact, repeat steps 1 to 2 above, tap the phone number (if needed) and then tap "Block number".

What about Caller ID?

If your service provider supports this feature, you may prevent your service provider from displaying your number(ID) when you call another person.

1. From the home screen, tap **PHONE app icon** .

2. Tap **menu icon** ⋮ located at the top of the screen.

3. Tap **Settings**.

4. Scroll down and tap **More settings**, **Additional settings** or **Calls**.

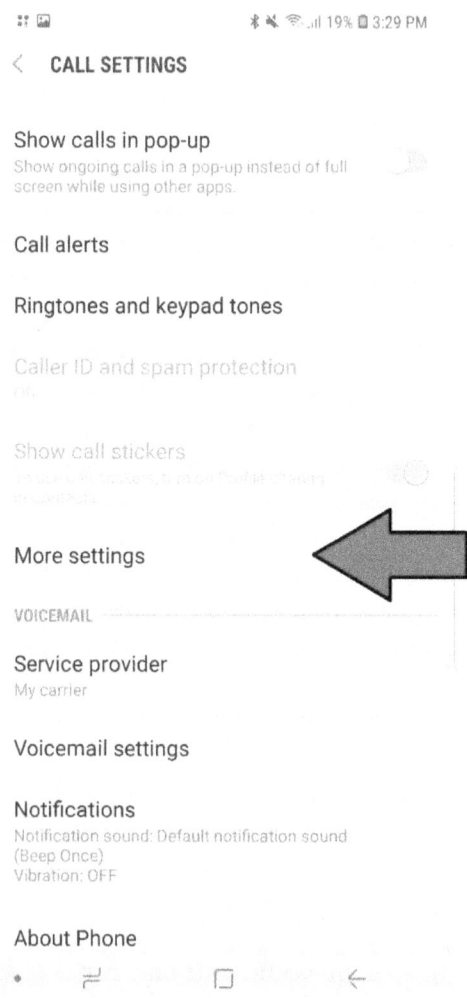

5. Tap **Show my caller ID** or **Caller ID** and then choose an option. If you don't see "Show my caller ID/Caller ID", tap **Additional settings** > **Caller ID**. Then choose an option.

Voicemail

Setting Up Voicemail

1. From the home screen, tap **PHONE app icon** .

2. Tap **menu icon** located at the top of the screen.

3. Tap **Settings**.

4. If needed, scroll down and tap **More settings**, **Additional settings** or **Calls**.

5. Tap **Voicemail**.

6. Tap **Setup** and follow the prompts. If you don't see setup option, please contact your network service provider.

Some Android phones also display Voicemail icon ⊙—⊙ at the top or bottom of the Phone app screen. If this is your case, tap this icon to setup or manage your voicemail.

Please note that you might need to contact your network service provider to successfully setup a voicemail. For example, you might need to contact your network service provider to get or create a voicemail password.

Listening to Voicemail or Call Your Voicemail

1. To listen to your voicemail, open the Phone app.

2. Tap the keypad icon .

3. Tap and hold number "1" (on the virtual keyboard) and
    follow the audio instructions to listen to your voicemails.
    Some Android phones also display Voicemail icon ○──○
    at the top or bottom of the Phone app screen. If this is
    your case, tap this icon to manage (or listen to) your
    voicemail.

If the instructions above do not work for you, please contact your
network service provider to know how to listen to and manage your
voicemails.

Managing Voicemail settings

1. From the home screen, tap **PHONE app icon** 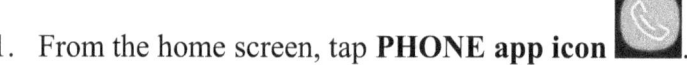 .

2. Tap **menu icon** ⋮ located at the top of the screen.

3. Tap **Settings**.

4. If needed, scroll down and tap **More settings**, **Additional**
    settings or **Calls**.

5. Tap **Voicemail**.

6. Tap a setting to manage.

Tip: If your network provider supports it, you might be able to divert you unanswered calls to voicemail. To learn how to manage call forwarding options, please see page 296. Please contact your network service provider to know how to divert calls to voicemail.

Using the Messaging app

This app allows you to send texts and images to other SMS and MMS devices.

To start or manage a conversation:

1. From the app screen, tap the **Messages** app or **Messaging** app icon.

2. Tap the new message icon or "+" located at the bottom of the screen.

3. Tap the "**To**" field and type in the first letters of the recipient's name. The list filters as you type. Then tap the required contact. Note; depending on your service provider, you can add up to 20 contacts (if not more). If you don't have the number on your contact, just key in the number in the "**To**" field or the "**Search Contacts or enter number**" field. To remove a contact from the send list, just tap the contact and tap the minus icon (-) or "**X**" next to the contact.

4. Tap the **Start** icon located at the top of the screen and write the text for your SMS/MMS. If you don't see "Start", tap the text input field (usually located at the bottom of the screen) and type the text for your SMS/MMS.

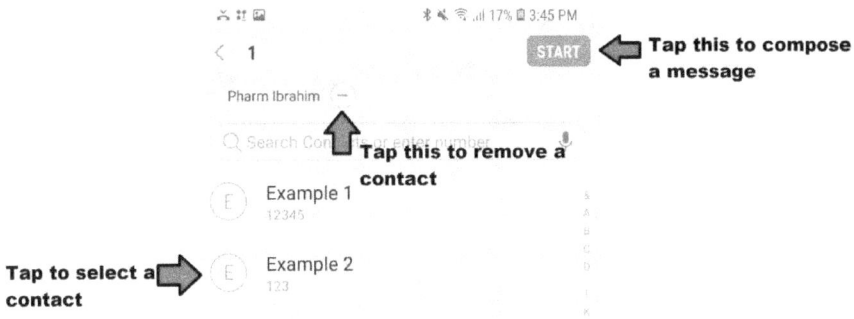

5. To attach a file such as audio, tap the plus (+) icon and tap the menu icon ⋮ (if needed). Then choose an option. If you can't see the plus (+) icon, tap the attachment icon ⫽ and choose an option.

6. When you are done, tap Send icon ⬈ . If prompted, tap **Send**.

7. To reply a message, tap the message and then enter a message in the reply field. Tap the send icon ⬈ when you are done.

8. To **Delete** a conversation, press and hold the message in question and tap on **Delete** icon ▢ .

9. On supported Android phones, in a conversation, you can press and hold a message to **forward, copy, share** or **delete** the message.

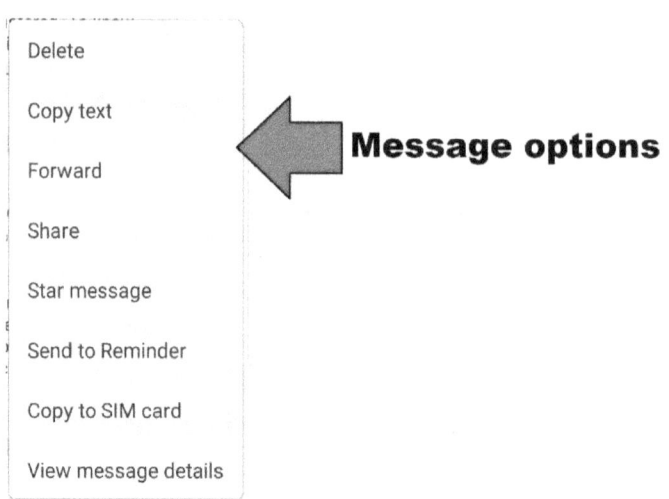

Delete

Copy text

Forward

Share

Star message

Send to Reminder

Copy to SIM card

View message details

Message options

Hints:

- If you receive an attachment, you can tap on the attachment to view it. To save an attachment, tap and hold the attachment and select **save attachment**. You can also tap the **Share** icon to share the attachment. To view saved attachments, go to the application screen and tap **My Files**. Then tap an appropriate category to view the saved attachment. If you don't have My Files (or similar app) on your Android phone, you may consider installing **Files Go by Google** from Google Play store.

- To customize your message settings, from the message screen, tap menu icon ⋮ and select **Settings**. Tap the desired setting to adjust. To access more settings, tap **More Settings** or **Advanced**. *Please note that the features available on message settings may differ from one service provider to another.*

Notifications

Block numbers and messages

More settings

Message settings menu

Emergency alert settings

Privacy

About Messages

- You can block text messages from certain numbers, if your service provider or Android phone supports this feature. To do this, Tap the menu icon ⋮ > **Settings** > **Advanced** or **More settings** (if needed) > **Block numbers and messages** > **Block numbers**. Then enter the desired number in the **Enter number** field and tap the + icon to add the entered number to the message block list. To go into your contacts/ message inbox, tap **Contacts/Inbox**. To remove a number from the message block list, tap the minus (-) or "**X**" icon.

- On some Android phones, when you receive a message, you can easily save the number if it is not yet saved in your contacts. To do this, tap the messaging app. Tap a conversation, tap the menu icon ⋮ located at the top right corner of the screen and tap the phone number in question (if needed). Thereafter, tap **Create contact**. Follow the on-screen instructions to complete the process.

EMAIL APP

Introduction

Android phones come with different forms of email apps. In this section, I would be talking about the common Google Gmail app.

Google Gmail App

How to Add Your Email Accounts to the Google Gmail App

You probably have many email accounts and you may wish to add these accounts to the Gmail app.

Note: You can download Google **Gmail** app from Google Play store.

The email accounts you can add to the Mail app include Google Mail, Yahoo Mail, Live, Exchange, Outlook among others.

To add an email account:

1. From the home screen, tap on **Gmail** . If you are using the app for the first time, please follow the prompts.

2. To add your first email account, tap "Add email address" or "Add another email address" and enter your email account information.

3. To add another email account, tap the menu icon 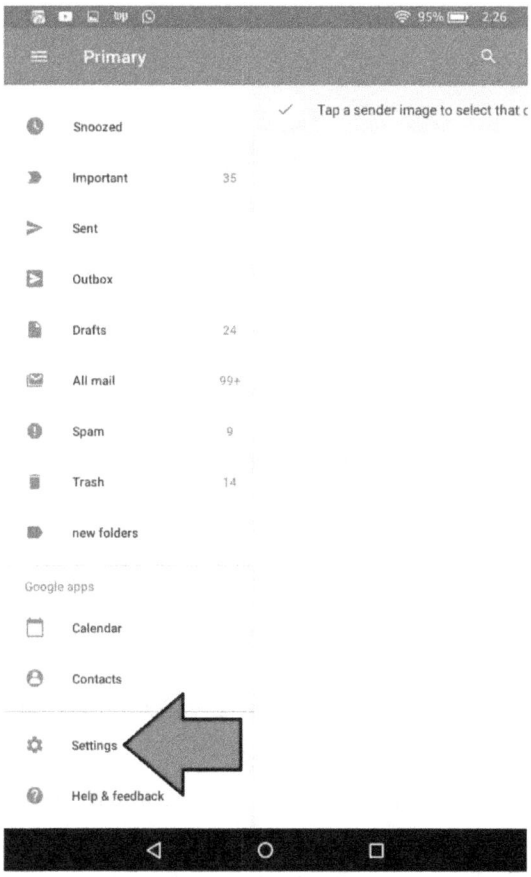. Scroll down and tap **Settings**.

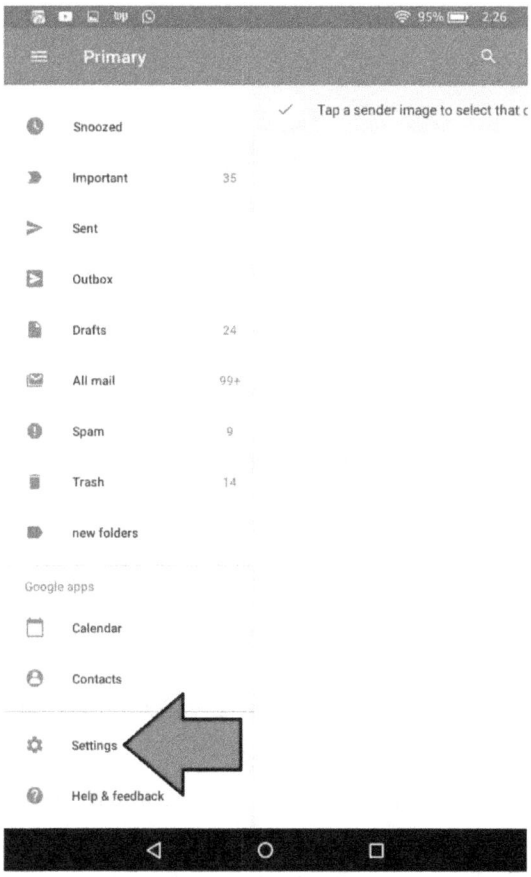

4. Tap **Add account** and follow the prompts.

Special Note on Adding Exchange Account to Gmail App

Following the instructions above might not be enough when you want to add your Exchange account to Gmail app and you may need extra information. You may need to obtain from your Exchange administrator or provider the account's server address, domain name, and username in addition to your email address and password.

How to Compose and Send an Email Message Using Gmail App

You can easily send an email message to your friends or organization using the Gmail app. In this section of the guide, we will be exploring how to compose an email message, and how to send an email message.

To send an email message:

- From the home screen, swipe up and tap **Gmail** 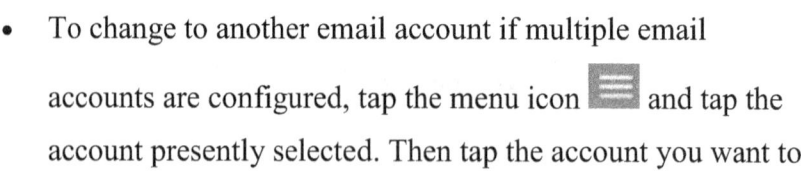.

- To change to another email account if multiple email accounts are configured, tap the menu icon ☰ and tap the account presently selected. Then tap the account you want to view.

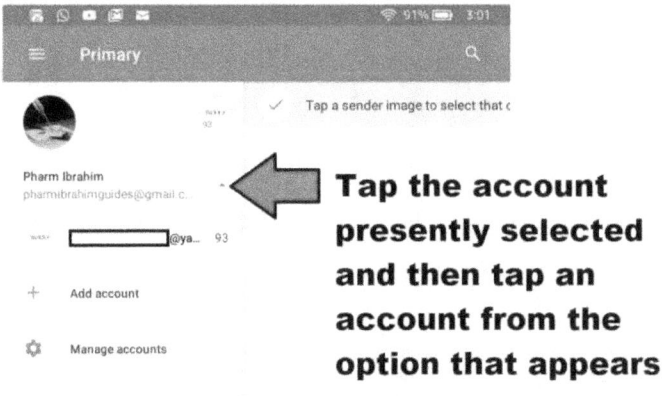

Tap the account presently selected and then tap an account from the option that appears

- To compose a new email, tap the new email icon  located at the bottom of the screen.

- Tap the field next to the "**To**" field and type in the email address of the recipient. As you type an email address, Gmail will suggest email addresses based on your contacts. To add another email address, simply type the email address into the "To" field. You may separate each email address with a coma. To delete/remove an email address from the "To" field, tap the email address and then tap the **X** icon.

- To send a copy to another person, tap the dropdown icon ∨ next to the "**To**" field and type the person's email address in the **Cc/Bcc** field.

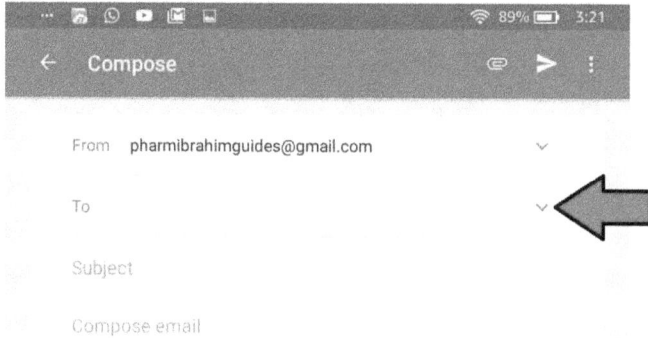

Tip: Cc means Carbon Copy. If you use the Cc option to send a message to many recipients, all the recipients will see the message and all other email addresses that have received the message. On the other hand, Bcc stands for Blind Carbon Copy. If you use Bcc option to send a message to many recipients, all the recipients will see the message, but will not see other email addresses that have received the message.

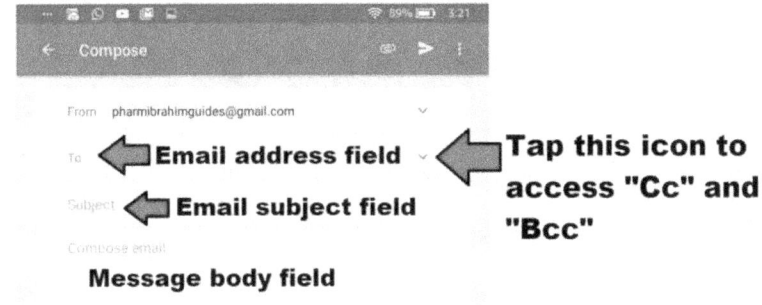

Email address field — **Tap this icon to access "Cc" and "Bcc"**

Email subject field

Message body field

- If you have more than one email account configured on Gmail app and you wish to send from a different email account, tap the dropdown icon next to "**From**" to choose a different email account. See the picture below.

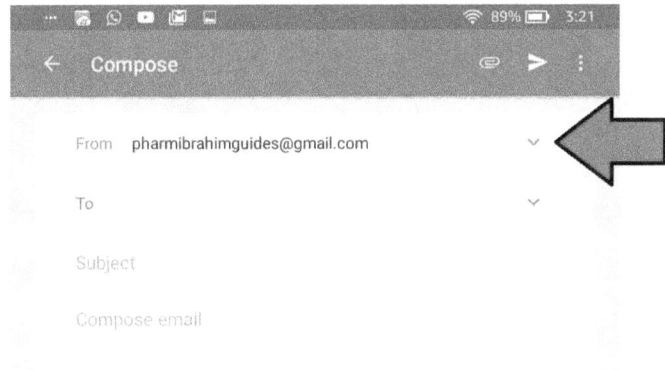

- Tap **Subject** field and key in the subject of your email.
- Tap the text input field and write the text for your email.

- To format a block of texts, select the texts by tapping and holding a word, and then dragging or to select the texts you want. Then select **Format** from the options that appear at the top of the screen.

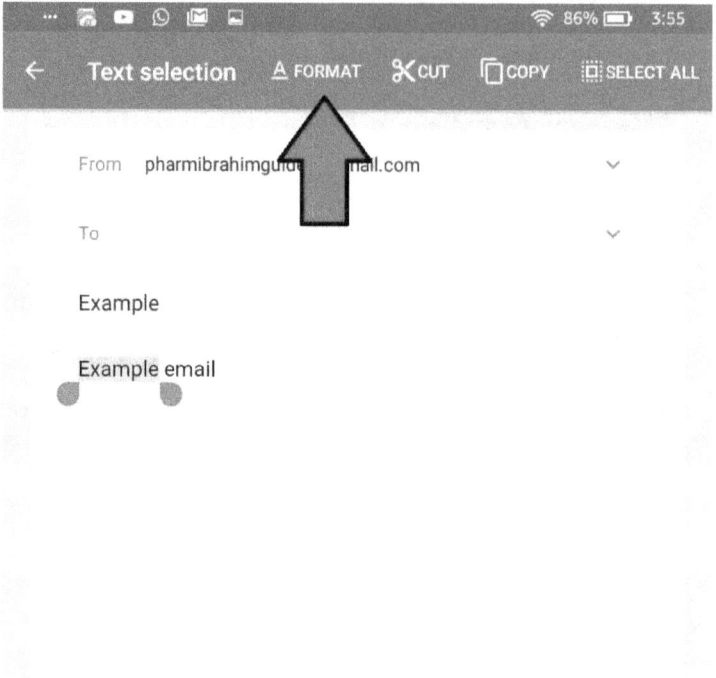

You can use the formatting tab at the bottom of the screen to perform the following actions:

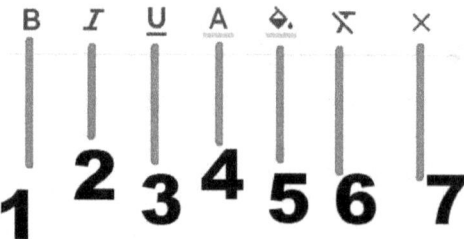

1. **Bold**: You can bold a part or your entire message using this feature. To bold a text, select the text(s) and tap the **B** icon.

2. **Italicize**: You can make your text appear italicized by clicking on the *I* icon.

3. **Underline**: Use the U icon to underline a text.

4. **Font color**: Tap this to change the font color.

5. **Font background color**: Tap this to change the font background color.

6. **Remove Formatting:** Tap this to remove any formatting you have given to a text or block of texts.

7. **Close:** Tap this to close the formatting dialogue box.

• When you are satisfied with the message and you are ready to send it, tap **Send** located at the top of the Gmail app screen.

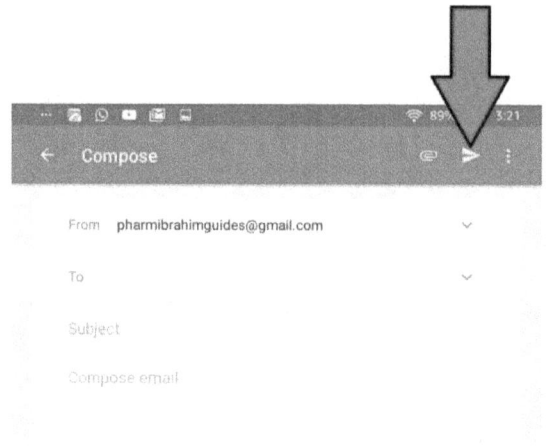

- To save a message as draft, tap the menu icon ⋮ located at the top of the screen and select **Save Draft**. Please note that you may need to fill the "To" field before you can save a message as draft. On the other hand, to discard a message, tap the menu icon ⋮ and select **Discard**.

Note: Before you can apply some of the formatting options above to a block of texts, you would need to select the texts. To do this, tap and hold a word, and then drag 🔵 or 🔵 to select the texts you want.

Attaching a File

You can insert an attachment into your message by clicking on the attachment icon ⌧ located at the top of the screen. This opens a dialog box. Select the type of files you want to attach. Then locate and tap on the file you want to attach.

Managing a Received Email

One of the most important functions of any email app is the ability to receive incoming messages. By default, Gmail app searches for new messages and alerts you when there is one.

New messages are either stored in Inbox or Junk/Trash/Spam folder and these are the places to check if you are expecting an email. To access Junk/Trash/Spam folder, tap the menu icon ☰ and tap a folder. Alternatively, swipe from the left edge of the screen towards the middle to access Junk/Trash/Spam folder.

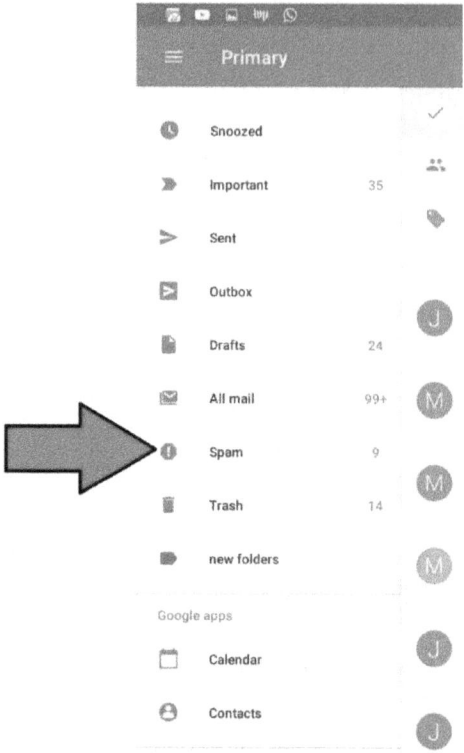

To see if there is a new message, swipe down from the top of the Gmail app's screen.

To read/manage a message:

Please note that some options discussed below might not be available on your phone. The options you see are dependent on the type of email account you are using. I have noticed that you will see a more robust options when you are using a Gmail account with Gmail app.

- Tap the subject of the message to open the message text in the preview pane.

- Those messages that you have not yet read should appear bold.

- The attachment icon ⬚ means that a message has an attachment.

- To make a message your favorite, tap the star icon ☆ located at the top right corner of the screen.

- To reply a message, scroll down on the message (if necessary) and tap **Reply**. If the email was sent to more than one person, you can tap **Reply all** to send the reply to all those who have received the message. To forward the message, tap **Forward**. While composing a reply message, you can tap the menu icon ⋮ (located at the top of the screen) to discard a message, save a message as draft or add an email address from Contact app.

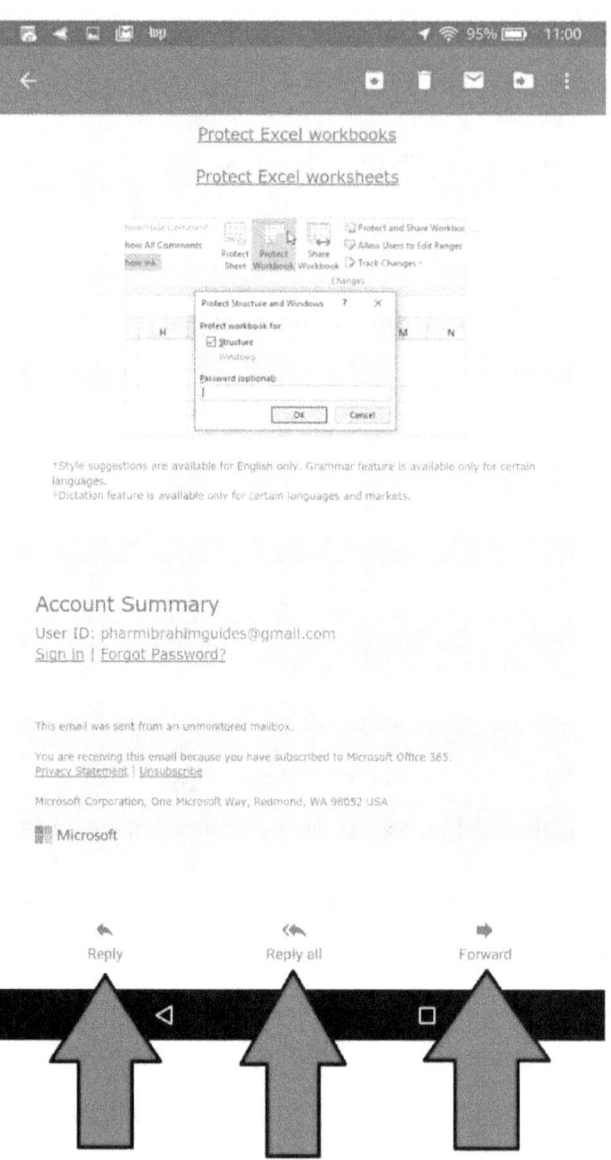

- To quickly delete a message, tap the delete icon located at the top of the screen.

- To move a message to another folder, tap the move icon ![move icon] and then select a folder

- To archive a message, tap the archive icon ![archive icon] located at the top of the screen. To access archived messages, tap the menu icon ![menu icon] (located at the top left corner of the screen) and tap **All mail**. Please note that when you archive a message, the message will come back to your inbox when someone replies to it.

- To access the details of a sender of an email, tap **View details** next to the sender name. This allows you to see details like email address.

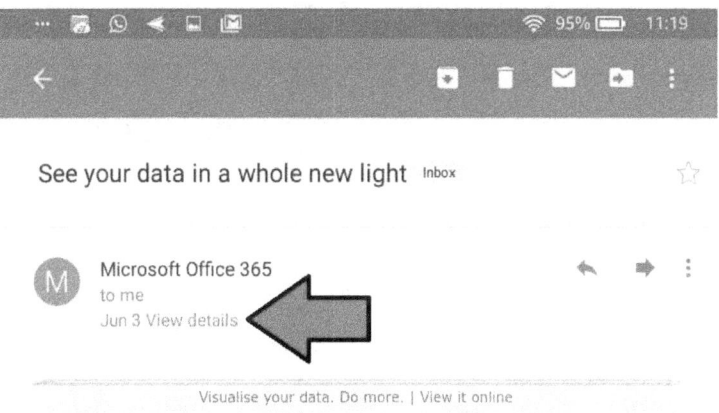

- To go back to inbox, while viewing a message, tap the inbox icon ![inbox icon].

Tip: You might like to customize what happens when you swipe the screen while viewing the message list in your inbox. To do this, please refer to the "Tip" on page 339.

Using the Gmail In-App Inbox Menu icons

When you tap a message in your inbox, you will usually see two menu icons. These icons allow you to customize your messages. To access these menu icons,

1. Open the Gmail app and tap a message from your inbox.
2. Tap a menu icon (see the picture below).

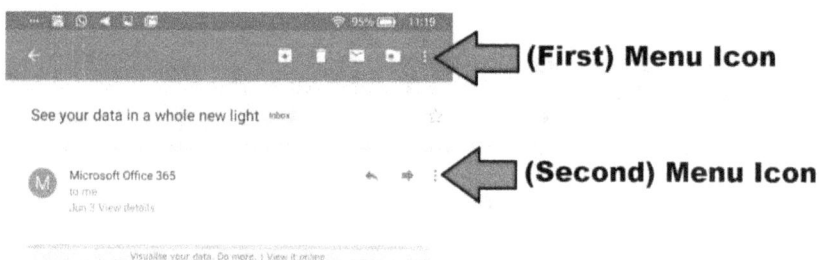

Tap the first menu icon to access the following:

Please note that the options you see when you tap the menu icon is dependent on the type of email account you are using. I have noticed that you will see a more robust options when you are using a Gmail account with Gmail app.

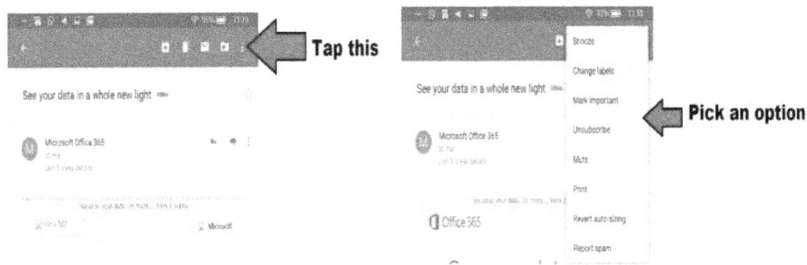

1. **Snooze:** When you tap "Snooze", you will be able to hide the message concerned in snoozed folder for a period of time. When you snooze a message, it is removed from the inbox and put inside the "snoozed" folder for a chosen time. To access Snoozed folder, tap the back arrow (if necessary) and then tap the menu icon (located at the top left corner of the screen). Tap **Snoozed**.

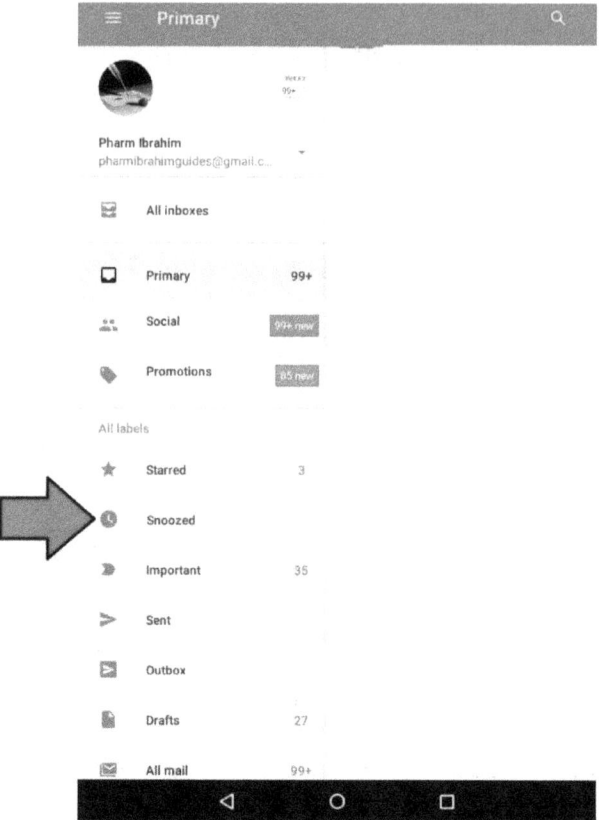

To unsnooze, open the snoozed folder, tap the message you want

to unsnooze and tap the menu icon ⋮ (located at the top of the

screen). Then tap **Unsnooze.**

Please note that you may not be able to use Snooze option if you
are not using a Gmail account.

2. **Change labels:** When you change the label of an email, you
    move/copy the email to a new location. To change a label,
    select **Change labels** and tick a folder you like (you can
    uncheck the label you don't want). Tap **OK.**

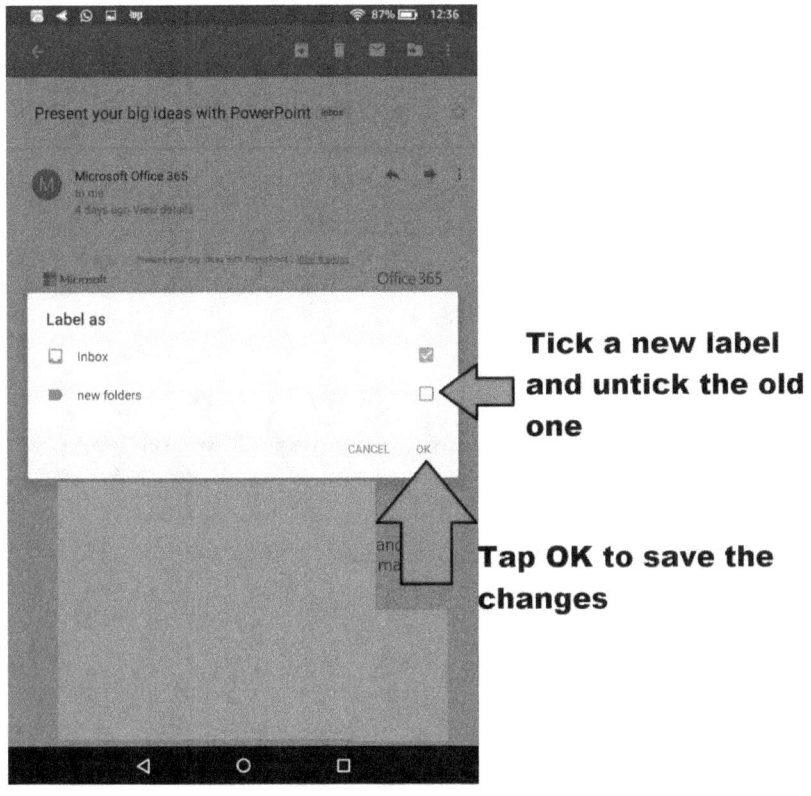

Tick a new label and untick the old one

Tap OK to save the changes

3. **Mark Important:** Any message you find very dear to you, mark it as important. To mark a message as important, tap **Mark Important**. To access "Important" folder, tap the back arrow ← (if necessary) and then tap the menu icon ≡ (located at the top left corner of the screen). Tap **Important**.

4. **Unsubscribe**: Gmail app allows you to unsubscribe from some emails using this option. To unsubscribe from an email list, simply tap **Unsubscribe**. Tap **Unsubscribe** again to confirm.

5. **Mute:** You can mute a message to prevent it from appearing in your main inbox. To access your muted messages, tap the menu icon (located at the top left corner of the screen). Tap **All mail**. Please note that when you mute a message, the message may not come back to your inbox when someone replies to it.

6. **Print:** Use this option to print a message or save an email as a PDF. To use this option to save an email as PDF, tap **Print.** Tap the dropdown arrow and select **Save as PDF** (if necessary). Thereafter, tap the yellow **PDF** icon and choose a folder. Then tap **Done/Save** to download.

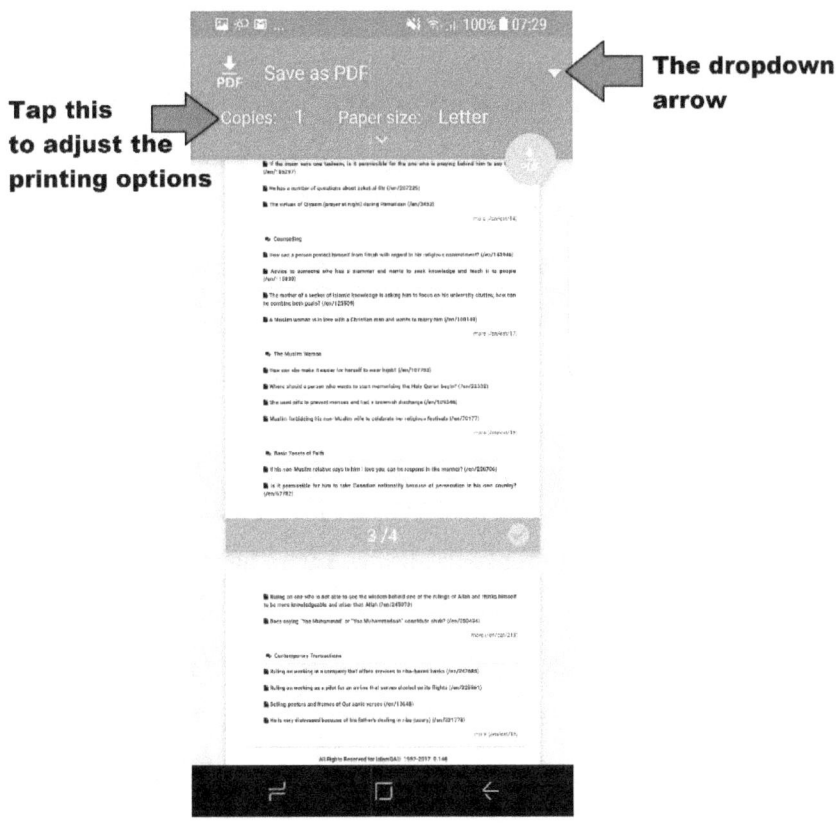

Tap this to adjust the printing options

The dropdown arrow

7. **Revert auto-sizing:** If you are viewing an email in your inbox and it is not appearing as it should, you can tap on **Revert auto-sizing** to see if this solves the problem.

8. **Report Spam:** If you believe that an email message is a spam, you can report it to Google using this option.

Tap the second menu icon ⋮ to access the following:

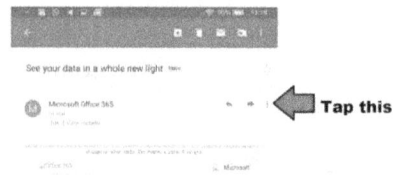 **Tap this**

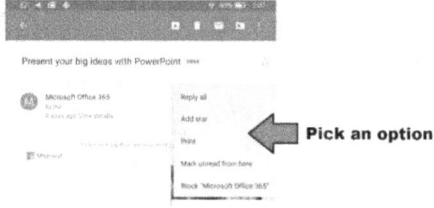 **Pick an option**

Please note that the options you see when you tap the menu icon is dependent on the type of email account you are using. I have noticed that you will see a more robust options when you are using a Gmail account with Gmail app.

1. **Reply all**: If an email is sent to more than one person, you can tap **Reply all** to reply to all those who have received the message.

2. **Add star (Make an email message your favorite)**: If you want to make a message your favorite, tap **Add star**. To view your starred message, tap the back arrow (located at the top of the screen) and then tap the menu icon (located at the top left corner of the screen). Tap **Starred**.

3. **Print:** Please refer to page 328 to learn how to manage print option.

4. **Mark unread from here**: If you want a message to appear bold (as if it is unread), tap "Mark unread from here".

5. **Block** ...: If you don't want future messages from a contact to be delivered to your inbox, tap **Block...**

Please note that any future message from a blocked contact will be marked as spam. To unblock a contact, tap the menu

icon ⋮ again and select **Unblock...**

How to Open and Save an Attachment in Email App

The email with an attachment should have a paper clip icon ⌀ displayed next to the address of the sender when you check your message inbox.

To open/manage an attachment:

1. Tap the message that has the attachment, as indicated by a paper clip ⌀ .

2. When the message opens, tap the attachment that you want to open and follow the prompts. If your device is not having an appropriate program to open the attachment, you may be unable to view the attachment. In a situation like this, you will need to install the appropriate program for the file type. You may ask the person that sent the message about the program to use to open the attachment.

3. To view saved/downloaded attachments, go to the download folder on your phone. Alternatively, you can double-tap the status bar (the bar at the top of the screen where icons such as

Wi-Fi icon usually appear) to view your recent downloads. Then tap the downloaded file you want to view.

In addition, if you are using an LG Android phone, go to home screen and tap **Management** then tap **File Manager.** Then tap a content category corresponding to the attachment you want to view.

If you are using a Samsung Android phone, go to home screen and tap **Tools** folder then tap **File Manager > Download**.

If you don't have a smart file management app on your Android phone, you may consider installing **Files Go by Google** from Google Play store.

Tip: You can prevent Gmail from automatically downloading an attachment when connected to Wi-Fi. To do this:

1. Open the Gmail app.
2. Tap the menu icon (located at the top left corner of the screen).
3. Scroll down the email options and tap **Settings.**

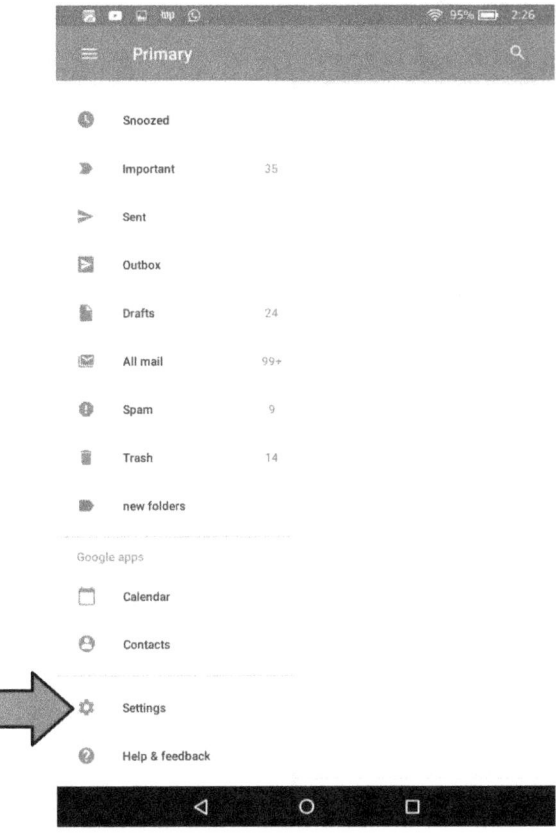

4. Tap an email account.

5. Uncheck the box next to **Download attachments.**

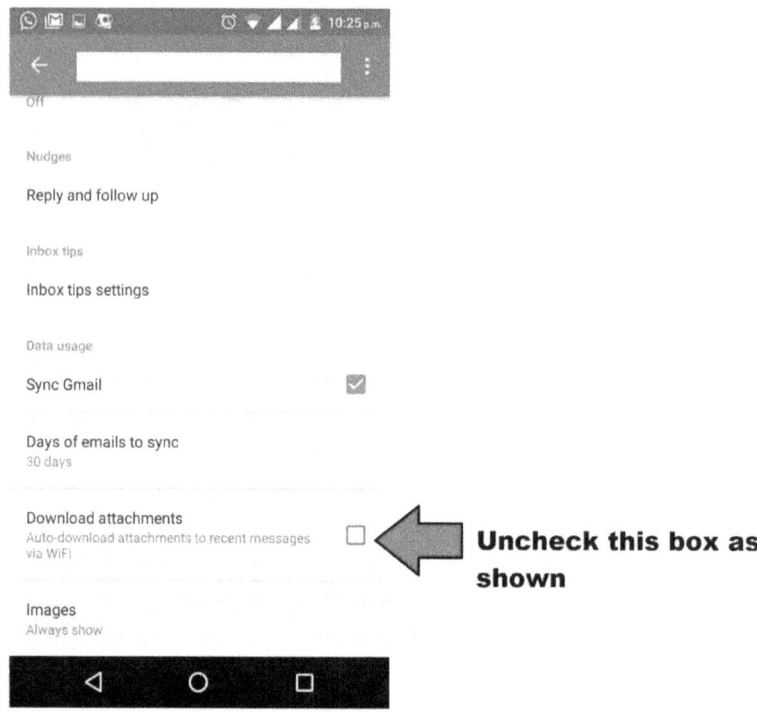

Unsubscribing from an Email List

If you will like to unsubscribe from any email list, please follow the steps highlighted below:

- Open the message you want to unsubscribe from.

- Tap the menu icon ⋮ .

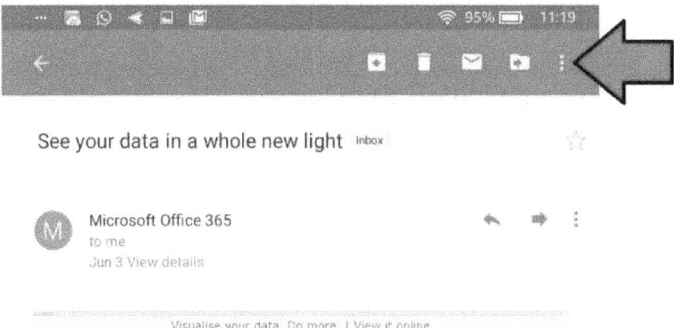

- Select **Unsubscribe.**

- Tap **Unsubscribe** again to confirm.

Blocking an email address

If an email address is disturbing you with unwanted emails, you can block the email address. To do this:

- Open the message in question.

- Tap the menu icon ⋮ .

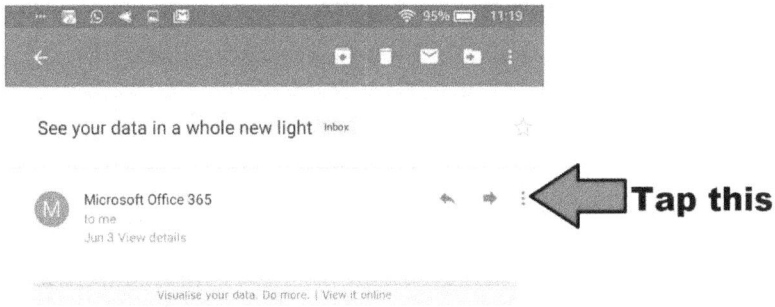

- Select **Block...**

Please note that any future message from a blocked contact will be marked as spam. To unblock a contact, tap the menu icon ⋮ again and select **Unblock...**

Cleaning Up Your Inbox

Overtime, inbox usually grows to contain thousands of irrelevant messages, if this is your situation, and you wish to clean your inbox so that it contains only the most important messages, please follow the instructions below:

1. Open the Gmail app and look for those email that contains the most irrelevant/unwanted messages. Open one of these emails and block the sender's address. Repeat this step for all the annoying email messages. Please see page 335 to know how to block a sender.

2. Then go back to your inbox and select all the irrelevant/unwanted messages. To select a message, tap and hold the message for one second and lift your finger. Repeat this method to select all the irrelevant/unwanted messages. If you mistakenly select a message, tap and hold the message for one second and lift your finger to unselect it. Then tap the delete icon 🗑 (located at the top of the screen) to send the selected messages to Trash folder. *Please note that items that have been in Trash folder for more than 30 days will be deleted (automatically).*

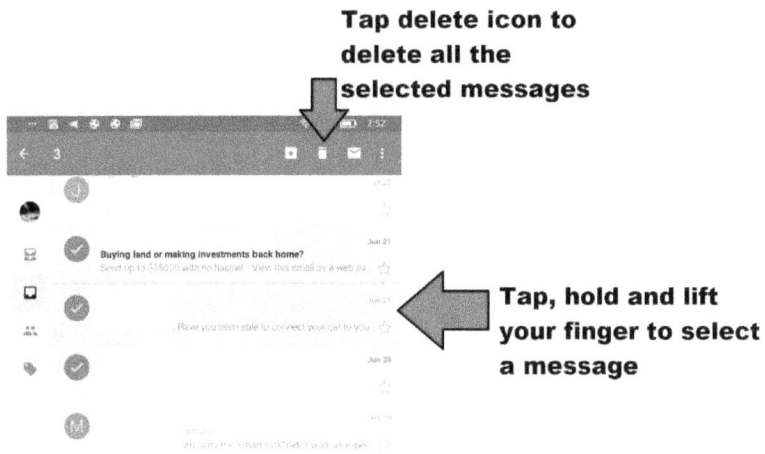

Tap delete icon to delete all the selected messages

Tap, hold and lift your finger to select a message

3. Go back to your inbox and select all very important messages following the method mentioned in step 2. Then tap the menu icon ⋮ (located at the top of the screen) and select **Mark important**. To access "Important" folder, tap the menu icon ≡ (located at the top left corner of the screen) and tap **Important**. Please note that if you mark a message as important, the message remains in your primary inbox.

4. Go back to your inbox and select all social/promotional messages following the method mentioned in step 2. Then tap the menu icon ⋮ (located at the top of the screen) and select **Move to**. Select Social or Promotions. To access Social or Promotions folder, tap the menu icon ≡ (located at the top left corner of the screen) and tap **Social/Promotions**.

5. Finally, go back to your inbox and tap the menu icon 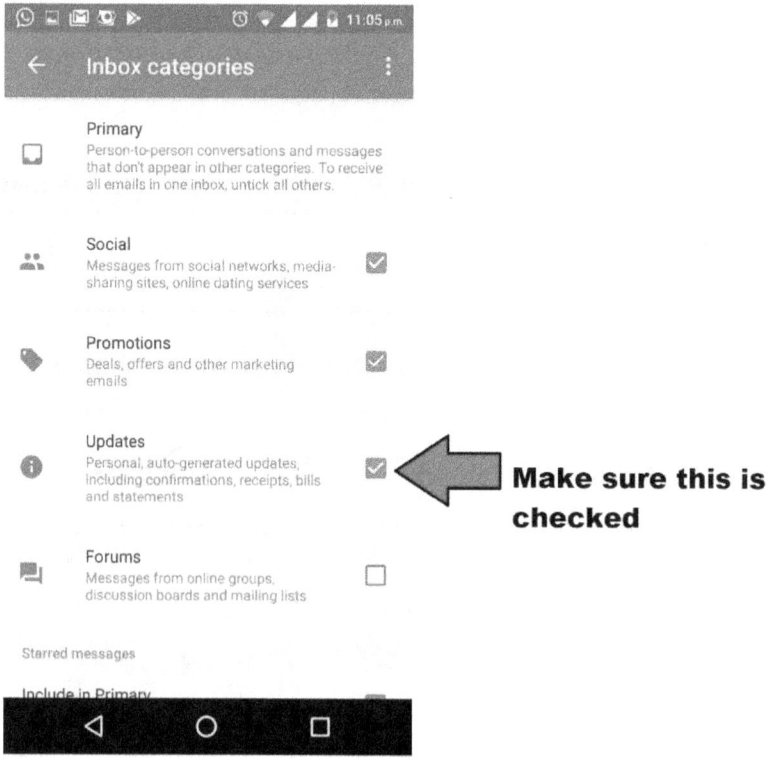 (located at the top left corner of the screen). Tap **Settings** and tap an account. Then tap **Inbox categories**. Make sure the checkbox next to **Update** is selected. When this is selected, Gmail will automatically put auto-generated updates including receipts, bills and statement in one (Updates) folder. This should allow you to find your bills and statement faster in the future.

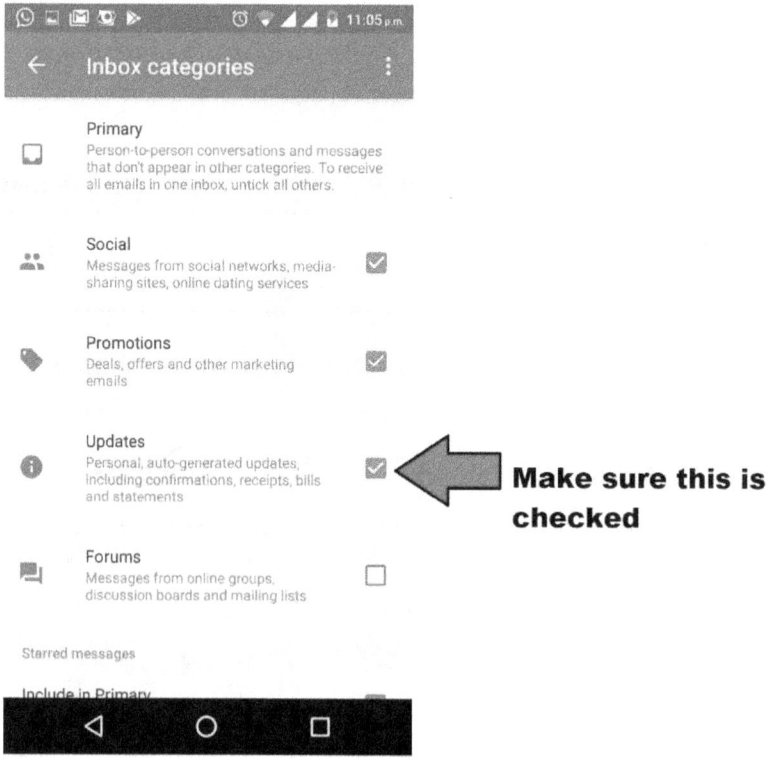

Make sure this is checked

Please note that, if you have several thousands of emails, it may take time before you can clean up your inbox. If this is your situation, I would advise you clean up your inbox little by little so as not to be overwhelmed. In addition, if you can, make sure you decide the fate of your future messages within 72 hours of receiving. Try to delete an unwanted message as soon as you read it. Don't wait for it to become a concern before you send a useless message to the trash bin.

Tip: You might like to customize what happens when you swipe the screen while viewing conversation list in your inbox, to do this:

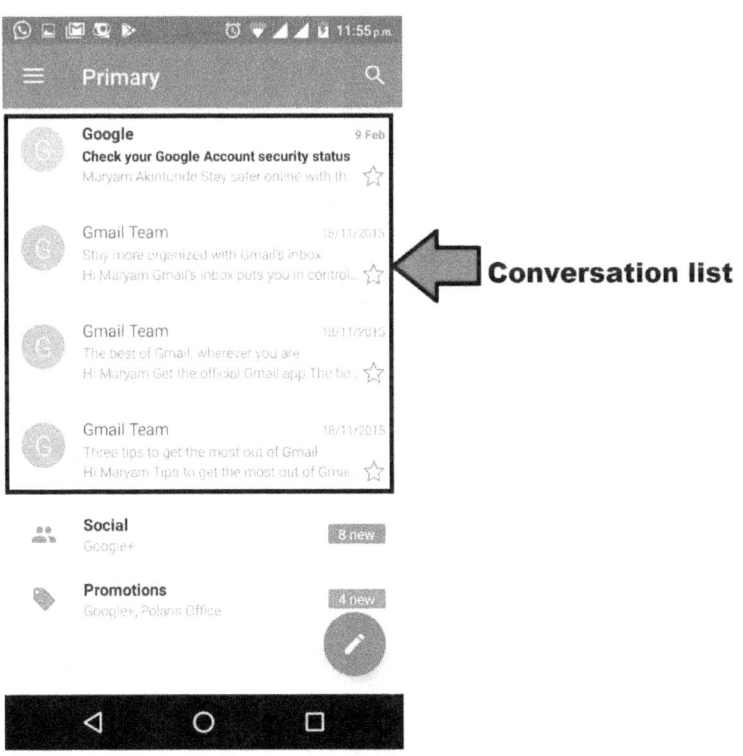

1. Open the Gmail app and tap the menu icon  (located at the top left corner of the screen). Tap on **Settings**.

2. Tap **General settings**.

3. Tap **Swipe actions**.

4. Tap **Change** next to **Right swipe** and pick an option.

5. Tap **Change** next to **Left swipe** and pick an option.

Searching the Gmail App

To avoid wasting time, you can use the search option in the mail app to quickly find emails. When looking for an email, using the search tab is usually the best option if you know the right search phrase to use.

To use the search feature:

1. Open the Gmail app.

2. Tap the search icon (located at the top of the screen).

3. Enter a search phrase and tap the lens icon or the done button on the virtual keyboard on your phone.

To delete your Gmail search history:

1. Open the Gmail app.

2. Tap the menu icon 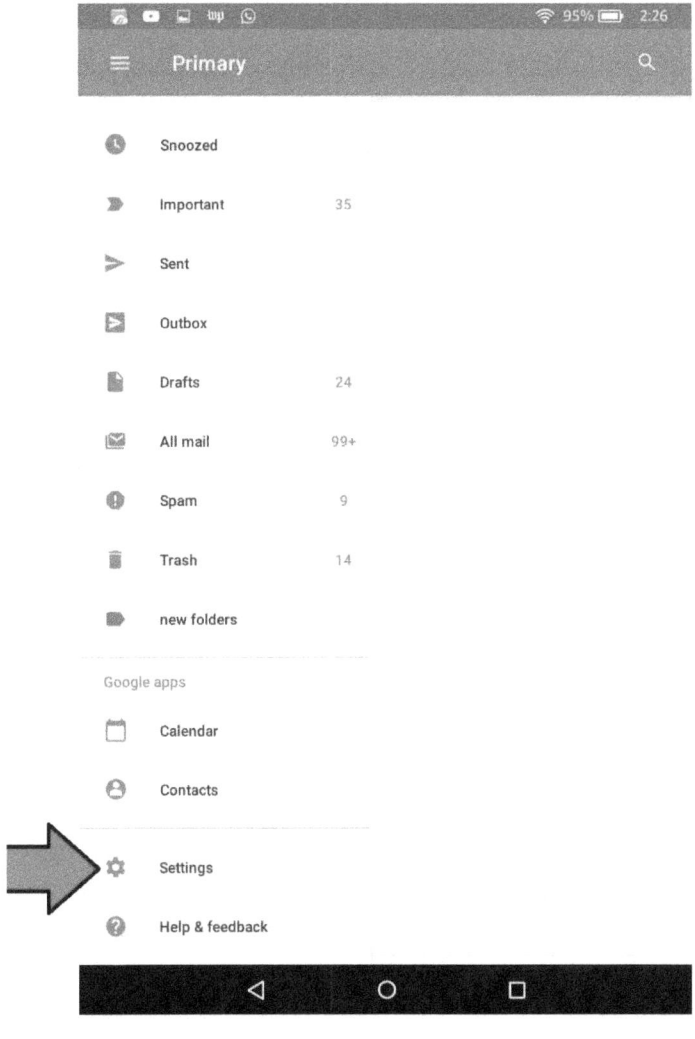 (located at the top left corner of the screen).

3. Scroll down the email options and tap **Settings.**

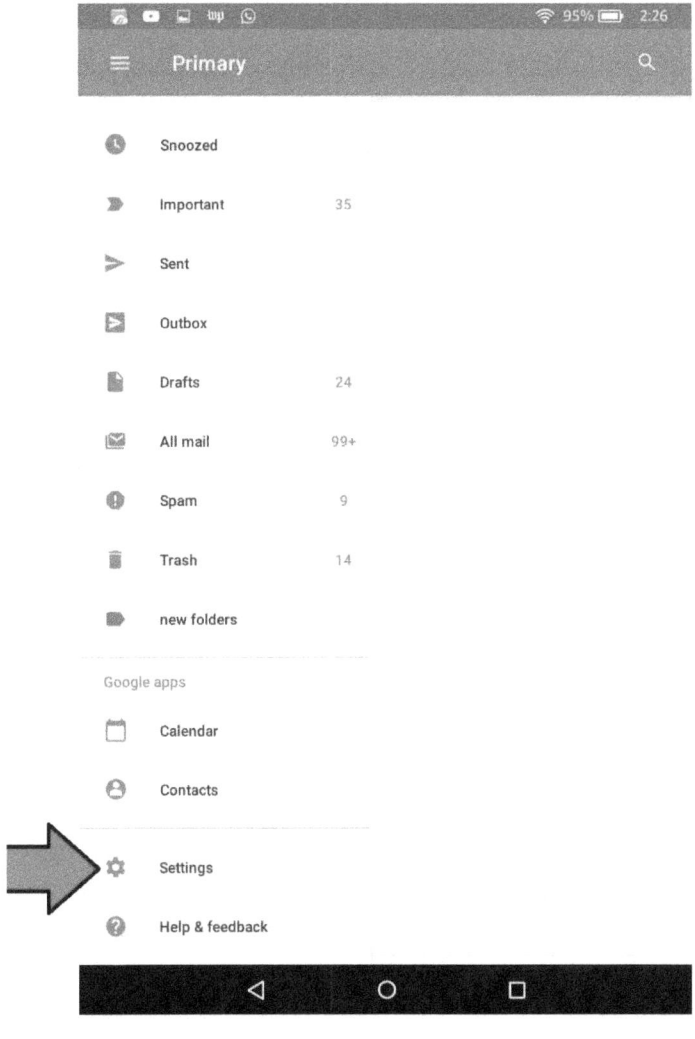

4. Tap **General settings.**

5. Tap the menu icon ⋮ (located at the top of the screen).

6. Tap **Clear search history**.

Stop Picture from Being Automatically Displayed

If you have allowed images to be displayed from a sender while viewing an email message, you can follow the steps mentioned below to remove this approval.

1. Repeat steps 1 to 5 under "To delete your Gmail search history" above.

2. Tap **Clear picture approvals**.

Tip: You can prevent images from being shown inside your email messages. To do this, repeat steps 1 to 3 under "To delete your Gmail search history" above. Tap an email account and scroll down and tap **Images**. Select **Ask before showing**.

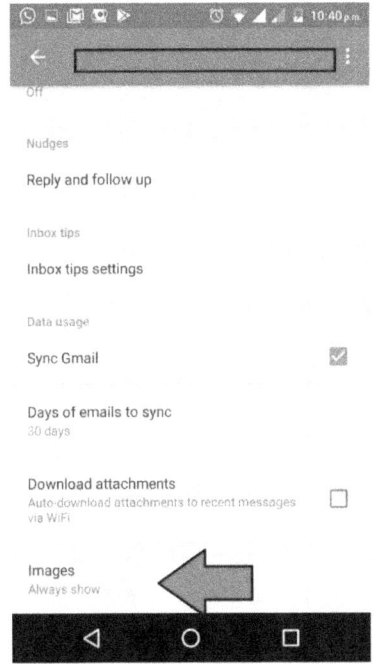
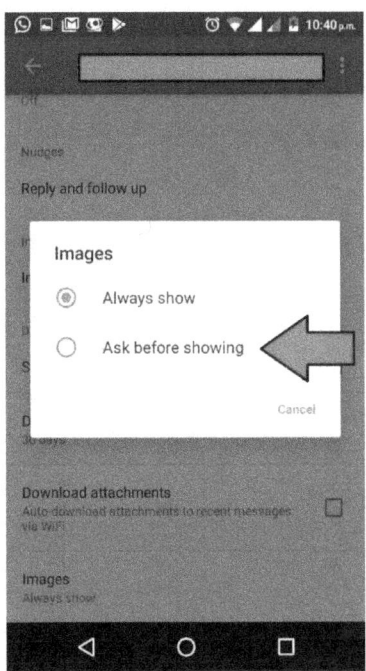

Using Vacation Responder

If you are on a vacation, you can enable Gmail to send an autoresponder to people that message you during this time.

Please note that the Vacation Responder might not be available if you are not using a Gmail account.

In addition, normally, messages categorized as spam and messages addressed to mailing list (you subscribe to) won't get response from the vacation responder.

To do this:

1. Open the Gmail app.

2. Tap the menu icon 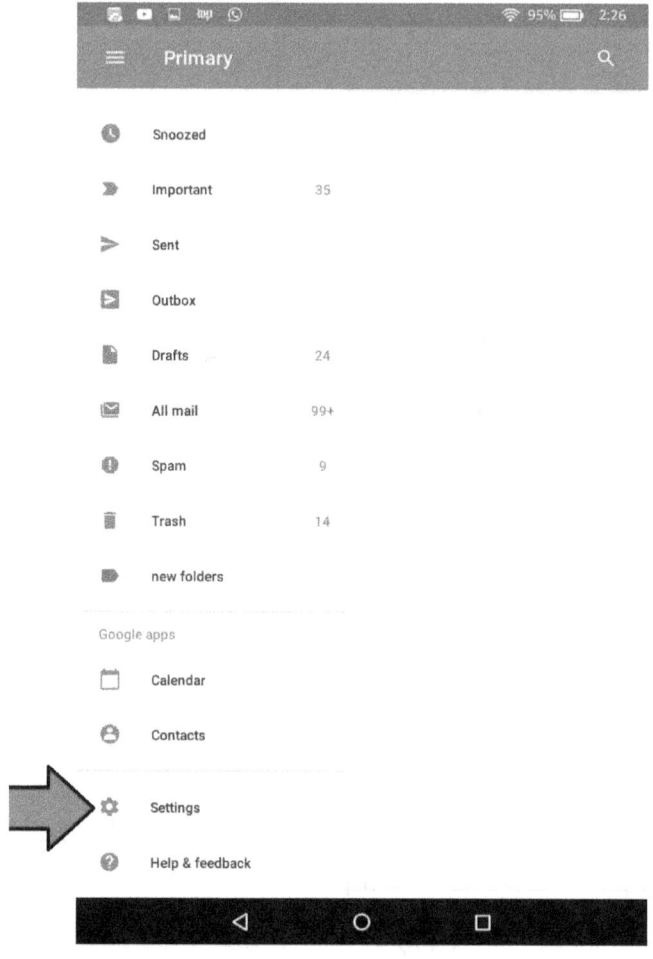 (located at the top left corner of the screen).

3. Scroll down the email options and tap **Settings**.

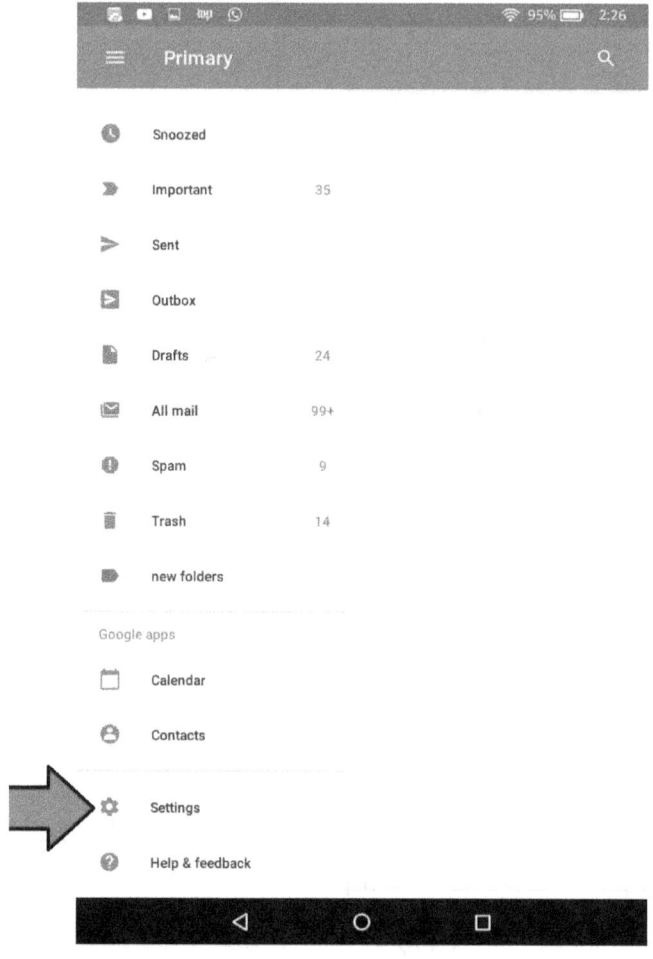

4. Tap an email account.

5. Tap **Out of Office AutoReply** or **Vacation responder**.

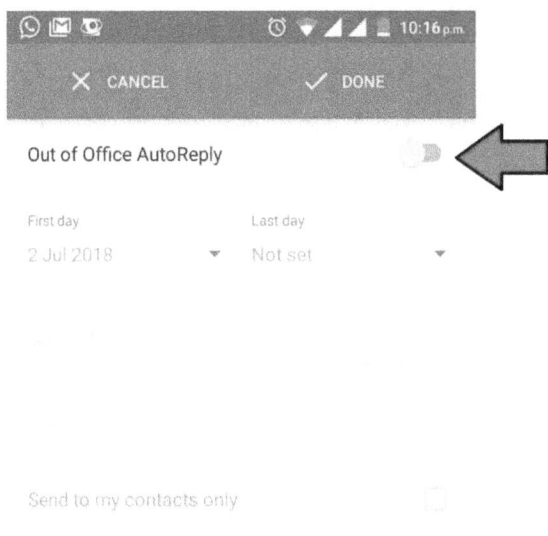

6. Tap the status switch next to **Out of Office AutoReply** or **Vacation responder** and fill in necessary information.

7. If you want Gmail to message only your contacts, tap the checkbox next to **Send only to my Contacts**.

8. Tap **Done** located at the top of the screen to save the changes.

Managing the Settings Options

Some of the options under Email Settings have already been discussed. But I would like to briefly mention few more things.

Please note that the options you see under settings is dependent on the type of email account you select. I have noticed that you will see a more robust settings options when you select a Gmail account.

1. To access the Email app settings, open the Gmail app and tap the menu icon ☰ (located at the top left corner of the screen). Tap on **Settings**.

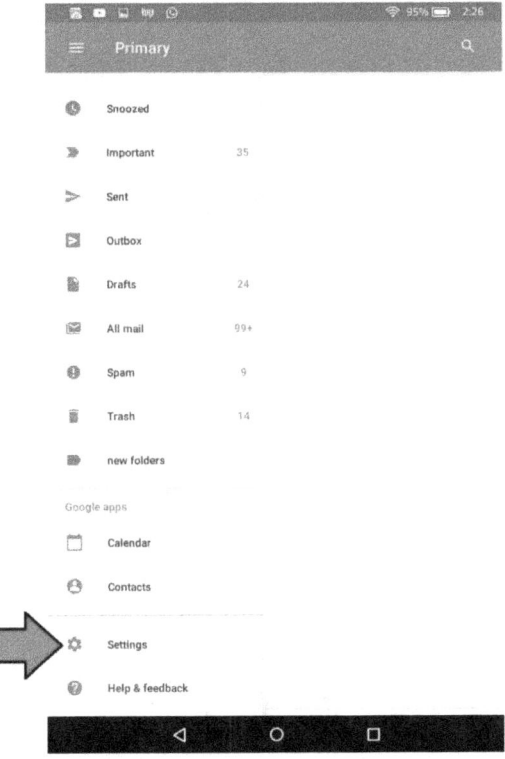

2. Tap an email account, and then tap an option of your choice.
   For example, to disable email notification, uncheck the box
   next to **Notifications**.

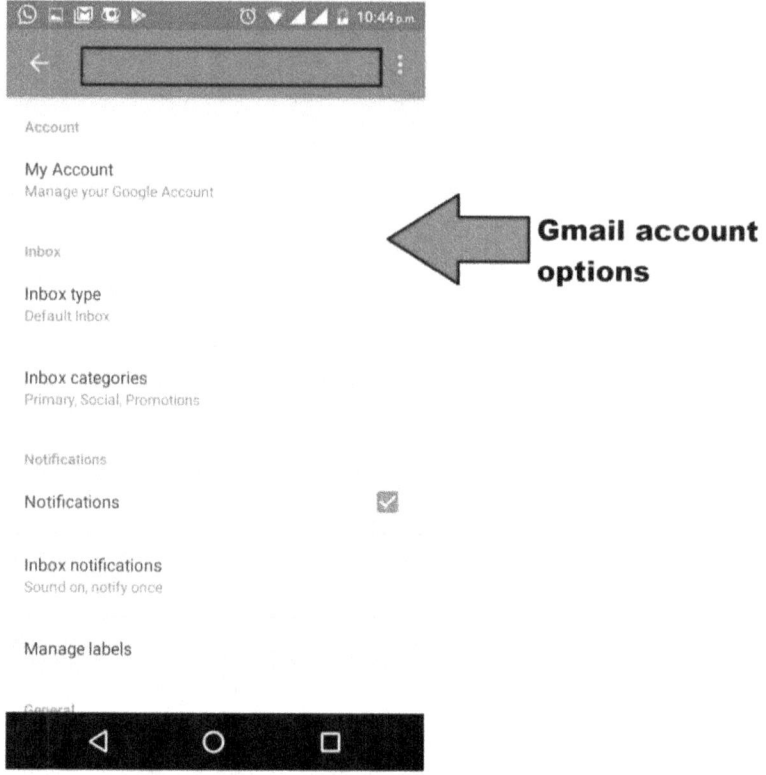

Gmail account options

Account

My Account
Manage your Google Account

Inbox

Inbox type
Default Inbox

Inbox categories
Primary, Social, Promotions

Notifications

Notifications

Inbox notifications
Sound on, notify once

Manage labels

General

Tip: You might notice that if you tap on weblinks while reading an email, it opens in Gmail app. If you want to disable this feature so that the weblink can be opened using a web browser, perform the following actions:

1. Open the Gmail app and tap the menu icon ☰ (located at the top left corner of the screen). Tap on **Settings**.
2. Tap **General settings**.
3. Uncheck the box next to **Open web links in Gmail**.

Deleting an Email Account

To delete an email account:

1. Swipe down from the top of the screen and select settings

   icon ⚙ .

2. Tap "Cloud and accounts," "Account" or "Users & Accounts".

3. Tap "Account" or "Users" (if needed).

4. Select the (Google) account you want to remove.

5. Tap "Remove Account". If you don't see "Remove account", tap the menu icon ⋮ and then select "Remove account".

Managing Email Signature

You can use the Signature tab to tell Gmail app what signature to include in a message. You can also edit signature message under this tab. To go to Signature settings, open the Gmail app and tap the menu icon ☰ (located at the top left corner of the screen). Tap on **Settings**. Tap the desired account and tap **Mobile signature**. Type in the signature you want and tap **OK.**

Note: An email signature is a text that appears by default after the body of your message. You may set your email signature to be your name or your brand.

Personal Information

Contacts App

This app allows you to create and manage personal or business contacts. With the Contacts app, you can save names, mobile phone numbers, home phone numbers, email addresses, and more.

Please note that there are different versions of Contact apps available on Android phones. In this guide, I will stick to the version of Contacts app developed by Google. You can download Google Contact app from Google Play store.

Creating a Contact

1. Go to application screen, and tap on the **Contacts** app. If you are using the Contacts app for the first time, follow the onscreen instructions to set it up.

2. Tap on **Add contact** icon located at the lower right corner of the screen.

3. To change the storage location, tap the dropdown arrow next to "Phone", "Device", "SIM" or email address (see below).

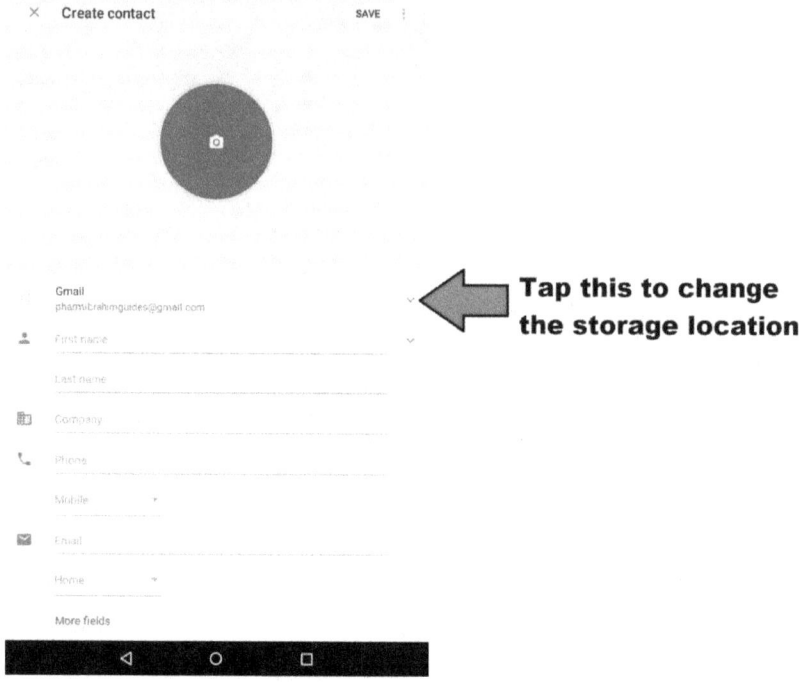

4. Fill in the details by tapping on each item on the screen.

5. To access more options, tap on **More fields** or **View more**.

6. When you are done, tap **Save** located at the top of the screen.

Please note that if you choose SIM Card as your storage location in step 3 above, you may not be able to fill more than a name and phone number.

Hint: To search for a contact, open the Contacts app and tap the

search bar (located at the top of the screen), and start typing a name. The list filters as you type.

Managing a Contact

1. From the app screen, tap on the **Contacts**  app.

2. To edit a contact, tap on the contact from the contacts list, tap

   the pen icon located at the bottom of the screen and then enter the new details. Tap **Save** when you are done.

3. To delete a contact, open the Contacts app, tap and hold the contact you want to delete and then tap on the delete icon

   located at the top of the screen. You can also use this method to delete many contacts at once. All you have to do is to select all the contacts you want to delete and then tap the

   delete icon .

4. To share a contact, open the Contacts app, tap and hold the

   contact you want to share and then tap the share icon .

5. To make a contact your favorite, tap the contact and then tap

   the favorite icon located at the top of the screen.

6. To call a contact, tap on the contact from the contacts list,

   and then tap the call icon .

7. To message a contact, tap on the contact from the contacts

   list, tap the message icon .

8. To email a contact, tap on the contact from the contacts list, tap the email icon 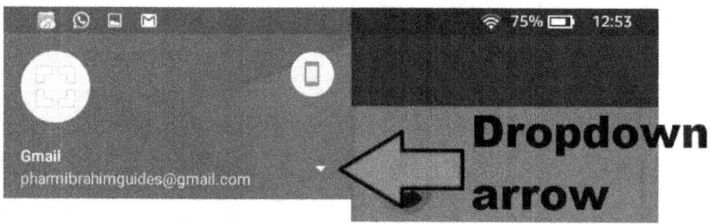. Please note that the email icon might not be available if you have not added the email address to the contact you are trying to email.

9. To view all the contacts available on your phone, open the Contacts app and tap the menu icon . Then tap **All contacts**.

10. To change your contact view (i.e. to view your contacts in other location such as SIM), open the Contacts app and tap the menu icon . Then tap the dropdown arrow next to "device", "phone" or email address and pick an option.

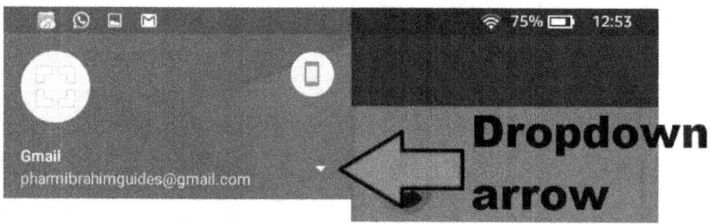

In addition, if you have another email address where your contacts are stored, and you wish to add it to the Contacts app so that you can access all your contacts, follow these steps:

1. Open the Contacts app and tap the menu icon . Then tap the small dropdown arrow (see the picture above) next to "device", "phone" or email address and select **Add account**.

2. Follow the prompts to complete this process.

Tip: To manage your contacts smartly and clean up duplicates, open the Contacts app and tap the menu icon ▤. Then tap **Suggestions** and follow the prompts.

Copy Contact(s)

If you have some contacts stored on your SIM card, you can copy them to your phone with some simple steps.

1. From the app screen, tap on the **Contacts**  app.
2. Tap the menu icon ▤.
3. Tap **Settings**.
4. Under "Manage contacts", tap **Import**.
5. Select where you are copying the contact(s) from (i.e. SIM card).
6. If you have multiple accounts on your phone, select where you are copying to and follow the prompts.

Tip: You can **export** contacts from your phone to other places by following the steps similar to the ones mentioned above. But don't forget that you will select **Export** (and not Import) in step 4 above.

Contact Group (Contact Label)

If you would like to send a message to several people at the same time, I would advise that you create a contact group. You can create a contact group for friends and family members in order to reach them easily.

To create a group:

1. From the app screen, tap on the **Contacts** app.
2. Tap the menu icon ☰.
3. Tap on **Create label**.
4. Enter a memorable name and tap **Ok**.
5. To add a contact to the created group, tap Add member icon located at the top of the screen (you may also tap the plus icon at the bottom of the screen) to add members to the newly created group and tap **Done**.
6. To add multiple contacts, tap and hold a contact and then lift your finger. Tap the other contacts you want to add. Tap "Add".

To remove members from a group:

1. From the app screen, tap on **Contacts** app.
2. Tap the menu icon ☰.

3. Tap on a Group or Label.

4. Tap the menu icon ⋮ located at the top of the screen.

5. Tap **Remove contacts**.

6. Tap Remove (**x**) next to the contact you want to remove.

Managing a group or label:

1. From the app screen, tap on **Contacts**  app.

2. Tap the menu icon ▤.

3. Tap on a Group or Label.

4. Tap the menu icon ⋮ located at the top of the screen and pick an option.

5. To send an email to a group, tap **Menu icon** ⋮ and tap **Send email**. Please note that you may not be able to send email to a group, if you have not added email addresses to the individual contacts in the group.

Deleting a group:

1. From the app screen, tap on the **Contacts** 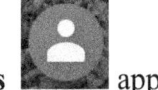 app.

2. Tap the menu icon ▤.

3. Tap on a Label or Group you want to delete.

4. Tap **Menu icon** ⋮ .

5. Tap **Delete label**.

Hint: To customize the Contacts app, tap on the **Contacts** app, tap the menu icon ☰ and then tap **Settings**.

In addition, please note that you can have a more robust management of your contacts by going to Google Contact's website at **https://contacts.google.com**. For example, you can undo changes you made to your contacts recently using this website.

To undo the changes you have made to your contacts:

1. Go to **https://contacts.google.com**
2. Sign in using your Google account (if necessary).
3. Click on **More** at left panel.
4. Click on **Undo changes**.
5. Select an option and click on **Confirm**.

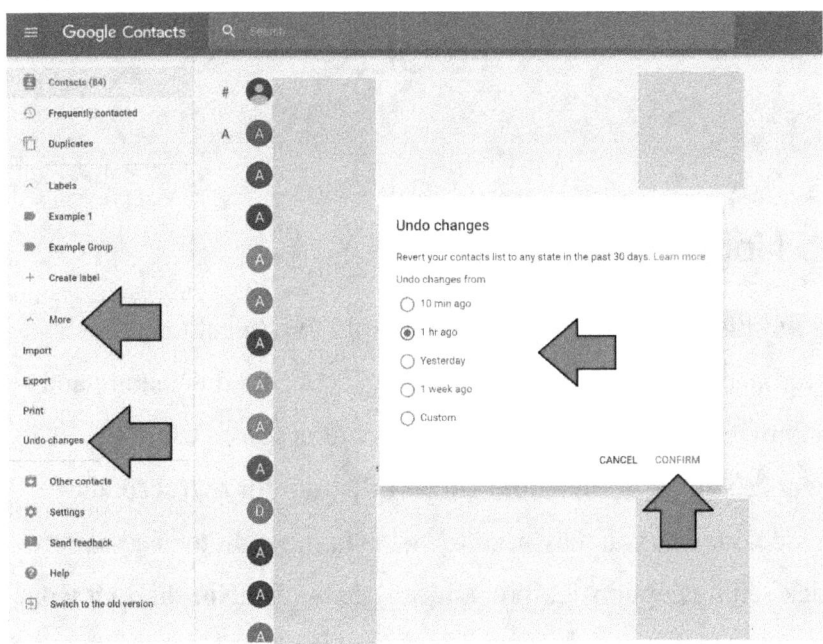

TOOLS

Do Not Disturb

Do not disturb gives you the opportunity to prevent unnecessary disturbances from your phone. To quickly access this feature and customize it, swipe down from the top of the screen using two fingers and then tap and hold **Do Not disturb** for two seconds. Please note that you may need to swipe to the right to access more quick settings options before you can see the **Do Not disturb** icon. For some Android phones, you may need to tap the text beneath "Do not disturb" icon to access Do not disturb settings. If you are using a Sony Android phone, tap **More Settings** to access a more robust settings of Do not disturb.

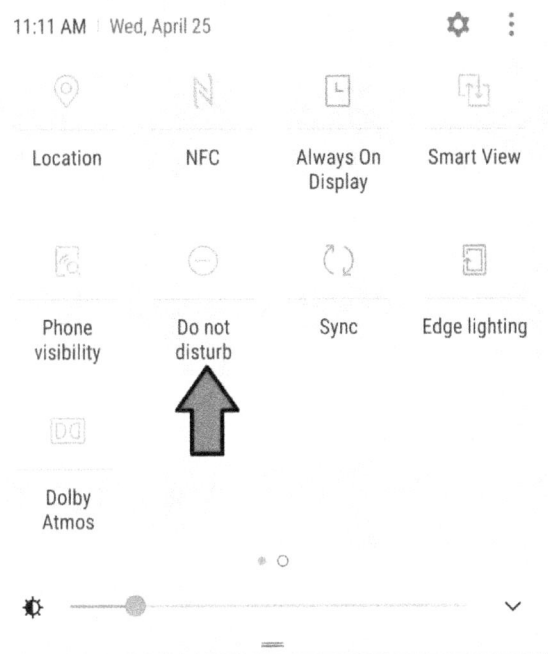

If you can't access "Do not disturb" on your Android phone using the method above, please try this:

Swipe down from the top of the screen and tap the settings icon

 .

Then tap on the search icon (located at the top of the screen) and start typing Do not disturb. The result filters as you type. In the search results, tap **Do not disturb**.

Please note that Samsung Android phone has been used in the (Do not disturb) example below. I have observed that if you understand the description of Do not disturb below, you should be able to customize Do not disturb on many other Android phones.

Then select an option.

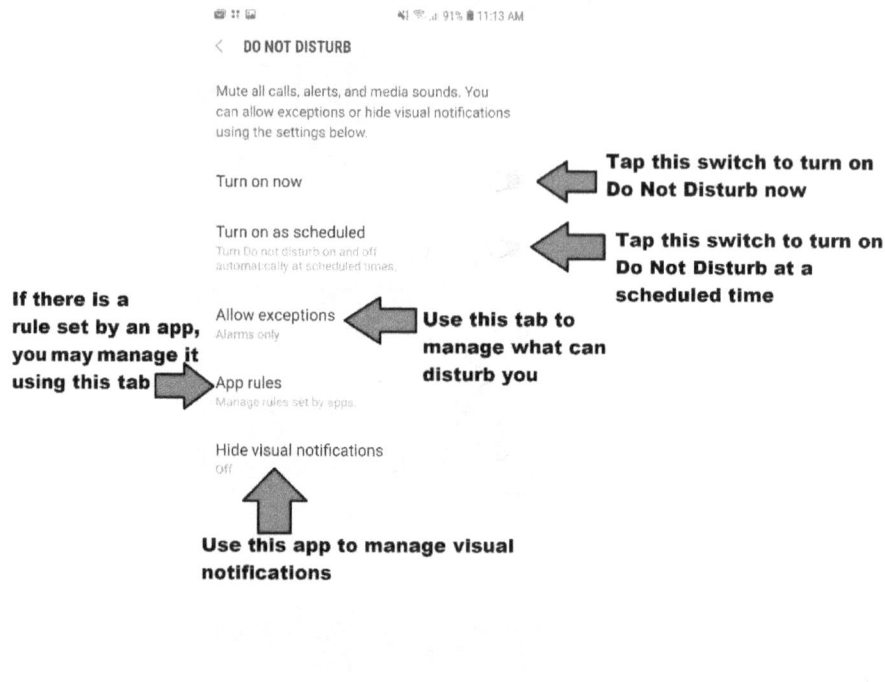

Tap this switch to turn on Do Not Disturb now

Tap this switch to turn on Do Not Disturb at a scheduled time

If there is a rule set by an app, you may manage it using this tab

Use this tab to manage what can disturb you

Use this app to manage visual notifications

If you choose to schedule Do Not Disturb, then use **Days, Start time** and **End time** to customize your experience. Thereafter, tap the back button to save the changes.

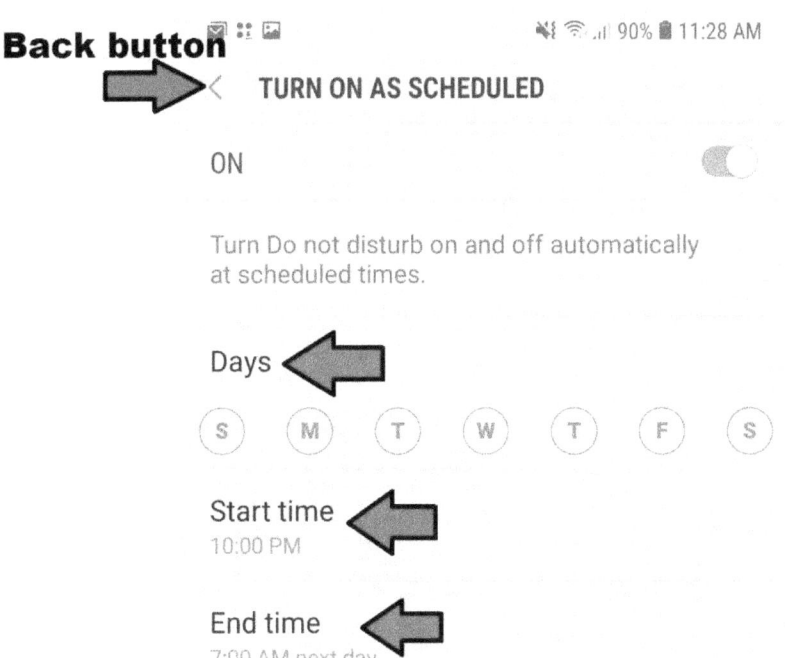

Back button

TURN ON AS SCHEDULED

ON

Turn Do not disturb on and off automatically at scheduled times.

Days

(S) (M) (T) (W) (T) (F) (S)

Start time
10:00 PM

End time
7:00 AM next day

If you are using a Samsung Android phone, please note that when Do Not Disturb is running, you may not get voice feedback from Bixby, instead you may only get text feedback.

To disable Do not disturb, swipe down from the top of the screen using two fingers and tap **Do Not disturb**. Please note that you may need to swipe to the right to access more quick settings options before you can see **Do Not disturb** icon. Do not disturb icon should appear grey when it is disabled.

For some Android phones, you may need to tap the text beneath "Do not disturb" icon to access Do not disturb settings. Then tap the status switch next to "Do not disturb" to disable it.

Google Calendar App

Your Android phone provides you with **Calendar** app to help you organize your schedules and tasks more conveniently and effectively. You can create schedules and add events.

Please note that there are different versions of Calendar apps available on Android phones, in this guide, I will stick to the version of Calendar app developed by Google. You can download Google Calendar app from Google Play store.

In addition, if you have already added your Google account to your phone, the calendar events from this account should appear in the Calendar application.

If you have not added your Google account to your phone, you can do so by following these steps:

1. Swipe down from the top of the screen and select the settings icon ⚙ .

2. Tap "Cloud and accounts", "Account" or "Users & Accounts".

3. Tap "Account" or "Users" (if necessary/available).

4. Tap **Add account** and follow the prompts.

Creating an Event

1. From the home screen, swipe up and tap on **Calendar** . If you are using the Calendar app for the first time, follow the onscreen instructions to set it up.

2. Tap the plus icon at the lower right side of the screen and choose whether you want to create a **goal**, a **reminder**, or an **event.** In this example, event is chosen.

3. To set the start and the end date of the event, tap onscreen date and adjust them accordingly. If the event is an all-day event, tap the status switch next to **All-day** to activate it. When you activate all-day, you would not be able to set a specific time for your event. To learn more about all-day event, please go to page 370.

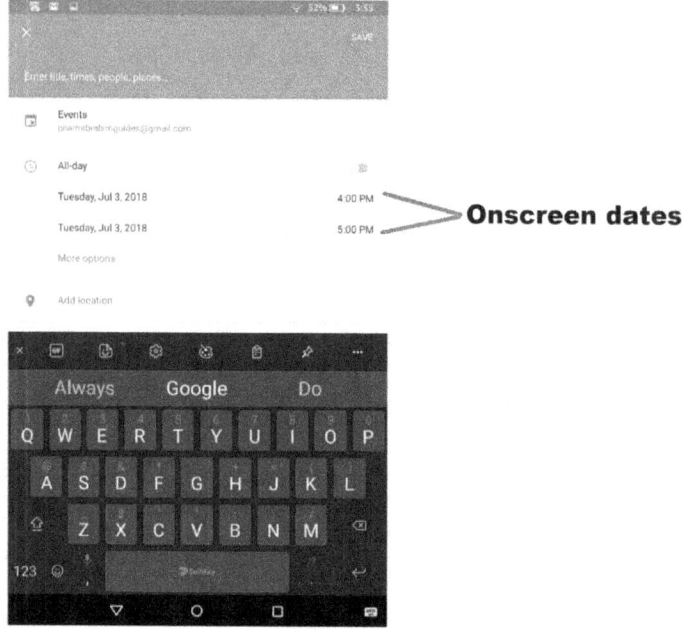

Onscreen dates

4. To enter a title for your event, tap "Enter title, times, people, places…" located at the top of the screen and enter a title. Tap **Done** to save the title. Fill in other details.

5. When you are done, tap **Save** (located at the top of the screen).

Hint: Your phone should give you a notification when the time for an event arrives.

Creating a Reminder

1. From the home screen, swipe up and tap on **Calendar**

    .

2. Tap the plus icon at the lower right side of the screen and choose whether you want to create a **goal**, a **reminder**, or an **event.** In this example, reminder is chosen.

3. Enter a title for your reminder or pick from the suggestions. Tap **Done** to save the title. If the reminder is not all-day (and you wish to set a specific time), tap the status switch next to **All-day** to deactivate it. When you deactivate all day, you would be able to set a specific time.

4. Tap the date to adjust the date. Tap the time to adjust it.

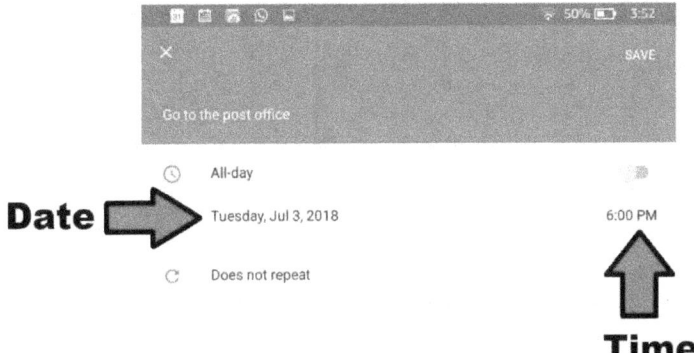

5. To choose when to repeat the reminder, tap **Does not repeat** and pick an option.

6. When you are done, tap **Save** (located at the top of the screen).

Creating a Goal

1. From the home screen, swipe up and tap on **Calendar**

.

2. Tap the plus icon at the lower right side of the screen and choose whether you want to create a **goal**, a **reminder**, or an **event.** In this example, goal is chosen.
3. Choose a goal and follow the onscreen instructions to complete the process.
4. Tap the checkmark to save your goal.

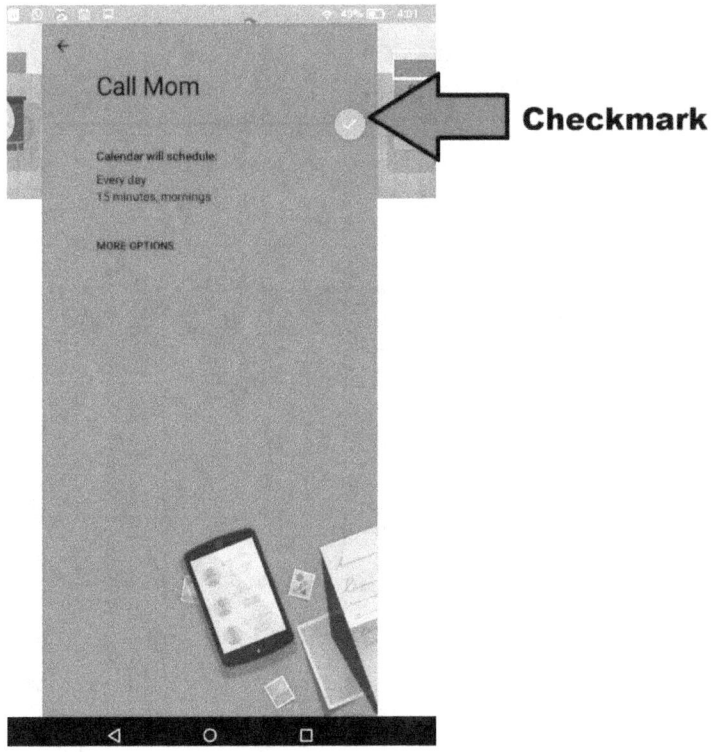

5. Wait for the saving process to complete. If prompted, tap **Looks Good,** if Google Calendar timing for your goal is OK, if not, tap **Adjust time**. Tap the pen icon and then tap the time and adjust it as you like. Tap **Save** (located at the top of the screen) to save the changes.

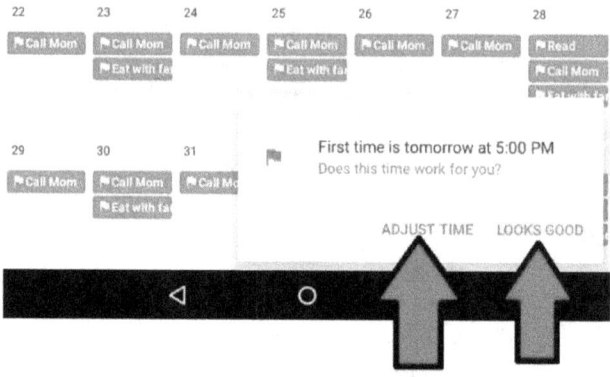

Understanding All-day Event

All-day event is a type of event that will take a lot of hours to complete. For example, if an event will begin by 9 a.m. and finish by 6 p.m., this type of event should be categorized as an all-day event. This will make it easier to see all other schedules (like reminders) happening during this time on your calendar. If you were to schedule an event between 9 a.m. and 6 p.m. on your calendar (and you don't select it as all-day event), it will block off a lot of time on your calendar. It may also overshadow other concurrent events.

In the picture below, the event is supposed to be an all-day event, but I have refused to do so.

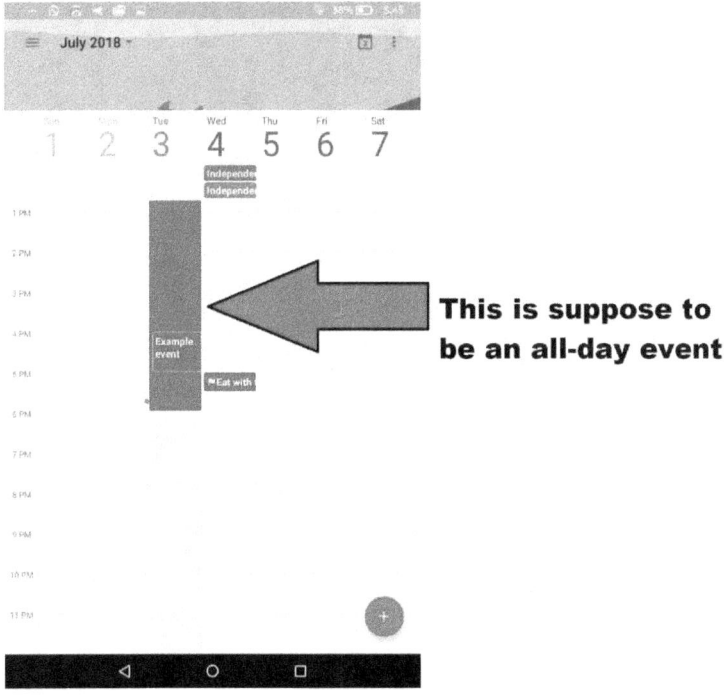

When I made the same event an all-day event, it becomes this (see below).

An all-day event

To make event an event an all-day event, please go to step 3 under **Creating an Event** (see page 365).

Viewing an Event, Reminder or Goal

1. From the home screen, swipe up and tap on **Calendar**

2. To change the calendar view, tap the menu icon ☰ (located at the top of the screen).

3. Select **Month**, **Week** or **Day**.

4. Then tap on an event, reminder or goal to view.

Editing an Event, Reminder or Goal

1. Repeat steps 1 to 4 above.

2. Tap the pen icon 🖊 and adjust what you want. Tap **Save** (located at the top of the screen) to save the changes.

Deleting an Event, Reminder or Goal

1. From the home screen, swipe up and tap on **Calendar** 📅

.

2. To change the calendar view, tap the menu icon ☰ (located at the top of the screen).

3. Select **Month**, **Week** or **Day**.

4. Then tap on an event, reminder or goal you want to delete.

5. Tap the menu icon ⋮ and select **Delete**.

Changing Calendar View

1. From the home screen, swipe up and tap on **Calendar**
.

2. To change the calendar view, tap the menu icon 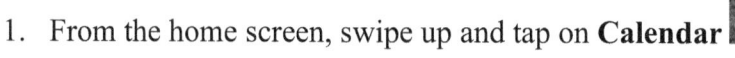 (located at the top of the screen).

3. Tap **Month**, **Week** or **Day**.

Inviting People to Your Events

If you have an upcoming event, you can invite people to it using the Google Calendar app. To do this:

1. From the home screen, swipe up and tap on **Calendar**
.

2. Tap the plus icon at the lower right side of the screen and choose **event**.

3. To set the start and the end date of the event, tap onscreen date and adjust them accordingly. If the event is an all-day event, tap the status switch next to **All-day** to activate it. When you activate all-day, you would not be able to set a specific time. To learn more about all-day event, please go to page 370.

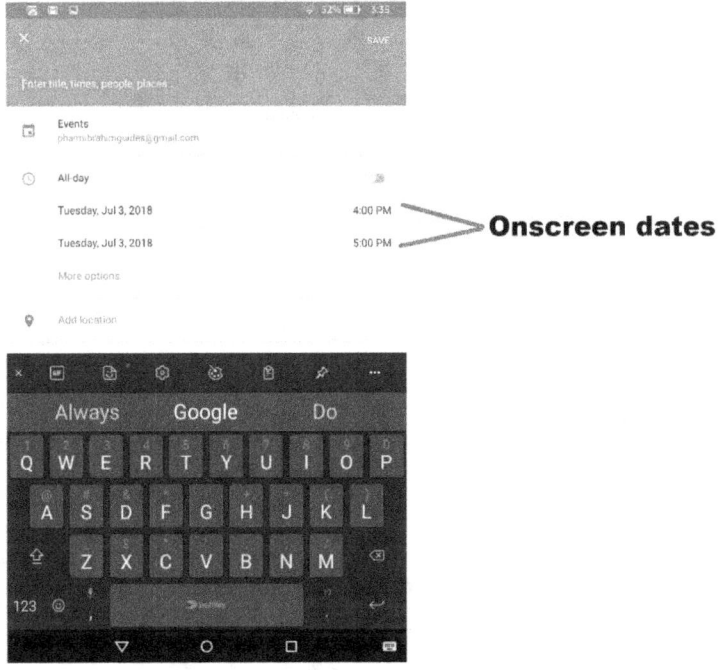

4. To enter a title for your event, tap "Enter title, times, people, places..." located at the top of the screen and enter a title. Tap **Done** to save the title.

5. To invite people to your event, tap **Invite people** and type the name of those you are inviting. The list filters as you type. To select any suggested name, tap it. You can also enter email address if you don't have the contact of those you are

inviting. In addition, if you have a Google group, you can enter the email address of the group to send invitations to the members of the group. Tap **Done.**

6. Fill in other details.

7. When you are done, tap **Save** (located at the top of the screen). If prompted, select **Send.**

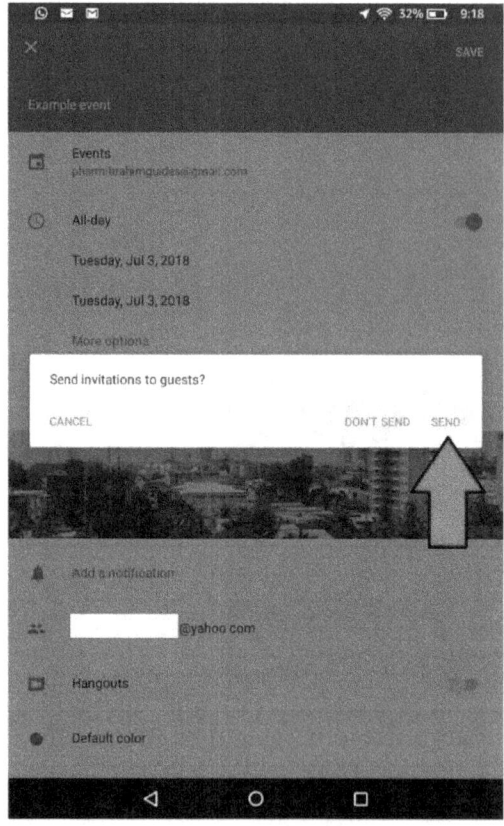

Generally, Google will send out email invitation to the invited guest/people after you save the event. The invitees will have the opportunity to respond to the request through their emails.

Tip: To see people coming to your event, simply open Calendar app, and tap on the event.

In addition, you can send invitation to thousands of people easily if you have Google group and you have these people (you want to invite) in your Google group. To create a group, visit groups.google.com

Controlling What You See in Your Calendar

You can choose what you see in your calendar. For example, if you don't want public holidays to appear in your calendar, you can block it. To do this:

1. From the home screen, swipe up and tap **Calendar** .

2. Tap the menu icon ≣ at the top of the screen.

3. Unselect those options you don't want to see in your calendar. For example, if you don't want your Reminder to populate your calendar, unselect it. Furthermore, if you don't want to see events from a Google account, you can use this method to unselect it.

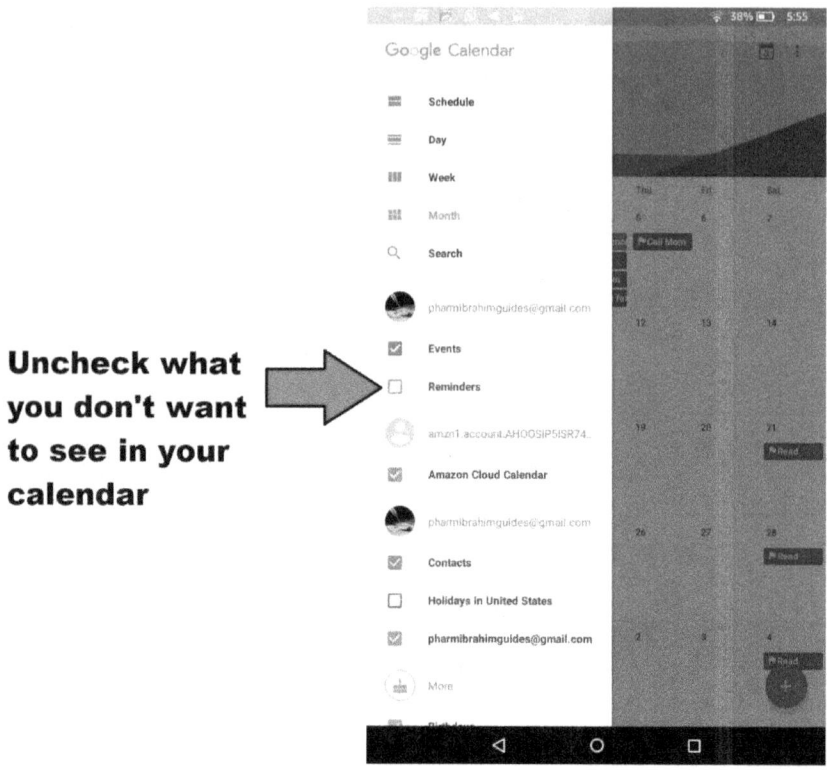

Uncheck what you don't want to see in your calendar

Managing Google Calendar App Settings

1. From the home screen, swipe up and tap **Calendar** .

   Tap the menu icon at the top of the screen.

2. Tap **settings** (located at the bottom of the screen) and choose an option.

3. To access general settings, tap **General**. General settings allow you to manage settings like time zone, notifications, quick response etc.

4. To adjust event's notification, tap **Events.** Tap a default notification (for example, tap "30 minutes before") and choose another one. To add another notification, tap **Add another notification**. To pick another color for your event, tap **Color** and choose one.

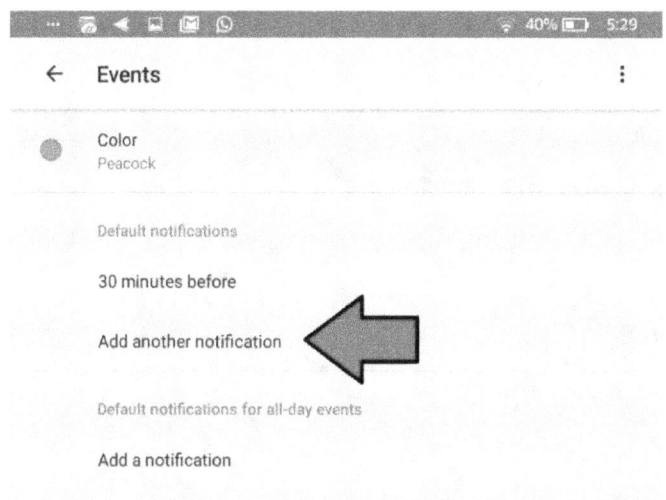

Accessibility Settings

Accessibility settings on Android phones allow you to manage options like vision settings, hearing settings, touch and interactions settings, talkback settings, font settings, display settings, shortcut settings, text-to-speech settings and more. I would advise you always visit Accessibility tab whenever you want to use your phone in a new way.

Interestingly, for many Android phones, complex accessibility settings usually have explanations/information beneath them. You can read these explanations to get what the options represent.

To access accessibility settings:

1. Swipe down from the top of the screen and select the settings

   icon ⚙ .

2. Tap **Accessibility**.

3. Tap an option to manage.

If you can't see accessibility settings following the method above, do these:

1. Swipe down from the top of the screen and select the settings

   icon ⚙ .

2. Then tap on the search icon 🔍 (usually located at the top of the screen).

3. Type **Accessibility** into the search bar. The result filters as you type. From the search results that appear, select "accessibility", "accessibility settings" or a similar phrase.

Using the Camera

Many Android phone comes with rear-facing camera(s), a front-facing camera and an LED flash. With these cameras, you can capture an image or record a video.

Note: Different Android phones have different camera features and it is difficult to have a discussion that would cut across all the types of Cameras we have on Android phones. In this guide, I would simply be explaining general camera options/features that are common with many/most Android phones.

To Capture a photo

1. From the app screen, tap **Camera**.
2. Aim the lens at the subject and make any necessary adjustments. To focus any part of the screen, tap that part of the screen.

3. To adjust the picture settings, tap settings ⚙ and then pick an option.

4. Tap the **front-facing/rear-facing icon** to switch between the front-facing and rear-facing cameras.

5. To zoom in, place two fingers on the screen and spread them apart. Do the reverse to zoom out.

6. Tap on **camera button** or when you are done adjusting the settings.

Tip: To change the picture storage location to SD card on supported Android phones, while on the camera app screen, tap the settings icon and then scroll down and tap **Storage Location**. Then select **SD card** from the option that appears.

To customize camera settings:

1. From the home screen, tap **Camera**.

2. Tap the settings icon .

3. Adjust the various settings as you like.

Hint: Camera settings consist of a lot of features, and you may not need to touch some of these features. In fact, the default settings are enough for many users/beginners.

On supported Android phones, if someone adjusts the camera settings the way you don't like, and you wish to restore the camera settings to factory settings, follow these steps. Tap the settings icon

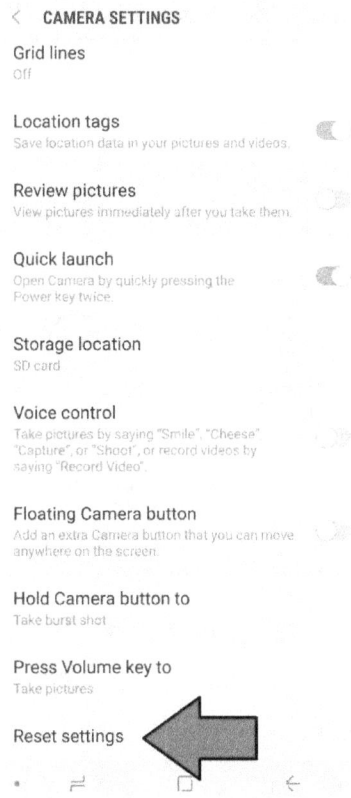 while on the camera app screen, scroll down and tap **Reset settings.** Tap **Reset** when prompted.

Recording a Video

1. From the app screen, tap **Camera.**

2 Tap on the video button or to start recording.

3. To zoom in while recording, place two fingers on the screen and spread them apart. To zoom out, move the two fingers closer together.

4. When done with the recording, tap the **video button** again.

6. To view your recorded videos, go to **Gallery/Photos** app.

Editing Your Photos

You can use your phone to edit photos.

1. Go to the application screen and tap on **Gallery/Photos**.

2. Tap on the photo you want to edit.

3. Tap the **Edit icon** (a pen icon) and then pick any editing tool(s). If

there is no edit icon, tap the menu icon and select **Edit**.

Getting Productive with Camera

Many people use the camera of their Android phone just to take pictures, but don't know that they can be more productive using the camera on their phones.

Interestingly, Android phone features a powerful camera that transforms the way you use a camera. In this part of the guide, we will be exploring ways you can be more productive with your phone camera.

Ways to be more productive with your phone camera are mentioned below:

- **Use your phone camera as a scanner for your documents**

You probably have many documents that are very important to you. Why don't you look for a time to take the pictures of all these documents and save them to your phone or have them stored in the cloud. There are times that you would want to check something inside a document, but you are not at home, saving your document on your phone should help you in a time like this. In addition, saving documents on your phone will save you time and stress because you have access to them on the go.

- **Take pictures of natural environment like waterfall and natural vegetation**

According to reports, looking at the pictures of natural environment like waterfall and natural vegetation gives people pleasure and serves as a coolness to one's eyes. In addition, it helps you appreciate the beautiful work of Almighty God.

- **Declutter your life**

Do you know that you can use the camera of your phone to declutter your life? You probably have many hand-written documents, business cards, to-do list etc. lying all over the places in your home. You can take the picture of these notes so that you can remove them from your house and give them to appropriate waste recycling company. This will create more space in your house and give you visual ventilation.

I would advise you properly label the pictures of your hand-written documents, business cards, to-do list etc. to help you easily find them in the future. In addition, you can consider saving the pictures of your hand-written documents, business cards, to-do list etc. on *Evernote*. I suggest Evernote because it gives you the opportunity to search texts inside images.

- **Use your camera as a barcode and QR (quick response) code scanner**

Barcode and QR code are machine readable codes that are used to store information. Barcode is linear or one dimensional in nature. It basically looks like a cluster of parallel lines. On the other hand, QR code is two dimensional in nature. An example of a QR code is shown below. Interestingly, Android phone is capable of reading QR codes and barcodes using "barcode scanner" apps. Many of us still take the long path of entering texts or links when we can get the same result by scanning barcode or QR code.

Example of a QR code

You can download and install a barcode/QR scanner from Google Play store, simply search for *barcode scanner* or *QR and barcode scanner*.

- **Take the pictures of notes in meetings and lectures instead of writing them**

Taking the picture of notes after a meeting or a lecture allows you to listen during the meeting or lecture instead of writing notes.

- **Use your camera to take pictures of valuable information/document in your life**

If you have any valuable piece of information that you can't afford to lose, use your camera to take its picture. That would serve as a backup in case of loss.

Connectivity

Computer Connections

Your phone can be connected to a computer with a USB cable. This would enable you to transfer items such as audio, document and image files to your phone from your computer.

Warning: Do not disconnect the USB cable from a computer while the device is transferring or accessing data. This may result in data loss or damage to your phone.

Transferring content via the USB cable:

1. Connect your device to a computer with an appropriate USB cable (like the one that came with your phone).

2. If prompted to allow an access to phone data, tap **Allow**. If you don't choose **Allow**, your computer may not access your phone data.

3. Slide down from the top of the screen and tap the USB option (**USB for...**). Tap it again, if needed.

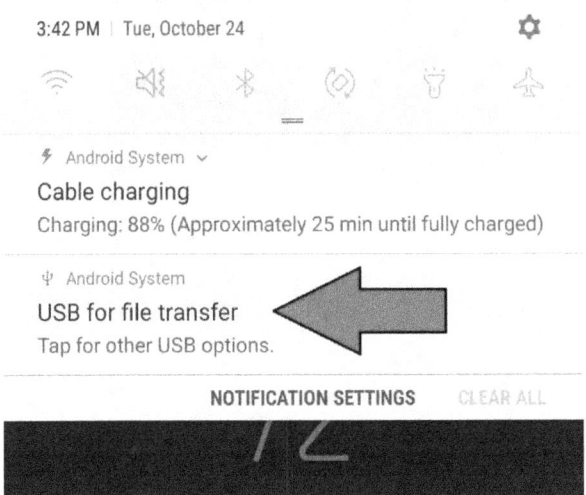

3:42 PM | Tue, October 24

⚡ Android System ⌄

Cable charging

Charging: 88% (Approximately 25 min until fully charged)

ψ Android System

USB for file transfer

Tap for other USB options.

NOTIFICATION SETTINGS   CLEAR ALL

4. Tap **Transfer Files** (if not selected).

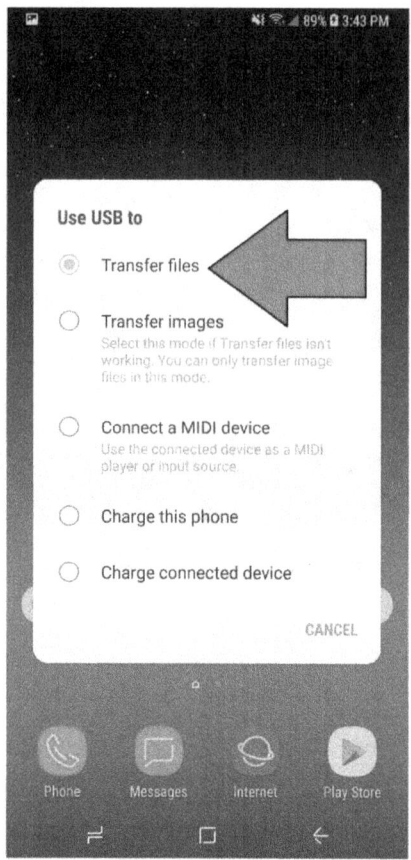

5. Your Android Phone should appear in the same location where an external USB drives usually appear. For Windows users, this is typically under "This PC/Computer" menu.

6. Open your device drive to see the different folders present. Note that you may not be able to access the folders if your phone is locked.

7. To transfer files from your computer to your phone. Locate the file you want to transfer on your computer. Then click, drag and drop the file into the corresponding folder on your Phone. For example, document files should be dragged to My

Documents folder. Alternatively, if you are using PC, right-click on the file you want to send, select **Send to** and then choose your phone from the options that appear.

8. *After the data transfer process*, disconnect your phone just as you would disconnect an external memory drive. If you are using Windows 10, you may just remove the USB cable from the phone when you are done with the transfer. You may not need to click any disconnect icon before you remove your phone if you are using Windows 10.

Note: After the transfer, your transferred files should appear under the corresponding content library on your device. To view any of the transferred files:

From the app screen, tap **My Files**. Then tap an appropriate category to view the transferred files or folders.

If you don't have My Files (or similar app) on your Android phone, you may consider installing **Files Go by Google** from Google Play store.

Note that your phone will only recognize the file you transferred if the file is a supported file type.

If you do factory reset to your phone, you may need to re-transfer the files again (unless you have them stored on a cloud storage like Dropbox).

Wi-Fi

Using your Android phone, you can connect to the internet or other network devices anywhere an access point or wireless hotspot is available.

To activate the Wi-Fi feature and connect to a network:

1. Swipe down from the top of the screen.

2. Tap and hold the **Wi-Fi** icon to access Wi-Fi settings. For some Android phones, you may need to tap the text beneath the Wi-Fi icon to access wireless settings.

3. Tap the switch next to Wi-Fi to turn it on.

4. Your device then automatically scans for available networks and displays them.

5. Select a network and enter a password for the network (if necessary). You may also manually add a network. To manually add a network, scroll down (if necessary) and tap **Add network**. Then follow the on-screen instructions.

6. To turn Wi-Fi off, swipe down from the top of the screen and tap **Wi-Fi** . Wi-Fi would appear grey when disabled.

Notes:

*   The Wi-Fi feature running in the background will consume battery. To save battery, put it off whenever you are not using it.

- The Wi-Fi may not connect a network if the network signal is not good.

- When Wi-Fi is connected, active, and communicating with a wireless Access Point, Wi-Fi active icon is displayed on the Status bar.

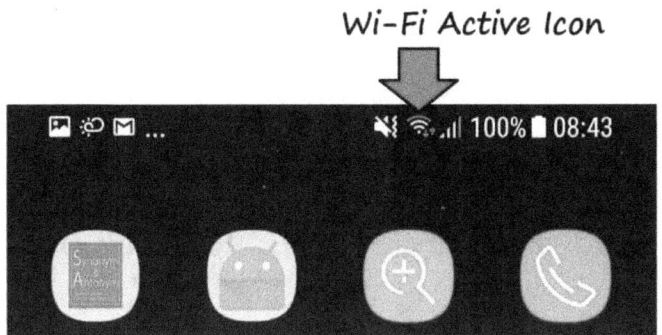

Mobile Data

Using your Android phone, you can connect to the internet or other network devices using the Mobile Data.

1. Swipe down from the top of the screen.

2. Tap and hold the **Mobile data** icon to access mobile data settings. For some Android phones, you may need to tap the text beneath the mobile data icon to access its settings.

3. Tap the switch next to "Mobile Data" to turn it on.

Alternatively, if the method above does not work for you, swipe

down from the top of the screen and select the settings icon ⚙ .
Tap "Network & Internet", "Connections", or "Wireless &
network". Tap "Mobile data". Tap the switch next to "Mobile Data"
to turn it on. If you don't see "Mobile data", tap "Mobile network"
and then tap the indicator switch next to "Mobile data" to turn it on.
Please note that you may incur charges when using mobile data.

Using Your Phone as a Mobile Hotspot

If your network provider supports it, you can use this feature to share
your mobile network with friends and family.

1. Swipe down from the top of the screen and select the settings

   icon ⚙ . Tap "Network & Internet", "Connections", or
   "Wireless & network".

2. Tap "Mobile Hotspot and Tethering", "Tethering & portable
   hotspot", "Tethering & mobile hotspot" or "Hotspot &
   tethering".

3. If necessary, tap "Portable Wi-Fi Hotspot" or
   "Mobile hotspot". If prompted to enable or disable Wi-Fi
   sharing, you can choose to disable Wi-Fi sharing. Wi-Fi
   sharing allows you to share your Wi-Fi connections with
   other devices, while mobile hotspot shares your mobile data
   with other devices. Please, before you share a Wi-Fi

connection with other devices, please ensure that you are not breaking any terms and conditions.

4. Next to "Portable Wi-Fi Hotspot", "Portable Hotspot" or "Mobile hotspot", tap **On** (or the status switch). If prompted, tap "OK". Please note that Wi-Fi may need to be turned off for you to turn on mobile hotspot.

5. Tap "Set up Mobile Hotspot", "Set up Wi-Fi hotspot" or "Configure Wi-Fi hotspot" and follow the prompts. If you don't see "Set up Mobile Hotspot" or "Set up/Configure Wi-Fi hotspot", tap the menu icon ⋮ (located at the top of the screen) and tap **Configure Mobile Hotspot.**
   If you are using Sony Android phone, tap "Portable hotspot settings" and then tap "Configure hotspot".

6. Enter a name for the network (this is the name that other devices searching for the network would see). Scroll down (if necessary) and tap **Password**. Then enter a password for the network and tap **Save**.
   If you are given the opportunity to pick the type of security you want, I would advise that you choose WPA2 (WPA2 is a highly secured encryption protocol).
   In addition, if you don't want your hotspot to require a password (and you don't want an encryption), pick "None" under "Security". Please note that for safety reason, using Security/encryption is strongly recommended.

7. After enabling the mobile hotspot, your friends and family should be able to connect to it just like they connect to other wireless networks.

8. To turn off mobile hotspot, repeat steps 1 to 3 above and next to "Portable Wi-Fi Hotspot", "Portable Hotspot" or "Mobile hotspot", tap **Off** (or the indicator switch).

Hints:

On a supported Android device, you can choose who connects to your mobile hotspot by creating the Allowed Device list. To do this:

1. Follow steps 1 to 4 above.

2. Tap the menu icon ⋮ > **Allowed devices**, and then tap **Add** to enter the device name and MAC address. The MAC address of many smart gadgets is found under **Wi-Fi settings** or **Wi-Fi Advanced settings.**

4. Tap **Add** to add the device.

5. Tap the status switch next to **Allowed devices only** to make sure only the allowed devices can connect to your mobile hotspot.

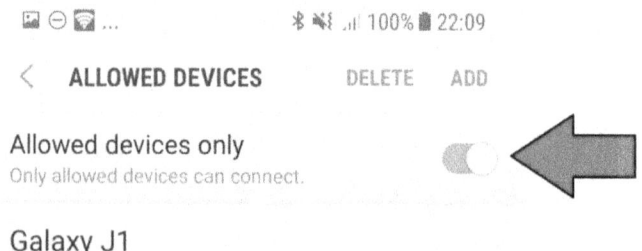

6. To delete an allowed device, tap and hold the device and select **DELETE.**

In addition, you can automatically turn off mobile hotspot if there are no connected devices. To do this, follow the step 1 above. Then tap the menu icon ⋮ > **Timeout settings**, and then select a time.

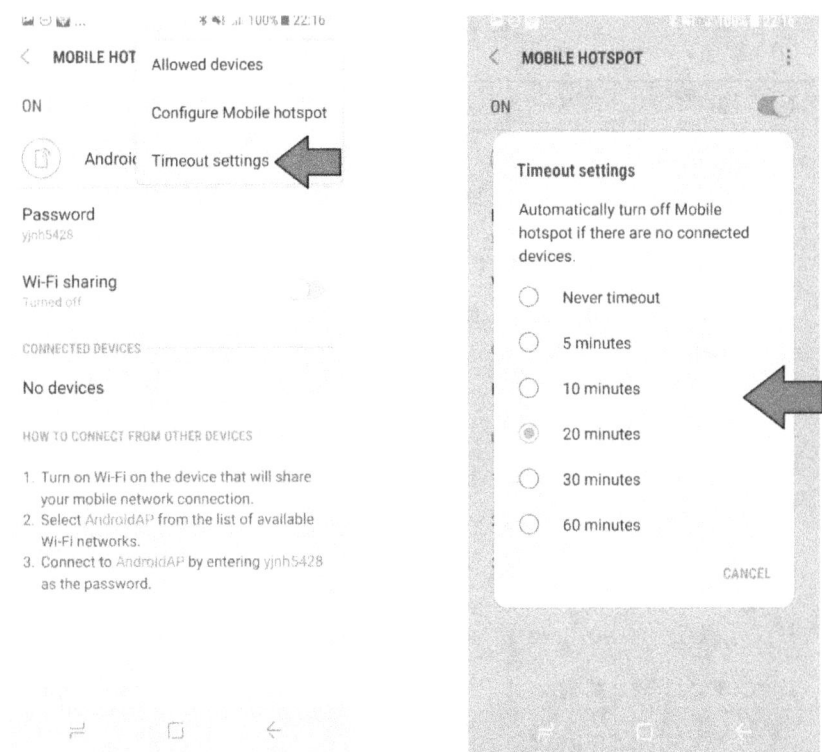

Alternatively, on some other Android devices, while on "Tethering & portable hotspot" page, tap "Portable hotspot settings" and then select "Power save".

Access More by Using Bluetooth

Bluetooth option allows you to connect to another Bluetooth device within range.

Note: If there are obstacles, the operating distance of the Bluetooth may be reduced. The Bluetooth communication range is usually approximately 30 feet.

To use the Bluetooth feature:

1. Swipe down from the top of the screen.

2. Tap and hold the **Bluetooth** icon .

3. Then next to **Bluetooth**, select **on** or tap the indicator switch. When Bluetooth is enabled, the indicator switch would appear bold.

4. Then Bluetooth automatically scans for nearby Bluetooth devices and displays them. Please make sure the Bluetooth of the device you are connecting with is turned on and discoverable.

5. Tap a device to connect with and follow the prompts to finish the connection. You may need to enter a pairing code.

6. When Bluetooth is enabled, the **Bluetooth icon** would appear next to the **Wi-Fi icon** on the status bar. Pairing between two Bluetooth devices should be a one-time process. Once two devices are paired, the devices may continue to

recognize this association and you may not need to re-enter a passcode.

7. To turn Bluetooth off, swipe down from the top of the screen, tap **Bluetooth** . The Bluetooth would appear gray when you turn it off (see the picture below).

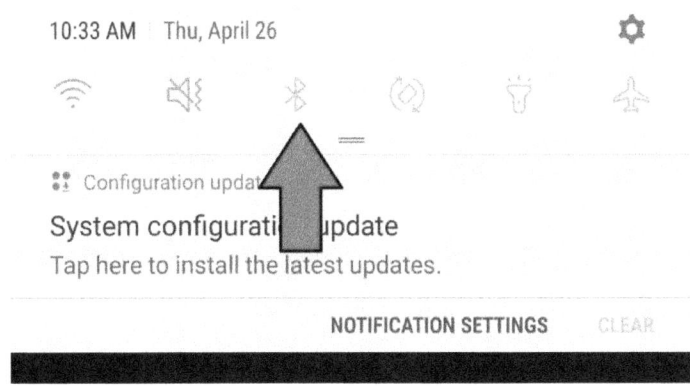

Unpairing a Paired Device

1. Swipe down from the top of the screen.
2. Tap and hold the **Bluetooth** icon.
3. Then next to **Bluetooth**, select **on** (if not already turned on).
4. Tap the settings icon next to the paired device, and then tap **Unpair** to remove the paired device.

Tip: On supported Android phones, once you have paired your device to another device, you can rename the paired device to make it easier to recognize. To do this, follow the steps 1 to 3 above and

tap the settings icon ⚙ next to the previously paired device. Then tap **Rename**. Enter a new name, and tap **Rename**. You can also use this method to customize many settings for a paired device. Simply select the appropriate setting (instead of selecting "Rename" as done above).

In addition, on a supported Android device, you can give your Android phone a new name. To do this, while on Bluetooth screen,

tap **Device name** or tap the menu icon ⋮ and select **Rename this device**. Enter a new name and tap **Rename**.

Location Settings

Enabling location service allows apps to serve you content/location related services.

To activate location services:

1. Swipe down from the top of the screen and select the settings

   icon ⚙ .

2. Tap "Security & location", "Connection" or "Lock screen & security".

3. Tap **Location**.

4. Next to the switch under **Location**, select **on**.

5. To put it off, tap the switch again.

Tip: If you want your phone to use the combination of Wi-Fi, GPS, and mobile networks to estimate your location, tap "Mode" or "Location Method" and then tap **High accuracy**.

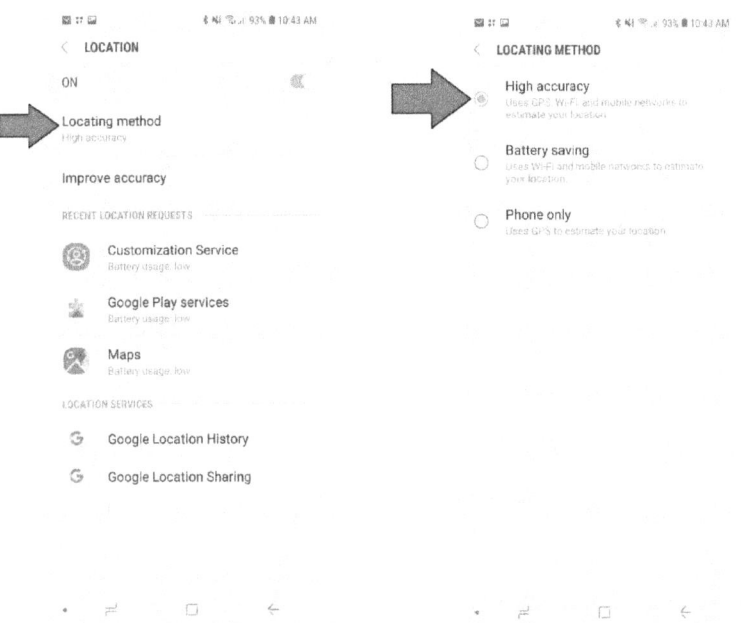

Finding Your Lost Android Phone

You can find your lost Android phone using Google "Find My Device". Please note that to use this service to find your lost device, your lost device must be turned on and connected to a Wireless network or mobile data. In addition, your lost device must have its location turned on (before it was lost). See page 400 to learn how to turn on location on your Android phone.

Tip: You can also use this method to erase your phone when you forget the lock screen password.

Note: It is dangerous to attempt to retrieve your lost phone by yourself. Please involve the attention of security operatives whenever you can.

To find your lost phone:

1. Visit **www.google.com/android/find**
2. Sign in using the Google account associated with your Android phone.
3. If prompted, read the information and tap **Accept** (if you agree).
4. If you have more than one device, select the lost device (at the top of the screen).
5. Use the onscreen map, to locate your device.
6. You can use the onscreen option to **play sound**, **lock**, or **erase** your device. Please note that you may need to click or tap "Enable lock & erase" before you see the option to lock or erase your Android phone.

Please note that if you use Google "Find My Device" to erase your phone, you would not be able to locate your phone again (using Google Find My Device).

Find My Mobile Feature (for Samsung Android Phone)

If you are using a Samsung Android phone, you can use this feature to locate your phone if lost.

Note: You must sign up for a Samsung account (as explained below), enable location service (as explained on page 400) and enable "Find My Mobile" feature (as explained below) to use the Find My Mobile option.

To add Samsung account (if you have not done so before):

1. Swipe down from the top of the screen and select the settings icon ⚙ .

2. Tap **Cloud and accounts**.

3. Tap **Account**.

4. Tap **Add account**.

5. Tap **Samsung Account**. Then enter your Samsung account information.

6. Or tap **Create Account** and follow the prompts.

Please note that if you have already added Samsung account, you can skip these steps.

To activate Find My Mobile Feature (for Samsung Android phones):

1. Swipe down from the top of the screen and select the settings icon ⚙.

2. Tap **Lock screen and security**.

3. Scroll down and tap **Find My Mobile**.

4. If required, enter your Samsung account's password and then tap **Sign In.** If you don't have a Samsung account, create one.

5. Make sure that the status switches beside **Remote Controls**, **Google Location Service** and **Send Last Location** are turned on.

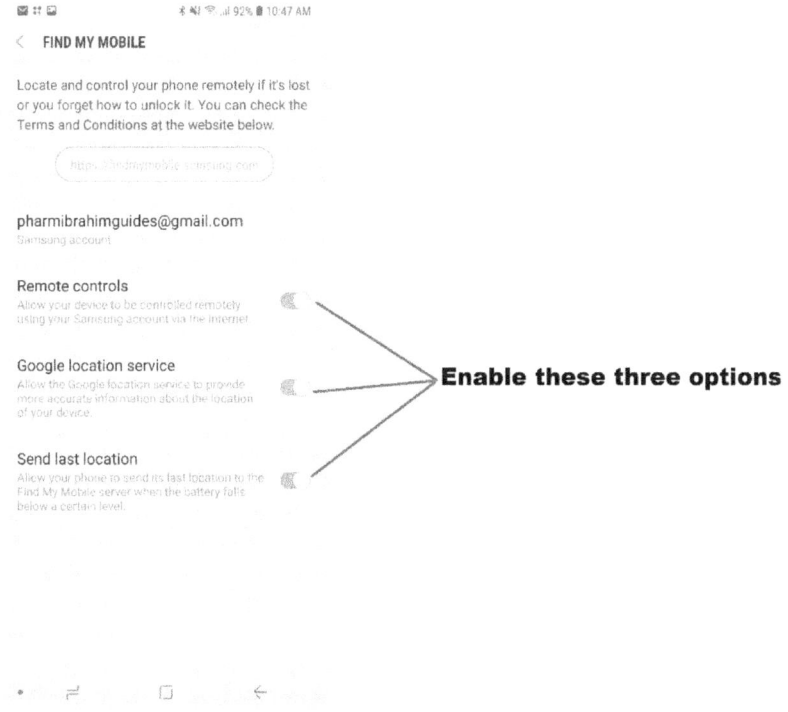

To find your lost phone:

Note: It is dangerous to attempt to retrieve your lost phone by yourself. Please involve the attention of security operatives whenever you can.

1. Open the web browser and go to **findmymobile.samsung.com**

2. Tap **Sign In**.

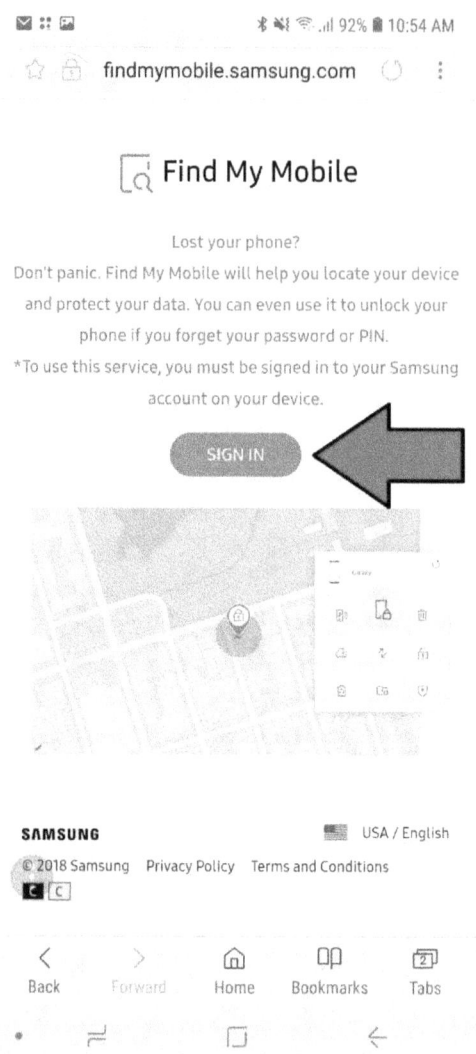

3. Enter the email address associated with your Samsung account into the email field and then enter your password. Click **Sign In.**

4. If you have more than one Samsung phone, you may need to select your lost Samsung Android phone (if it is not currently displayed). To do this, tap the menu icon ≡ next to the current device name and select your device name.

5. Tap the dropdown icon to access the map.

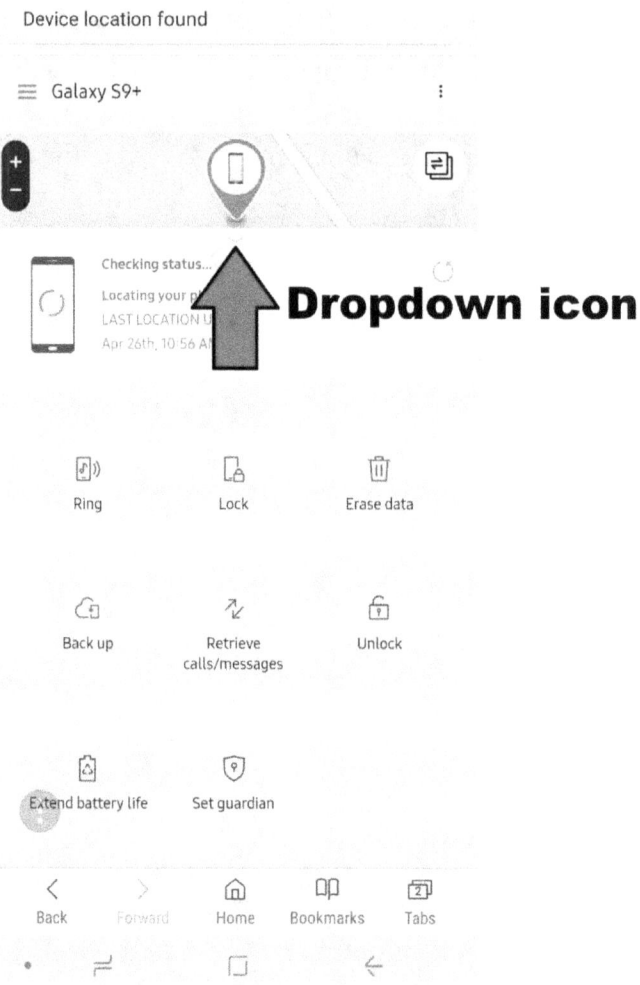

6. To close the map, tap the V-shaped icon.

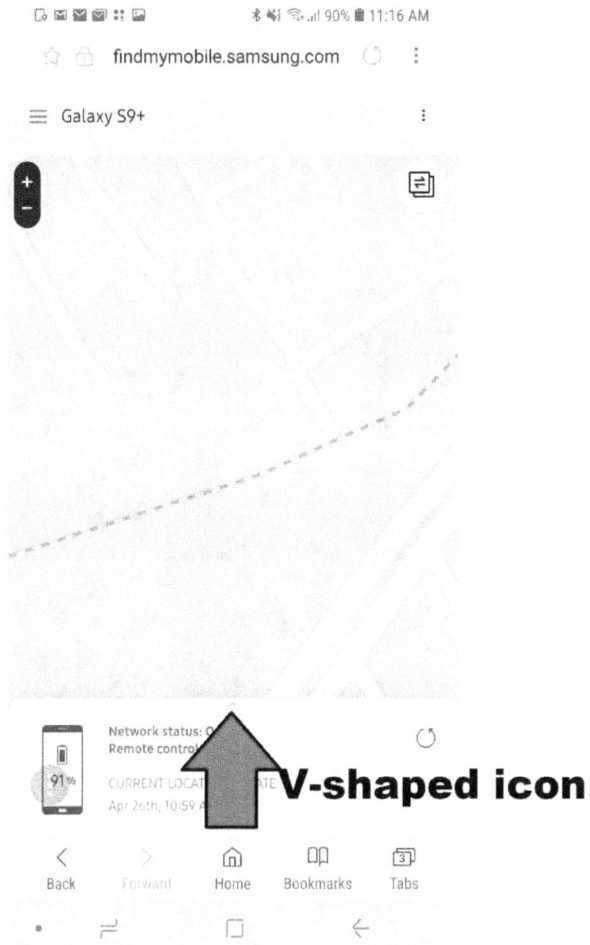

The current location of your phone will be displayed on a map.
You can use the options on this website to **ring your device, lock
your device, back up your device, extend battery life, set
guardian and wipe/erase your device**.

Tip: You can use **Samsung Find My Device** to unlock your device when you forget your log in information. To do this, follow the steps 1-4 above and tap **Unlock** and enter your Samsung account password.

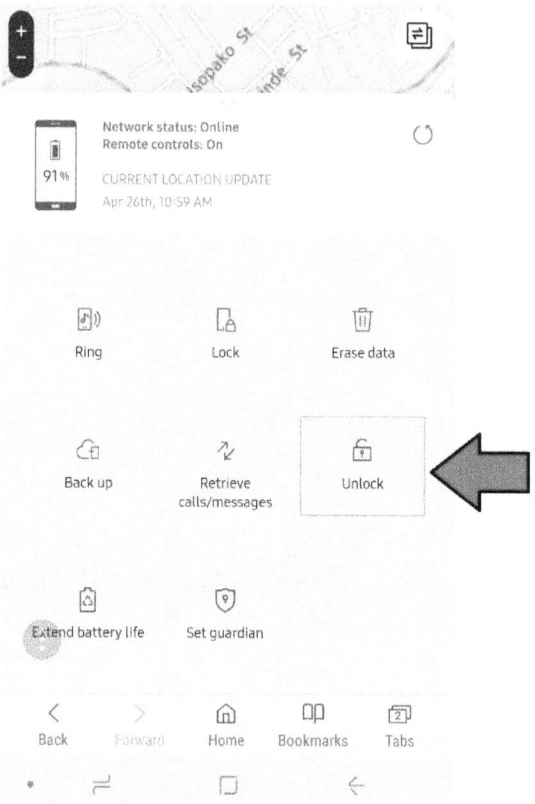

Note: Please note that your phone may need to be connected to a wireless or mobile network to be able to use the **Samsung Find My Mobile** feature to manage your phone. However, you may still be able to know the last known location of your phone.

In addition, if you use Samsung Find My Mobile to erase your phone, you would not be able to locate your phone again (using Samsung Find My Mobile).

Using the NFC (Near Field Communication)

This is a technology like the Bluetooth and Wi-Fi. It utilizes electromagnetic radio frequency. Devices using NFC may be passive or active. A passive device is not powered by battery but contains information that other devices can read but does not read any information itself. An example of a passive NFC is the NFC tag. On the other hand, an active NFC device can read information and send it. An example of an active NFC device is your Android phone.

If supported, you can use the NFC feature to send files from your Android phone to other NFC supported devices.

Please note that not all Android phones support NFC.

To turn on and use NFC:

1. Swipe down from the top of the screen using two fingers then tap and hold the **NFC** icon for two seconds. Please note that you may need to swipe to the right to access more quick settings options before you can see the **NFC** icon. If your Android phone does not have an NFC icon (under the quick settings menu), then swipe down from the top of the screen and tap settings . Then tap "Connected devices" or "Device connection".

2. Under "NFC and payment", "Device connection" or "Connected devices" tap the switch next to NFC. When NFC is turned on, the indicator switch should appear bold.

Also, make sure the status switch next to **Android Beam** is turned on.

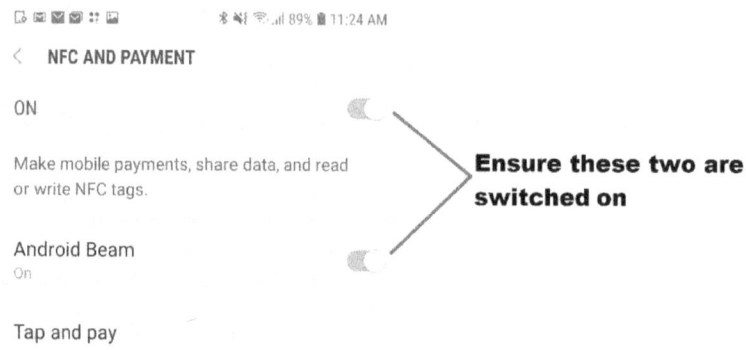

3. To use NFC to send a file to another device, ensure both devices involved have their NFC turned on. Then open the file you wish to send and tap **Share**. Tap **Android Beam**. Hold your mobile phone and the receiving device back to back. Then tap the screen to send the file.
4. To turn off NFC or Android Beam, repeat steps 1 and 2 above.

It may not be very effective in sending large files because it may be slow.

Using NFC to make payment

In recent times, NFC is finding more usage in payment system.

To make payments with the NFC:

1. Follow steps 1 and 2 above (under **To turn on and use NFC).**

2. Place the back of your device against the NFC card reader.

Usually, after you have enabled NFC payments on your phone, you should be able to make payments for items by tapping your phone against a participating store's NFC reader.

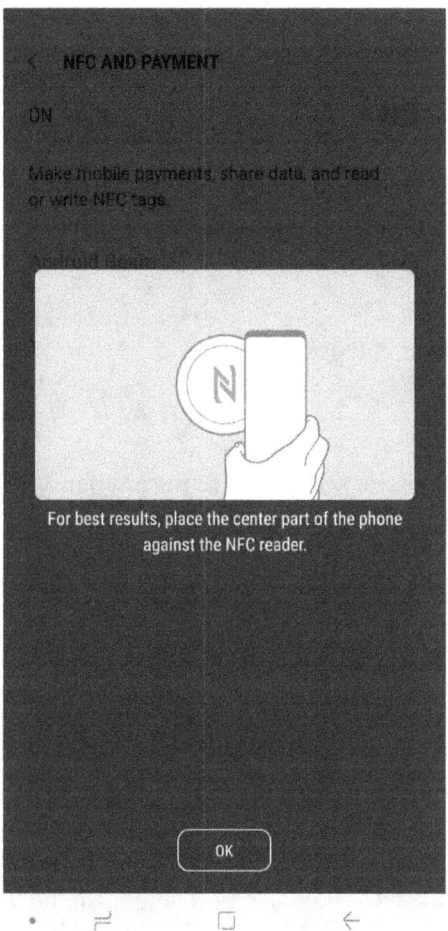

Settings

Settings menu give you the opportunity to customize your device as you like.

To access the settings menu

1. Swipe down from the top of the screen and select the settings icon ⚙ .

2. Alternatively, go to the application screen and then tap **Settings**.

3. Tap a setting category.

Search for Settings

It is advisable to use the searching feature when you are not sure exactly where to find a certain setting.

1. Swipe down from the top of the screen and select the settings icon ⚙ .

2. Tap Search bar.

3. Enter a word or a phrase in the Search field. The list filters as you write.

4. Tap an option (make sure you select the best match).

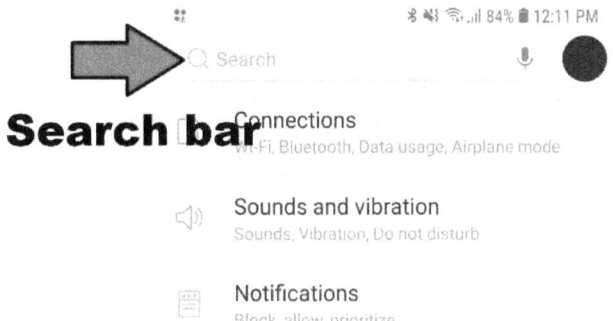

Search bar

Connections
Wi-Fi, Bluetooth, Data usage, Airplane mode

Sounds and vibration
Sounds, Vibration, Do not disturb

Notifications
Block, allow, prioritize

Hint: There is a tip to getting what you want from your Android phone. From time to time, you would want to customize your phone in a special way. All you need to do in a period like this is to open the settings as described above. Then tap the search bar and enter a search word or phrase corresponding to what you want to do.

What You Must Know About Android Phone

How to Find Your Phone When lost

As a human being, it is not impossible that you may misplace your phone. If someone else (a thief) has not taken custody of it, there are steps to follow to find it. These steps have been discussed at length in the preceding chapter; please refer to page 402 for details.
Note: It is dangerous to attempt to retrieve your lost phone by yourself. Please involve the attention of security operatives whenever you can.

Staying Productive While Using Your Android Phone

Smartphones are cool things to have, but if you are not careful, you may get entangled by it. Many people spend less time with friends and family because of their phone. They enjoy pressing their phones all the time even if it adds little or no meaning to their lives.

The truth is that if you want to stay productive, you must know when to drop your phone and do things that are more important to you. You must know when to switch off your phone or avoid using the internet. I have noticed that it is easier said than done. For most of us, it is difficult to drop our phones (and avoid online chats) to attend to other important things. What I have personally observed is that many of us need an outside help. One of the beautiful things we need is a good software (application) to make us accountable and prevent internet/app access when we are tempted.

Cold Turkey app is one of the apps out there that can help you block apps on your phone (for a specified time) so that you can concentrate on other things. You can download **Cold Turkey** app on Google Play store.

In addition, if you are looking for an accountable app that will enable you to know how you spend your time, you can try RescueTime Time Management app. This app will let you know how you spend your time on your Android phone. It will also let you know how productive you are. You can learn more and download **RescueTime Time Management** app from Google Play store.

Finally, one application that has personally helped me in my life is Freedom application. This application has helped me to avoid internet or apps when I need to do other important things. Unfortunately, as at the time of writing this guide, this app is not available on Android. However, it is available on Windows and iOS. You can learn more about Freedom at **https://freedom.to**

How to Reduce Your Mobile Data Usage on Android Phone

If you realize that you are using more MB/Data than normal, there are steps to follow to reduce your data consumption.

1. The first thing is to make sure that you update apps on Wi-Fi only. To do this:

    a. Go to application screen and tap Google "Play Store".

    b. Tap the menu icon.

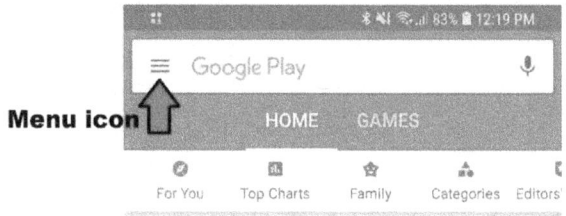

    c. Tap **Settings**.

    d. Tap **Auto-update apps** and select **Auto-update apps over Wi-Fi only.**

2. Consider using a data friendly browser: Browser like **Opera Mini** gives you the opportunity to save data through their **data saving** feature. You can also control the picture quality of webpages when you are using Opera Mini browser and thereby saving data. To download Opera Mini, please visit Google Play store.

3. Enable Data saver: On supported Android phones, you can enable data saver. To do this, from the home screen, tap the

settings icon ⚙ . Tap "Network & Internet",
"Connections", or "Wireless & network". Tap "Data usage"
or "Mobile Data". Then tap "Data saver", if you don't see

"Data saver" tap the menu icon ⋮ and select "Data saver".
Tap the status switch next to **Data saver**.

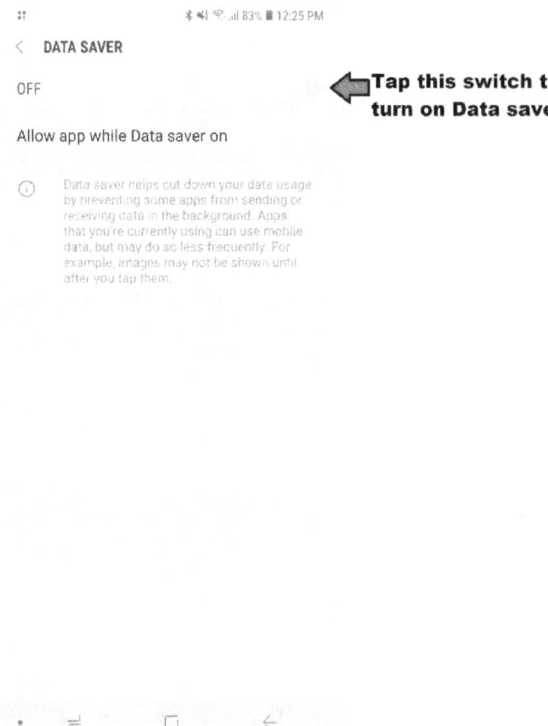

On supported Android phones, to control the number of apps
that have unrestricted access to your data, tap **Allow app
while Data saver on.**

4. Use the **Datally** app. This app allows you to save and control the use of your data. To download **Datally**, please visit Google Play store.

Solution to Non-Responding Apps

Sometimes an app may start misbehaving and may even refuse to close. The first thing you can do in a situation like this is to tap on the recent button or . This gives you an access to all opened/running apps on your phone. Locate this app and tap **X** icon to close it. Try launching the app again.

If it is still misbehaving after closing it or it refuses to close, then you may try these steps:

1. Swipe down from the top of the screen and select the settings icon .

2. Swipe up and tap "Apps".
   If you don't see "Apps", tap "Apps & Notifications" and then "App info" or "Apps".

3. Then tap on the misbehaving application from the list of applications.

4. Select **FORCE STOP**. This will stop the app from carrying out any process on your phone. To enable the app again, just launch the app.

Note: Please restart your device if stopping an app causes your device to stop working correctly. *In addition, force stopping an app may cause error(s).*

Tip: If you believe the misbehaving app has some errors, you can clear the cache or data, please go to page 92-95 to learn more.

How to Conserve Android Phone's Battery Life

You may notice that you have to charge your Android phone twice in 24 hours to keep it on. There are steps to follow to ensure that your phone serves you throughout the day with just a single charge.

1. **Reduce the screen brightness and turn off the automatic brightness:** I have realized over time that screen brightness consumes a lot of energy. There is usually a substantial difference between using a phone with a maximum brightness and using it with a moderate brightness. As a rule, don't use your phone with a maximum brightness unless you can't see what is on the screen clearly. For example, if you are outdoor. Make sure you reduce it immediately when it is no more needed.

   To reduce the screen brightness, swipe down from the top of the screen using two fingers. Then use the small circle (shape) on the slider to adjust the brightness.

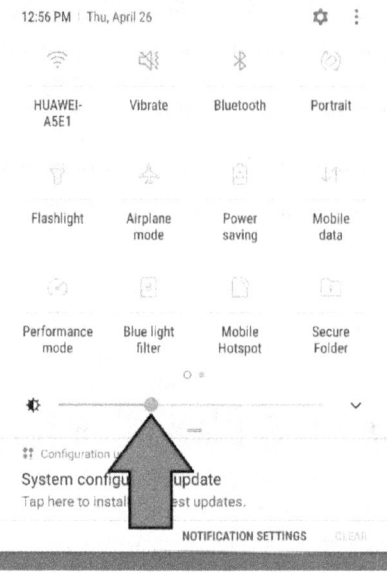

To manage more brightness settings on your Android phone, swipe down from the top of the screen and select the settings

icon ⚙ . Tap **Display** and then tap an option corresponding to what you want to do.

2. **Shorten the Screen timeout:** If you really want to save your battery life, you must try to shorten the screen timeout. Reducing how long your phone would stay lit up after you finish interacting with it will help you to save your battery. To manage screen timeout setting:

a. Swipe down from the top of the screen and select the

settings icon ⚙ .

b. Tap **Display** > **Screen Timeout.** Then choose an option. Alternatively, tap **Display** > **Advanced** > **Sleep** and then

choose an option. For other Android phones, tap **Display**
> **Sleep** and then choose an option.

3. **Turn off Wi-Fi and Bluetooth:** When you are not using Wi-
   Fi or Bluetooth, please always remember to put them off.
   These features really consume energy and they are better off
   when not in use.

4. **Reduce number of notifications:** There are two benefits of
   doing this. The first is that there will be less distractions and
   the second benefit is that notification consumes energy. Limit
   yourself to those notifications that are important to you. To
   manage notification setting:

a. Swipe down from the top of the screen and tap the

settings icon ⚙ .

b. Swipe up and tap "Apps". If you don't see "Apps", tap "Apps & Notifications" and then "App info" or "Apps". Please note that if you are using an LG Android phone, you may need to tap **General** tab, before you see "Apps & notifications".

c. Tap the app you want to manage.

d. To manage the notification of an app, tap **Notifications** and choose an option.

5. **Close all unnecessary apps:** The truth is that any app you are accessing is consuming out of the limited battery energy. It is important to close any app you are not using from time to time. To access all apps currently running on your phone, tap on the recent button ▣ or ⊐ and then tap **X** icon next to the application you want to close. Alternatively, swipe left or right to close an app.

6. **Use a correct charger:** Using a wrong charger can endanger the health of your phone/battery, and it is better to avoid such practice.

7. **Consider switching off your phone:** If you are not going to use your phone for an extended period, you may consider switching off your phone.

What to Do if You Forget You Device Lock Screen Password/Pin

If you forget your lock screen pattern or password, the only option I know for many Android phones, is to erase the phone. Please note that if you erase your phone, you are going to lose all the data stored on it, but you can still access any data you have backed up in the cloud (e.g. Google Cloud). To learn how to erase your phone when you forget your lock screen password or pattern, go to page 402.

On the other hand, if you are using a Samsung Android phone, you might be able to unlock your phone (without erasing it) by following the steps below:

1. Open a web browser and go to **findmymobile.samsung.com**
2. Tap **Sign In**.

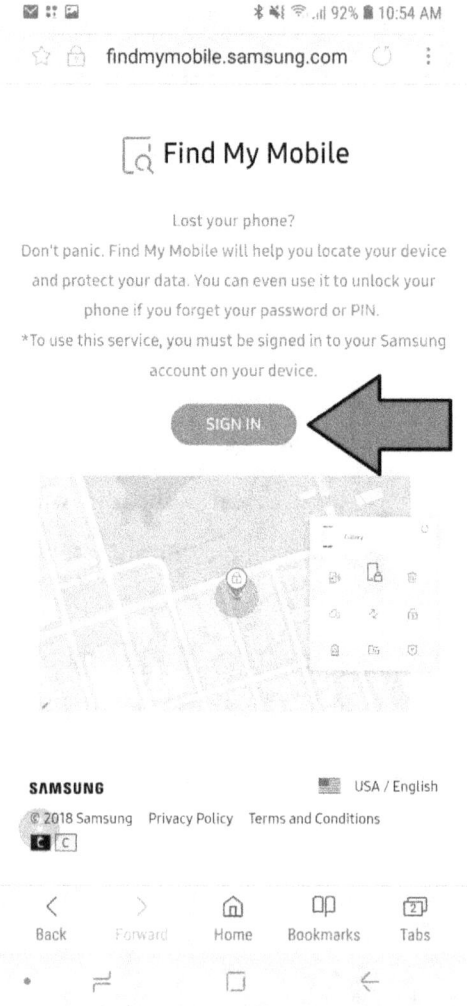

3. Enter the email address associated with your Samsung account into the email field and then enter your password. Click **Sign In**.

4. If you have more than one Samsung phone, you may need to select your Android phone (if it is not currently displayed). To

do this, tap the menu icon next to the current device name and select your device name.

5. Tap **Unlock** and enter your Samsung account password.

Note: Your Samsung Android phone may need to be connected to a wireless or mobile network to be able to use the **Find My Mobile** feature to unlock your phone.

In addition, please note that if you have disabled **Remote Controls on** your Samsung Android phone, you would need to activate it before you can use the method above. To do this:

1. Swipe down from the top of the screen and select the settings

   icon ⚙ .

2. Tap **Lock screen and security**.

3. Tap **Find My Mobile**.

4. Enter your Samsung account information and then tap **Sign In**. If you don't have a Samsung account, then create one.

5. Make sure that the status switches beside **Remote Controls**, **Google Location Service** and **Send Last Location** are turned on.

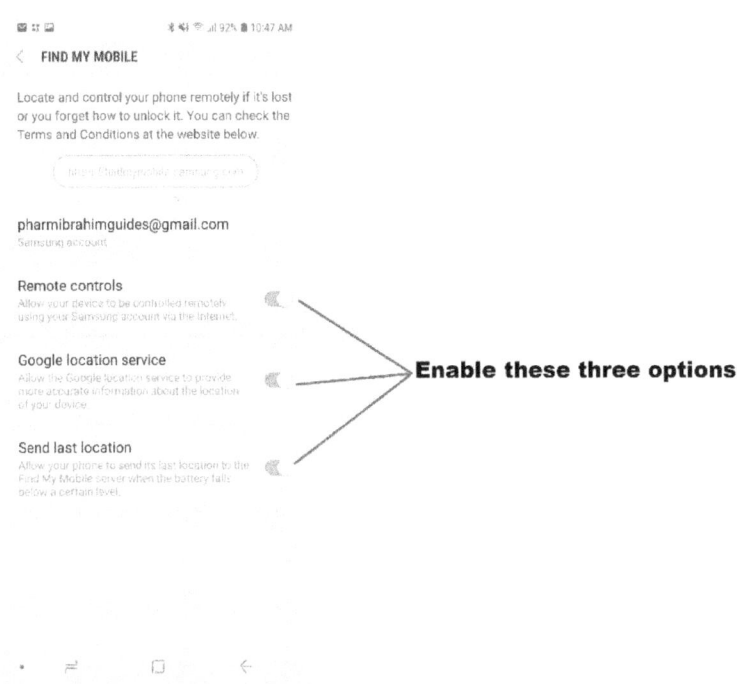

How to Take Screenshots on Your Device

Another task you can perform on your device is taking a screenshot. To take a screenshot with your device, please follow the instructions below:

Press and hold the volume down key and the power key simultaneously until you hear a small sound/vibration (you will press it for around 2 seconds). You can view captured images in Gallery. To view the screenshot, double-tap the status bar (the bar at the top of the screen where icons such as Wi-Fi icon usually appear) and then tap the screenshot.

Extras

What You Must Know Before Selling or Giving Away Your Android Phone

A time would probably come when you may need to give away or sell your Android phone. There are few things you must know before this time comes.

Some time ago, BBC reported that Avast (an antivirus giant) was able to use publicly available forensic security tools to extract naked selfies from second-hand phones bought on eBay. Other extracted data were emails, text messages and Google searches.

It is usual for many users to perform factory resets before selling their phones. The truth is that with the advent of sophisticated software, factory reset is no more enough. In fact, you have to go a step further.

So, what can you do to save your privacy? The simple answer is to go a step further by always encrypting your files. You should encrypt all your data before performing factory reset when you are considering selling or giving away your phone.

However, you must know that encrypting your device before doing the factory reset may not give 100% protection to your privacy. Who knows if programmers will develop a software that will be a step ahead of that in the nearest future? The best way to completely protect your privacy is to destroy your phone when you don't need it again. But as you know, this is not feasible many times and may not be advisable.

Finally, encrypting your phone before performing factory reset is an efficient way of protecting your privacy. At least it makes it much more difficult for people to retrieve your files.

Interestingly, most (if not all) Android phones automatically encrypt data stored on it. However, you would need to encrypt data stored on memory card yourself. To do this:

- Swipe down from the top of the screen and select the settings icon ⚙ .

- Tap the search icon 🔍 located at the top of the screen.
- Begin to type encryption, and tap the result that best matches what you want to do.
- Tap "Encrypt SD card" or similar phrase and follow the prompts.

If you don't see any option to encrypt your SD card, make sure your external memory card is properly installed/inserted.

When you encrypt your memory card, you may need a numeric PIN or password to decrypt your SD card when you first access it after switching on your device.

Tip: You will need to reset your Android phone to factory setting before you give it out. To do this:

Consider backing up your data before doing a factory reset.

- Swipe down from the top of the screen and select the settings icon ⚙.

- Tap "System", "General Management" or "Restart & Reset".

- Tap "Reset" (if needed).

- Tap "Factory data reset" and follow the prompts.

Travelling with Your Phone—What to Know

While travelling abroad with your Android phone, there are few things to know. These things are discussed below.

1. **Unlock your phone and plan to get a local SIM card**

If you are travelling abroad, it is important you consider unlocking your phone to use foreign SIM cards on your phone. Generally, you can unlock your phone by contacting your network service provider. If your phone is already unlocked, then have a clear plan to get a local SIM card when you get to the foreign land. Generally, using a local SIM card for your calls will save your money than roaming. **Note**: If you are unable to unlock your phone and you want to stay several months abroad, consider buying a cheap unlocked phone.

2. Get to know about roaming

If you are not planning to unlock your phone or get a local SIM card, then I would advise that you know about roaming plans. You can easily do this by contacting your network service provider.

3. Set up a lock screen

It is important to set up a lock screen while going abroad. This would save you a lot of stress if you lost the phone. Security in some places in the world is bad and your phone can easily be snatched from you. Even if your phone is not stolen, you can misplace your phone while moving from one place to another. If you have set up a screen lock, you can be sure that it would be extremely hard (if not impossible) for people to access your data from the lost phone. To know how to set up a lock screen, see page 136. I would advise you to use a lock screen password (if you can) for your device. A lock screen password appears more secured than pattern or PIN.

Tip: If you mistakenly misplace your phone, you may locate it by following the steps on page 402.

4. Get a power bank (USB Battery Pack)

Charging your phone might not be easy while abroad. I would advise you consider getting a power bank to charge your phone. You can get cheap and reliable power bank from Amazon.

5. Monitor and save your data

Data are quite expensive in some countries of the world. I would advise you monitor and save data as much as you can. To know how to save data on Android phone, please see page 418.

6. Be careful when using Wireless network

Using a wireless network in a foreign country needs an extra care. There are some countries that are notorious for hacking. I would advise you research about any country you are visiting to know how to prepare for it. To learn how to stay secured when connected to wireless, see page 437.

7. Get familiar with Google Translate

If the country you are going is not speaking your language, then you need someone or something to help you with language translation. Interestingly, Google Translate might provide some help in this regard. To start using Google Translate, visit

https://translate.google.com

8. Get familiar with the Google Map application

Google Map is one best map applications in the world. You can easily know the route to your destination using this app. I would advise you familiarize yourself with Google Map before traveling. This application can save you a lot of stress and time. You can download **Google Map** from Google Play store.

Getting an Antivirus for Your Phone -- Is It Necessary?

Many people may not really take the issue of antivirus seriously because they think that virus software targets PC much more than phones. The truth is that things are changing every now and then. The best thing you can do is to always keep a guard.

Interestingly, there are many reputable free antiviruses on Google Play store. My favorite antiviruses are AVG, Lookout and Norton Antiviruses. You may check Google Play Store to download any of these.

In addition, some Android phones come preloaded with an antivirus or device security, if this is your situation, you may not bother installing additional antivirus.

Note: The best way to protect yourself from a virus attack is being proactive. For example, I don't expect you to click the links present in an unsolicited email. So, having many antiviruses on your phone may not help if you are not prudent in your actions.

Safety Precautions When Using Android Phone on Wi-Fi (Wireless Network)

With many free Wi-Fi hotspots, it is likely that you are going to find yourself using Wi-Fi more on your Android phone. There are few things to keep in mind when using Wi-Fi.

1. Confirm the Network Name

Hackers sometimes set up a fake Wi-Fi network in order to tap into the information of unwitting public users. To avoid this, make sure you are sure of the name of the network you are connecting to. You may ask any trusted individual around you if you doubt the name of a network.

2. Connect to a Secured Site

Whenever you are sending a sensitive information, always make sure that the site is a secured website. You can know whether a website is a secured site or not by checking whether the *url* address of the website starts with **HTTPS.** If it starts with https, then it should be a secured site.

3. Run an Antivirus Software

As earlier mentioned, using an antivirus is very crucial in today's world. You may consider installing a genuine antivirus. There are many of them on Google Play store.

4. Get a Virtual Private Network (VPN)

It is highly important you use a virtual private network when using a public wireless network. There are both free and paid VPN providers. My favorite is **Hotspot Shield VPN.** It is available on Google Play store. They offer both free and paid versions. You may also check out other VPN apps to pick the best.

5. Avoid Automatic Connection

Make sure your Wi-Fi is off when not using it to avoid your phone automatically connecting to an open network. Turning your Wi-Fi off when not using it will also save your battery.

I am Having a Dwindling Love for my Android Phone; What Should I Do?

It is possible that after buying an Android phone, you realize that it performs below your expectation. It is likely that you dislike your phone because of its hardware or software issue. Generally, the hardware has to do with the design, the phone make up, the weight of the phone etc. While the software has to do with the OS and applications.

If your love for an Android phone is reducing because of the software, there is a way out. You can take your time to look for beneficial apps to install on your device.

If your love for an Android phone is reducing because of the hardware, then it is either you learn how to live with it (you may have to force yourself to love it), give it away or you sell it. If you are considering selling your phone or giving it away, then make sure you read the article on page 431.

TROUBLESHOOTING

If the touch screen responds slowly or improperly or your phone is not responding, try the following:

- Remove any protective covers (screen protector) from the touch screen.
- Ensure that your hands are clean and dry when tapping. In addition, ensure that the screen of your phone is not wet. If wet, use a soft dry towel to clean it.
- Press the power button once to lock the screen and press it again to unlock the screen and enter a PIN/password/pattern if required.
- Switch off your device and on it again.

Your phone doesn't charge

- Make sure you are using a recommended charger (like the one that came with your phone) to charge your Android phone.
- If the Android phone does not indicate that it is charging, unplug the power adapter and then restart your device.
- Make sure you are using the USB cable that came with the Android phone or anyone that has similar specs.

Your device is hot to the touch

When you use applications that require more power or use applications on your device for an extended period, your phone may be a bit hot. This is normal, and it should not have much effect on its performance. You may just allow your phone to rest for some time or close some applications.

Your phone freezes or has fatal error

If your phone freezes or it is unresponsive, press and hold the Power key until the phone restarts. Please note that you may need to press the Power key for several seconds (for 10 to 20 seconds for Sony Android phones, and for up to 30 seconds for Google Pixel phones) before the phone will restart.

If the instruction does not work for you, try this. Press and hold the volume up button (or volume down button for some Android phones) and the power button for about 5 seconds or until it restarts. The process described above is also called soft reset.

Phone does not connect to Wi-Fi

Make sure you don't have a limited network connectivity in that area. If your network signal is good and you still cannot connect, you may perform any of these actions.

- Make sure your Airplane Mode is off.
- Try restarting the Wi-Fi.
- Move closer to your router and scan for the available networks. If the network still does not show up, you may add the network manually.

- Restart your router and modem. Unplug the modem and router for few minutes and plug the modem in, and then the router.

- Try restarting you phone.

Another Bluetooth device is not located

- Ensure Bluetooth feature is activated on your phone and the device you want to connect to.

- Ensure that your phone and the other Bluetooth device are within the maximum Bluetooth range (usually approximately 30 feet).

A connection is not established when you connect your phone to a PC using USB cable

- Ensure that the USB cable you are using is compatible with your device.

- Ensure that you have the proper drivers installed and updated on your PC.

Audio quality is poor during a call

- Ensure that the network signal is strong. When you are in an area with a weak or poor network/reception, you may lose reception. Try moving to another area and then try again.

Safety precautions

A. To prevent electric shock, fire, and explosion

1. Do not use damaged power cords or plugs, or loose electrical sockets.
2. Do not touch the power cord with a wet hand.
3. Do not bend or damage the power cord.
4. Do not short-circuit the charger.
5. Do not use your phone during thunderstorm.
6. Do not dispose your phone by putting it in fire.

B. Follow all safety warnings and regulations when using your device in restricted areas.

C. Comply with all safety warnings and regulations regarding mobile device usage while operating a vehicle.

D. Proper care and use of your phone

1. Do not use or store your phone in very hot or cold areas. For many Android phones, it is recommended to use your device at temperature from 5^0C to 35^0C.
2. Do not put your phone near magnetic fields.
3. Do not use camera flash close to people's eyes or pets' eyes because it can cause temporary loss of vision or damage the eyes.
4. When speaking on the phone, speak directly into the mouthpiece.

5. Avoid disturbing others when using your phone in public.

6. Keep your phone away from children because they may mistakenly damage it as it may look like a toy to them.

Just Before You Go (Please Read!)

Although I have put in tremendous effort in writing this guide,
I am confident that I have not said it all.
I have no doubt believing that I have not written everything possible
about Android phones.
So, I want you to do me a favor.
If you would like to know how to perform a task that is not included
in this guide, please let me know by sending me an email at
pharmibrahimguides@gmail.com. I will try as much as possible to
reply you as soon as I can.

You may also visit my author's page at
www.amazon.com/author/pharmibrahim
And please don't forget to follow me when you visit my author's
page, just click or tap on **Follow** button located below the profile
picture.

Index

www.ingramcontent.com/pod-product-compliance
Lightning Source LLC
Chambersburg PA
CBHW070322220526
45467CB00001B/3

9 781717 813091